THE
BEST
WOMEN'S TRAVEL
WRITING

Volume 12

TRUE STORIES
FROM AROUND THE WORLD

TRAVELERS' TALES

THE BEST
WOMEN'S TRAVEL
WRITING

Volume 12

TRUE STORIES
FROM AROUND THE WORLD

Edited by
LAVINIA SPALDING

Illustrated by Colette Hannahan

Travelers' Tales
an imprint of Solas House, Inc.
Palo Alto

Travelers' Tales and Solas House are trademarks of Solas House, Inc.,
Palo Alto, California, travelerstales.com I solashouse.com

Credits and copyright notices for the individual articles in this collection are given starting on page 319.

Art direction and cover design: Kimberly Nelson
Cover photograph: Hans Vivek, New Delhi, India
Interior design and page layout: Howie Severson

ISBN: 978-1-60952-189-9
ISSN: 1553-054X
E-ISBN: 978-1-60952-190-5

First Edition
Printed in the United States
10 9 8 7 6 5 4 3 2 1

For Helen Prothero, who always steers toward love.

Perhaps travel cannot prevent bigotry, but by demonstrating that all peoples cry, laugh, worry, eat, and die, it can introduce the idea that if we try to understand each other, we may even become friends.

—MAYA ANGELOU

We are volcanoes. When we women offer our experience as our truth, as human truth, all the maps change. There are new mountains.

—URSULA K. LE GUIN

Table of Contents

Introduction

*L*ast year, I spent a week in Fez, Morocco, teaching a writing workshop. It was my second visit to the city, and I stayed in the old, walled medina. A UNESCO World Heritage Site, "Fès-el-Bali" is a maze of more than nine thousand narrow, winding pedestrian streets filled with homes, schools, mosques, restaurants, *hammams* (bath houses), *riads* (guest houses), and *souks* (markets). The medina was a clogged, chaotic blur, an ever-swirling kaleidoscope of color and sound and scent—and while mesmerized, I tried hard to keep my bearings.

I didn't stand a chance. I got lost every two minutes: any time I unbolted the heavy door of my *riad* and stepped outside, or exited a café, or craned my neck to gaze at a thin bookmark of blue sky above the peeling paint of an orange wall. I got lost because the medina's serpentine byways are mostly unnamed, and because I had no cell service (and thus no GPS) and neglected to orient myself by obvious landmarks, and because the meticulously detailed map my *riad* host annotated and explained thirteen times looked more to me like a brain than a map.

It didn't help that I have a poor sense of direction; wherever I go in the world, I become at least temporarily misplaced. Still, the version of disorientation handed to me in Fez was extreme, and multiplied by the men who materialized whenever I looked confused (again, every two minutes) to insist I was heading the wrong way, down a dead-end street, and needed to follow them. I'd been warned about these false guides who pretended to show tourists to their hotels but steered them instead to their shops, and I knew how to respond: *"La, shukran,"* I'd say firmly, *No, thank you,* then quicken my pace, perhaps turning a corner with confidence, and wind up even farther off course. At which point they'd request payment for their services.

Finally, I received some advice.

"Let yourself get lost," a friend said. "You're *supposed* to get lost."

"And when I no longer wish to be lost?"

"Ask a woman for directions. Women won't steer you wrong."

In the days that followed I surrendered to the labyrinth, turning this way and that, wholly absorbed. I meandered through shops stocked with dainty glass teacups, ankle-length *djellabas* (traditional robes), silver teapots, and tall, tidy cones of saffron and cinnamon. I admired brass lamps the size of beach umbrellas and touched the soft leather of purses dyed Pepto pink and parakeet green. I watched craftsmen weave linens on giant hand-operated wooden looms, ate *chebakia*—sesame-honey-rose-water cookies—and held mint to my nose at the phenomenally pungent eleventh-century Chouara Tannery. I whispered Buddhist prayers for caged chickens, live snails, and a camel head hanging from a hook. Then, when I tired of being directionless, I asked a woman for directions. And somehow, with women pointing the way, the way felt more familiar.

This wisdom, of both leaning into lostness and seeking guidance from women, was still on my mind six months later when I began work on *The Best Women's Travel Writing, Volume 12*, and faced 1300 submissions (800 more than usual). My mind tumbled to it in the following months, as I found myself adrift in the new Covid-riddled world. It came to me whenever I called my best friend in Canada, her voice a clasped hand across a closed border, and during long chats with my mother, who was spending her quarantine drawing portraits of fierce goddesses and brilliant female scientists. I contemplated it when I began helping my son with online preschool (in French; I don't speak French) and found sanity among a new group of mom friends. And I reflected on it at the threshold of an essential anti-racism reckoning, when I realized I didn't know how to discuss race and turned to my older sister, a longtime activist and lifelong mentor. I clung to it when I began my anti-racism work by reading articles and books by Black women.

And it's on my mind now, because the truth is, attempting to pen an introduction about travel today—in the midst of a global pandemic during which our passports lie fallow; in an era of climate change and catastrophic natural disasters; and at the dawn of a four-hundred-years-overdue revolution brought on by systemic racial injustice—I've never felt more lost as a writer.

"Let yourself get lost. You're *supposed* to get lost."

"And when I no longer wish to be lost?"

"Ask a woman for directions. Women won't steer you wrong."

This book marks the twelfth volume of *The Best Women's Travel Writing* series, and the sixth I've edited. Over the years, I've occasionally been asked, "What *is* women's travel writing, and why is it different or special?" I never quite nail the answer—it's complex—but I do know that in meandering through women's essays, I always seem to trip across something I'm not even aware I'm seeking, but vitally need. These "somethings" run the gamut from escape to inspiration to connection to catharsis. And always, lodged sturdily in there among everything else, is the truth. I always find truth. Or more accurately, I am guided to it.

The collection you hold in your hands is rife with these necessary somethings. Ranging in locale from a ferry on the stormy Adriatic Sea to a hostel lounge in Bolivia to the back seat of a police car in Colombia, and covering topics as motley as a train robbery in Italy, an amateur autopsy in Ireland, and a fairytale romance in Indonesia, the thirty-four essays I selected led me to a secret corner of a place and an emotion, and shone lights on precisely what needed to be illuminated.

Kaitlin Barker Davis's essay, "Come and See," for instance, about visiting the remains of an Indonesian village scorched by the volcanic eruption of Mt. Merapi—offered unexpected insight into my own editorial process, as I found myself drawn toward story after story of strength and survival: "Here is the uncomfortable truth," she writes, "of disaster tourism: we want to get close to danger without actually being in danger. But maybe there's something more. Maybe it isn't the tragedy that we are really drawn to. Maybe what we crave is evidence of human resilience. We want to see it with our own eyes, hope it exists within us should we ever need it."

Likewise, Eva Holland's remarkable essay, "A Strange Ambition," about learning to survive in the Arctic regions of Canada, reminded me that even in the darkest times (or, in her case, the coldest), we all possess not only hidden reserves of grit, but also of grace, which enable us to recognize the beauty arising from the struggle. Holland writes: "Here was that same lesson I had learned and relearned over these two weeks. Joy and awe would always win out, if I let them. The Arctic had an alchemical ability to transform my fears and suffering into raw wonder. If I kept coming back, kept flinging myself onto the ice, moments like these were the rewards."

I believe in travel. I believe that by disorienting us, it rearranges us. Travel builds character and ignites imagination, nurtures independence and humility, catalyzes curiosity and self-examination. It can be a bulwark against stagnation, and a call to action. It widens our worldview and brings us face-to-face with our privilege, as it forces us to reassess entrenched beliefs and long-held concepts. Of course, travel is no magical elixir. I've stopped believing it's "fatal to prejudice," as Mark Twain famously declared (if only it were that simple), but I do hold that it's a solid start toward upending our biases and assumptions, because it compels us to see beyond the abstractions of a foreign land to its humanity.

But travel has a shadow side, too: there's the environmental impact of flying and cruising, the crowding of our planet's most wondrous places, the littering of sacred sites, the pricing-out of locals. And it has dreadful roots (colonialism, capitalism) and gruesome side effects (exploitation, exoticism, saviorism).

I wrestle with this duality. How do I reconcile the damage travel does with the awareness that it profoundly enriches my life; that it is not only my livelihood but also, at times, my sanity? It's another area in which I get hopelessly lost. And while I may never navigate this ethical tangle, I recognize that travel itself is what helps me make sense of—or at least pay more attention to—a world both exquisite and unbearably cruel.

For this volume of *The Best Women's Travel Writing,* I included narratives that explore some of the questions and contradictions we face as travelers. Alongside accounts of thrilling quests, epic pilgrimages, abundant hospitality, hilarious escapades, kinship, and communion—stories that point to my ultimate faith in the transformative power of travel—are essays that made me sad and mad and deeply uncomfortable. Essays that asked me to pay more attention. There are journeys told through the lens of genocide, slavery, injustice, and climate change. And disasters—two fires, a couple of volcanic eruptions, an earthquake—not to mention near-deaths, misdeeds, regrets, and loneliness.

I wasn't seeking any of these journeys, but I vitally needed them. I needed to get lost in their questions and steered toward awareness.

In Christina Ammon's essay, "Convivencia," about a revelatory trip to Spain, she asks a probing question we must all address. "With maturity, my political consciousness had evolved. I looked at the world with all of its violence and inequality and now wondered: *Why did evil exist, and why was it allotted so unjustly?*"

In "Key Change," Rahawa Haile explores what it means to love a place that's disappearing due to climate change. She writes, "We may very well be living in the dismantling, you and I, whether we choose to watch or not. And how does one build among constant erosion? Where do we go?"

In "Wade in the Water," Alexandria Scott rows a boat through Maryland's Chesapeake Bay, reflecting on the indelible strength of her enslaved ancestors. "Enslavement was meant to define and overpower my people," she writes, "but they resisted. Like the water that surrounded them, they carried on with strength, stalwart consistency, and beauty."

And in "Why I Took My Daughter to Auschwitz," Peggy Orenstein puts forth the painful essence of human character. "We are all capable of evil, big and small. We all have within us the monstrous, the conniving, the cruel." But then she pivots with the words I needed to hear. "Yet we are also capable of selflessness, bravery, and resilience."

It's no great mystery why I was attracted to stories of strength, resistance, and resilience in these times. The pandemic has taken so much from us. Lives and loved ones lost. Mental and physical health compromised. Weddings, graduations, and funerals canceled. The absence of touch. Jobs, businesses, and homes lost. Economic disaster. Unspeakable heartache.

The act of living always comes with suffering. (In Buddhism, this is called *samsara*, or the cyclical nature of life.) Mercifully, it also contains tenderness, fortitude, and renewal. Times of despair turn up unexpected treasures. As I've sheltered in place, for instance, I've been buoyed by accounts of mountain goats reclaiming the Welsh town of Llandudno and a kangaroo hopping through the city center of Adelaide, Australia; reports of the smog lifting over Los Angeles and the Himalayas becoming visible from hundreds of miles away; stories of Italians singing on balconies and Spaniards banging pots for health-care workers, and citizens of mega-metropolises and tiny towns across the globe rising up together to fight for justice and equality.

The world has changed in immeasurable, inconceivable ways, and it continues to shift. I wonder, as you're reading this, what is the state of our fragile, fractured world? Are we traveling yet, or still ensconced at home, experiencing the faraway via books and virtual reality?

In Susan Orlean's essay "Zooming in on Petra," she recounts a trip to Jordan to watch a technology company create a virtual model of Petra, which will allow those who can't travel there to experience it digitally. "But visiting a place," Orlean writes, "—breathing in its ancient dust, confronting it in real time, meeting its residents, elbowing its tourists, sweating as you clamber up its hills, even seeing how time has punished it—will always be different, more magical, more challenging."

I agree. And while I'm restless at my core, I'm oddly content to wait. Because I know that eventually, when it's safe to resume all that elbowing and sweating, and honor both the magic and challenge of travel, it will be worth it. And perhaps we'll be more worthy of it.

Though the pandemic has taken much from us, it's also offered something to those fortunate enough to have survived it: a reset—a chance to wake up and see, for a minute, what it would look like to preserve our imperiled planet, species, and cultures, along with irrefutable proof of the interdependence and equality of humans. Will we accept the reset and correct course? Begin making more ethical, sustainable, inclusive choices? And, with the reminder that travel is an incalculable privilege, stop taking it for granted? I have no answers, only aspirations. I hope that when we find our way out of the morass, we'll emerge gentler and kinder, more tolerant and aware, with great and wild gratitude for all who have helped us along the path.

Which brings me back to Fez.

By the end of my week in the medina, I continued to get lost every two minutes, and one afternoon, I had an errand to run—my husband had asked me to return to a specific shop and purchase a small rug to match one we'd bought there a few years before. When I showed the address to my local friend Zakia and asked for directions, she laughed at me.

"You'll never find it," she said.

Zakia was aware of my underdeveloped sense of direction and, having grown up in the medina, insisted on accompanying me. Inside the shop, while the owner unfurled carpets across the tiled floor, Zakia and I chatted and sipped mint tea. I kept telling her she needn't stay, and she kept ignoring me. By the time I found my rug, it was near dinnertime. I was embarrassed.

"I'll be fine," I said. "Just point me in the right direction."

"No way," she said, laughing again. "You need a babysitter."

Then she took my arm and shepherded me through the medina's infinite turns and bends, back to my *riad*. I was grateful. Though I'd accepted by then that there *was* something rewarding in the surrender of letting myself get lost, her guidance steadied my dizzy spirit. As she turned to go home, I placed my hand on my heart, and she waved goodbye cheerfully.

In this collection of essays, you will meet more people like Zakia—golden-hearted souls who come from places like Azerbaijan, Bhutan, Canada, Cuba, The Czech Republic, France, Germany, India, Indonesia, Ireland, Japan, Jordan, Mexico, Nepal, Spain, and Tanzania. People who become the heroes of our stories because they show the way or deliver joy, care for us when we're vulnerable, help us navigate meaning, or propel us when we're stuck. They are custodians of travel; they keep us believing in its magic.

Consider this anthology a guidebook to take with you down the unnamed, unmapped road ahead, into a medina-like world of untold twists and turns. I hope that in these thirty-four true travel tales you will find something you weren't aware you were seeking but vitally need—and I hope you'll let yourself get lost in them.

You're *supposed* to get lost.

And as your guides: thirty-four women who won't steer you wrong.

—Lavinia Spalding
New Orleans

ℳ ℳ ℳ

Finding El Saez

She went back to set things right.

We head west out of Havana in the early afternoon, my husband Kevin behind the wheel of our circa-1990 rented Geely sedan. The air feels like the inside of a mouth, and even though third gear sounds like an opera singer warming up and the stereo doesn't work, we're grateful for air conditioning. The highway winds through coastal Artemisa, a tranquil, verdant province of farmland and gleaming seascapes. Exquisite scenery. But I have an ulterior motive for returning.

I've come to settle an old debt.

I last saw the man I seek thirteen years ago, as I rode away from the town of Bahía Honda in a Volkswagen Kombi packed with agricultural workers. He raised one hand in an open-palmed goodbye. The truck rounded a corner and I lost sight of him. There's no reason to think he's still in Bahía Honda, except that it's the kind of town where people live from birth until death. A place where no one is a stranger.

Except me. I was a stranger.

I have forgotten this man's name in the intervening years. I remember a one-room shack with a dirt floor and an outdoor kitchen, no plumbing. The exterior may have been robin's egg blue. He didn't have a telephone, much less email, and I never wrote down the home address.

For the longest time, I had a photograph of him and his wife sitting on a plank bench, regarding the camera with frank, unsmiling expressions. Her hand rested casually on his knee. I'd planned to use this snapshot to ask around in town like they do in movies—*Have you seen this man?*—but though I ransacked my house before leaving California, the photo seemed to have vanished.

So I'm looking for a memory, a wispy one. I have two specific details: He is unusually tall, and he used to play volleyball for the Cuban national team.

"You know your chances of finding this guy are basically nil, right?" Kevin says.

"If it doesn't work out, we'll move on."

I figure I can count on an hour of Kevin's patience if we catch a lead, or half an hour if we don't.

Out here in the boonies, we share the road with horse-drawn carts, tractors, dirt bikes wobbling under three or four people, wandering livestock, and potholes the size of open graves. The much abused *Why did the chicken cross the road?* joke takes on new life, as one seemingly suicidal chicken after another darts perilously in front of the car. Kevin grips the wheel, his red Pharaoh beard jutting forward with concentration as he swerves around them.

We travel with an endless rotation of hitchhikers in the back seat: mothers with small children, students returning from school, laborers heading home from work. Some ride for dozens of kilometers, others for a couple minutes. On an island where few people own cars, this is public transportation. Locals are expected—sometimes legally required—to stop for hitchhikers. Tourists aren't obligated, but if your car isn't at capacity at all times, you're basically a jerk. Besides, the road maps are so lousy that driving anywhere besides the Carretera Central, you need directions.

And we are way off the map.

When a passenger mentions she's from near Bahía Honda, my ears perk up. "I'm looking for someone I used to know," I say in Spanish. "I don't remember his name, but he's super tall."

She shrugs, shaking her head.

Kevin's right; it's a long shot.

At a sharp curve in the highway, the vista unfolds, revealing the slingshot-shaped bay from which the town draws its name, a deep teal inlet framed by steep green hills. In the distance, *mogotes*—gigantic limestone mounds shaped like bread loaves—rise from the steaming jungle.

We let the woman out at her driveway and soon pick up a medical student in his early twenties. He's from Bahía Honda itself, and he has a thick regional accent. When I describe the man, he says, "Like really, really tall? That has to be El Saez."

"El Saez . . . that's his name?"

"It's what everyone calls him. Like a handle. If you're looking for the tallest guy in town, it has to be him."

Kevin's Spanish is limited, so I translate. "He knows him," I beam.

"You're kidding me."

"El Saez hangs out at the kiosk," the kid says. "I'll show you."

My stomach jitters as we enter Bahía Honda. What will I say? I now realize I hadn't really expected to find him.

The kiosk is a crumbling cinder-block store, shelves bare save for a meager selection of knock-off sodas and beer, doughy street pizza, and botulism sandwiches. Clearly a hangout. Men drape themselves languidly on the front steps or stand in loose groups. Laughing, smoking, holding up the walls.

When we exit the Geely, people pause to give us the once-over. Kevin and I are both pale redheads; my long red curls match his beard. We're obviously foreign.

"*¿Dónde anda El Saez?*" the medical student asks the group. "*Éstos yanquis lo buscan.*"

A confused chorus of "Yankees looking for El Saez? Why?"

"*Yo sé donde está,*" one guy booms from the steps. He saunters over. "I always know what he's up to. I'm his best friend."

I explain that I knew El Saez thirteen years ago and want to see him.

"*¿En serio?*" He climbs into the Geely's backseat without waiting for an invitation. "*Vámonos.*"

Our new passenger wears a baseball cap with the brim flipped up, plastic sandals, board shorts, and a tank-top, his arm muscles bulging. He introduces himself as Tabaco.

"You must smoke a lot," I laugh.

"Only when I was a little kid," he grins. Before day's end, Kevin and I will watch Tabaco burn through three packs of cigarettes.

He guides us through town to a manicured park with rows of giant banyan trees, their large rubbery leaves clacking in the breeze.

"*¡Oye, El Saez!*" Tabaco hollers out the window.

A man stands from a white marble bench. He is indeed tall, maybe 6' 5", dressed entirely in white. His skin and eyes are a rich chestnut brown, and his hair is beginning to gray.

He wears a quizzical expression.

In my memory, the guy was lanky, more of a string-bean; this man has a bit of a paunch. I'd expected to recognize him, but now I feel uncertain. It's been too long.

I plunge ahead anyway, hoping I won't make us both feel foolish. "I was here a long time ago," I say. "I stayed in your home. Remember that?"

His face is impassive. He regards me for what feels like a long time, betraying no recognition.

Then he says, very quietly, "I never thought you'd come back."

———

When I first met Misael Saez—a.k.a. El Saez—I'd been living in Cuba for nearly a year, studying Sociology at the University of Havana as part of the first wave of American exchange students since the Revolution. Though I was supposed to return to the U.S. upon completing the program, I planned to head for Colombia or Brazil instead. I had fallen out of love with my home country, and madly in love with travel.

One phone call flipped my life upside down. My mom rang the student house on a Friday afternoon to tell me that her Hepatitis-C had taken a turn for the worse. She'd been putting off treatment for years, but now her viral count was spiking into the millions; she was careening toward liver failure. Her only option, she explained, was an experimental chemotherapy cocktail. She'd have to commit to a year-long drug trial in Los Angeles, during which she'd be virtually bedridden—as much from medication side effects as the illness itself. The prognosis wasn't good. But despite the 40 percent success rate, the treatment was her only shot.

My mom had no savings, no other immediate family. Just me. I'd have to drop out of school and move to Los Angeles—a city I disliked. The walls of the student house seemed to tighten around me, the wooden slat blinds like the bars of a cell. Sweat streamed down my face and back. Outside, Havana pounded. A smoggy vortex of desire and need and too much time on people's hands. I had to get somewhere quiet, somewhere I could think.

I didn't even pack a bag. I left the house in the clothes I was wearing, walked to 5ta Avenida, and started hitchhiking out of the city, toward the rural western provinces. I knew I'd return to Havana later and coordinate my travel plans. I would do the right thing. I just needed time to shake the panic.

I brought only the cash in my pocket—a fistful of *moneda nacional*, the cheap Cuban currency of the day, and US$10.

Not even enough for one night in a state-authorized *casa particular*, but I didn't care. All I could think of was escape.

If it moves, it's transportation was a popular quip in Cuba, and on that day, I hitched rides on tractors, motorcycles, truck beds, and an empty livestock hold with manure in one corner. There were hours standing by the roadside, swatting flies, waiting for someone to stop. Sunset found me squeezed into a claustrophobic Volkswagon with two dozen commuters returning to the provinces after the workweek in Havana. The truck snaked high into jungle-cloaked mountains, pot-holes knocking people against one another. A foreign woman hitchhiking alone sparked curiosity, and I could feel people ogling, but I wasn't in the mood to talk. I watched the road recede from the back of the truck through a lattice of arms braced against the ceiling.

In Los Angeles, everyone would have cars. Cell phones, new clothes, lacquered nails, bleached teeth. I imagined spending days in a windowless cubicle—despite having promised myself I'd never be an office drone again. How else would I support two of us? I didn't know what nursing someone through chemo entailed. Would I have to mop up vomit? Give injections? Did I have what it took to be a good nurse? What if I became resentful?

Over everything loomed the unimaginable: My mom might die on me. I tried to picture a world without her. It felt like a violation of natural law.

A soft voice interrupted my silence. "*Te ves infeliz,*" said a man sitting beside me. "*¿Estás bien?*" You look unhappy. Are you okay?

Misael Saez. Even when he was seated, his height was intimidating. The long fingers and knobby shoulders. But his voice was calm and gentle, his expression open. Before I knew it, I was telling him about my mom, and with the words came tears.

Most Cubans I knew, especially men, were boisterous, loud, opinionated, fond of drama. Misael seemed different.

He looked solemnly at his hands while I aired my fears. "My mom died last year," he said quietly. "Breast cancer."

I gleaned from his tone that he missed her, that the wound was still fresh. I wondered dizzily if this would be me in a year or two. I didn't believe in fate, and yet meeting Misael felt fateful, like I had fled the student house specifically to find him. A man who had already survived the unthinkable.

When Misael debarked the Kombi in the town of Bahía Honda, I followed him.

He asked where I was staying. "No plans," I said, trying to act casual.

"If you want, you can come with me. We don't have anything, but my wife is a good cook."

There were many things we didn't discuss. Like the fact that it was illegal to house a tourist without a license from the state, and he was putting himself at risk. Or that a night in someone's home usually cost US$20, which I didn't have on me.

Misael shared a humble home with his wife Yadira and her two children. One room with a dirt floor, two small beds, and an outdoor kitchen and latrine. Yadira seemed understandably concerned about her husband bringing home a stray American. But he explained the situation, and she made me feel welcome, preparing an extraordinary meal of diablo shrimp with black beans, rice, and fried yucca.

After dinner, the kids slipped behind a curtain and took turns bathing with a bucket of water and a ladle. Feeling like an intruder, I excused myself for a walk. Misael trailed me out of the house. A paranoid voice in my mind told me to be on guard, that he might make a pass. But he didn't, and I soon understood that he was watching out for me. I felt safer than I had in a long time. The town was dark, the moon not yet risen. We walked side by side under a great heap of stars, not talking, listening to crying insects and night birds.

Later, I shared a single bed with Yadira's two kids. Even though I was twenty-three, I felt like a child. We slept feet to head, three of us smashed together, surrounded by a gauzy mosquito net.

I awoke before dawn, disoriented, and turned to see a child's feet on the pillow beside my face. Light snores rose and fell through the room. My mind was churning.

In Havana, everyone hustled. The average income was around US$10 per month. Free education, health care, and basic foodstuffs were provided by the government—but not enough to survive. The nicest people, including those I considered real friends, constantly angled for foreign money. It was nothing personal, a matter of necessity. But after several months in Havana, I was exhausted from being worked over. Tired of being followed, catcalled, asked for help, offered help, and sold bicycles, cigars, informal tours, salsa lessons, and love. Nothing came for free in the city, not even friendship.

What would be expected of me in return for food and lodging?

I thought about the US$10 folded in the pocket of my jeans across the room. This family seemed poor even by Cuban standards. What I had wasn't much, but it could only help.

Then another thought tangled with that one. Would Misael take offense if I offered him cash—as if his kindness had monetary value? I didn't want to turn our human connection into a financial transaction. I decided to slip the bill under a pillow, where someone would find it after I'd left, but I couldn't reach my jeans without waking my bedmates. Then, once everyone was up, there seemed no way to do it subtly.

Misael walked me to the main road and waited with me for a Kombi out of town. I kept fretting over money. Was he waiting for me to offer him something for the family? Should I pull out the bill and see if he would accept?

In the end, I froze. When the truck came, I climbed aboard and waved goodbye.

———

I have stewed over this for years. Though no one asked for money—so unusual in Cuba—my US$10 might have eased their way a little. A small kindness in return for a large kindness. But I hesitated and clung to my dumb American money.

In the photo I snapped of Misael and Yadira, their faces looked gaunt. Yadira had prepared a special meal that night, probably spending more on ingredients than usual, and I had brought nothing to the table but my problems.

This moment has stayed with me. A confluence of beauty and shame, a treasured memory I don't like to think about. The time when I felt most in love with humanity and least in love with myself.

Now, thirteen years later, face to face with Misael Saez again, I find myself rambling, talking too much under his gaze. I feel awkward and exposed. It occurs to me, not for the first time, that maybe I don't deserve to tie up this loose end. Every traveler makes mistakes, but all that most people get to do is pay it forward, try to be more thoughtful toward others in the future.

"I can't believe you came here," he says, still staring like he's seen a ghost. "I thought you forgot me."

"You helped me out when I was having a hard time," I say, "and I wasn't in . . . the right state of mind to thank you properly."

He nods, and I cringe inwardly. Had he noticed when I left without a gesture of gratitude, without leaving him anything to give his wife for her trouble? Had they argued about it after I was gone? Now I have American money burning a proverbial hole in my pocket. I'm not going to miss the chance to make this right. "Do you have time for a drink?" I ask.

"*Está bién,*" he says. "*Un roncito.*" A little rum.

We pile into the rental car. Tabaco guides us to a bar at the edge of town—a tin trailer with a single outdoor table and umbrella in the middle of a paved lot. Kevin buys a bottle of Havana Club Añejo Especial and a round of beers. We're shy on glasses, so Tabaco uses a knife to saw an empty beer can in half and pours a shot into the makeshift cup.

"Cuban glassware," he says. Everyone laughs.

Though Kevin and Tabaco don't speak the same language, they're both so animated that they manage to entertain each other while Misael and I catch up.

"I can't believe you came back," he says again and again, touching his fist to his heart. "This is incredible."

I'm sorry to learn that he and Yadira have divorced and their marriage ended bitterly, but glad to hear he's coaching a high school volleyball team, a job he loves.

Misael tells me he's often wondered what became of my life. This surprises me, though it shouldn't. Why should our brief friendship have mattered only to me?

"You were very depressed when we met," he says. "You cried all the time." He runs his fingers over his face, miming tears. "Your mom was sick. What happened to her?"

I beam. This is where I get to tell him she's all right. That I nursed her through twelve hard months of chemo, and it worked. Thirteen years later, she's doing well.

We both get misty. Misael takes my hand and squeezes.

One bottle becomes two. Tabaco grows increasingly rambunctious, commandeering the trailer's tinny sound system and starting a small dance party in the paved lot. He yells to everyone who passes on foot, vehicle, or horse: "These crazy Americans came to find El Saez after thirteen years! Can you believe that?!"

Tabaco obviously relishes the attention he's getting from hanging out with foreigners in this untouristed town. Meanwhile, Misael remains steady and thoughtful, speaking only when he has something to say. They are a study in opposites, but their friendship also makes sense. A man of few words doesn't have to talk much with Tabaco around.

People come and go through the afternoon, including Misael's brother and nephew who pull up on a horse-drawn cart. We rent a room for the night, and in the evening, Tabaco invites everyone to an open-air bar on a muddy beach crowded with locals. There's eating and dancing and an unreasonable amount of rum.

I stay beside Misael all night, and we talk while the party swirls around us. Even drunk, he is the eye of a hurricane, his voice low and calm, and it's so clear why I clung to him, why his company grounded me when I felt dislodged from my life.

"People talk," he says, making a yapping mouth with his fingers. "People say all kinds of things. But as soon as you're out of sight, they forget. Not you."

This makes me feel so full.

I'd thought of this trip as my chance to settle a debt that was bothering my conscience. Like removing an old splinter. It was, in a way, a selfish agenda. I didn't expect this to mean so much to Misael. Money didn't seem like the right currency back then, and it still doesn't. What matters more is that I can show Misael the impact of his generosity on one person's life.

As a traveler, I often frame relationships in terms of gratitude. For hospitality, lessons learned, paths opened. But the exchange is reciprocal. To the people who stay put—especially in a place like Cuba where it's difficult for locals to leave—travelers are the outside world coming to town. We will not be forgotten, and our gestures and attitudes will be keenly observed by the people we meet. It's a huge responsibility.

On my way out of town the next day, I lay US$40 on Misael. The money isn't necessary—I'm sure of that now—but I imagine it will come in handy anyway. The moment is a little awkward, but not as bad as I fear.

"I'd like to give you this," I say. "You helped me back then. Now I can help you a little."

He protests mildly, but tucks the folded bills into his pocket with a shrug and a smile.

I leave understanding that what we've exchanged has nothing to do with cash; it's the shared certainty that neither will forget the other. Even if our paths never intersect again, we will always be friends.

Kevin climbs behind the wheel. I look back as we drive away. Misael Saez is standing in the road, one hand raised high over his head, palm open.

♍ ♍ ♍

Alia Volz is the author of the memoir Home Baked: My Mom, Marijuana, and the Stoning of San Francisco, *which was recently featured on NPR's* Fresh Air. *Her work appears in* The New York Times, Salon, Bon Appetit, *and* The Best American Essays. *Alia has crossed Spain on foot, seen Fidel Castro orate in a downpour, and made love at the feet of Easter Island's Moai. But she keeps rolling back to her hometown of San Francisco.*

Naomi Melati Bishop

ॐ ॐ ॐ

Stolen Tickets

Chasing truths and spreading ashes.

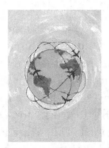

Dad created myths and lived them. He'd take me on three A.M. walks in strange cities and tell me wild stories about how he helped overthrow the Suharto regime; how he was blacklisted in Indonesia; how my mother's death when I was seven years old was a possible murder plotted by the regime, and that's why we had to sleep with a baseball bat under our pillow.

But recently, I learned this: Gordon, a.k.a. Dad, and his ex-girlfriend Uta, a countess and a model, traveled the world on stolen plane tickets. If it weren't for these stolen tickets and the journey they took him on, I wouldn't exist.

He told me about all of his adventures—including the crime of the stolen tickets—again and again like bedtime stories, though I'm aware that just because his self-fulfilling folk tales were vivid doesn't mean they were necessarily accurate. I gathered them from the memory bank he shared, as well as from the journals and photos he left behind.

I've spent the years since my father's death traveling across the world chasing truths about his life and spreading his ashes. That was his dying wish: for me to deliver him across oceans and continents—smack dab in the heart of every city, every beach, and every memory.

The stolen plane tickets arrived on a rainy summer evening in 1971, when a Black Panther showed up at his doorstep in Berkeley, drenched and desperate for a place to hide. A gun was tucked inside the sleeve of his leather jacket. Gordon invited him in for coffee and a joint.

"Can I crash here?" the Black Panther asked.

"Sure, man. You got money to chip in?" Gordon asked.

"I've got something better than money," the Black Panther said. He drew a lockbox from his wet backpack. Inside were sixty, ninety, maybe one hundred sets of blank airline tickets. "So-and-so's friend works for Qantas. She brought these home," he explained. "These are good for getting you anywhere in the world. You go to the airport and have the agent write out the ticket. One destination at a time. But you can't stay longer than three weeks. You have fun. You lose track of time. If that happens, tear up the first pack and start over with a fresh pack. Don't let anyone catch on. You see, these tickets are…."

"I catch your drift," Gordon said.

"Take as many as you'd like. But be careful, man, that's how folks end up having three babies in each continent."

Gordon smirked, snatched four blank ticket books, and built a makeshift bed for his new guest in the walk-in closet. He spun a globe he kept to watch where his finger would land—a nightly routine that calmed his frenetic thoughts.

"Let's run away," his girlfriend Uta said, shortly after my dad received the tickets. "Somewhere new. Somewhere far and exotic."

So, my father and Uta zigzagged across nations and time zones and cultures. Gordon's charm and Uta's regal beauty opened doors; together, they befriended royalty, politicos, artists, businessmen, shamans, and indigenous folks around the world. On the stolen tickets, they'd eventually hop to France, Italy, Mexico, Australia, Tahiti, Fiji, Nepal, Brazil, Afghanistan, Singapore, and Indonesia. At each destination, Gordon would buy a small souvenir and slip it into his pale green attaché case, which he eventually gave me.

At LAX in 1971—prepared for their first journey—my father let Uta do all of the talking while he hid. Uta wore a floor-length cream dress and hoop earrings. She spoke to the agents without hesitation. Her English, tinged with French and German overtones, made her seem worldly, and she was quick on her feet—handy traits for negotiating at international airports. Meanwhile, my father, with his long hair and blue eye shadow (which he wore almost daily), hid in a kiosk, sweating profusely, in a velvet bellbottomed tuxedo and cowboy boots, one gold and the other silver.

"The next flight to Paris is in six hours," the agent said, handing Uta two tickets.

"You're a sorceress," Gordon said to his partner. "Just like all the other fairytale witches from the Black Forest."

They made it through security without raising an eyebrow, and shared a high from the rush of not getting bagged. Onboard the plane, they ordered champagne and toasted, "To Utzarella and Gordonzolla."

Gordon added, "Don't things taste better when they're free?"

In Paris, they hitched a ride to Hotel Le Meurice to pay an unannounced visit to their mutual friend, Salvador Dalí, with whom they'd lived in an artist commune years prior.

"Ahh, it's *The Man Who Plans to Eat a Car!* Enter," Dalí said, twisting his wispy, gelled mustache into tiny knots. He was referring to the title of the collage book Gordon had made for Dalí: a pictorial story about a German auto enthusiast who planned to eat a car. It was still prominently displayed on Dalí's coffee table, its pages now browned from touch. "It is a masterpiece," Dalí said.

My father let Dalí in on the secret about the plane tickets.

"Go to Bali," Dalí said decisively. "There's magic there."

Dalí tore out some drawings and handed them to Gordon. "For you."

Gordon put the sketches in his pale green attaché case, wedged between the blank tickets.

Next stop: Kabul.

Afghanistan, at the time, was facing a wave of freedom—a golden era of modernity and democratic reform. Women attended universities (often in miniskirts) and worked for Parliament. Tourists flocked to Kabul, curious about the "mystic east" and lured by the beauty of the city's ancient sculptures, sprawling gardens, and surrounding snowcapped mountains.

Gordon and Uta followed the Silk Road and visited the Bamiyan Buddhas. They frequented Sigi's on Chicken Street to exchange ideas with fellow travelers. They bathed in the Kabul River. They slept in a large room on thick carpets, along with twenty or thirty other tourists. They made love in secret. Hedonistic hippies, freaks, heads, and other tourists came to Afghanistan for spiritual quests and adventure, or else to escape the humdrum of convention. Painted VW vans purred down the streets. Kabul was a destination on the infamous overland hippie trail, deemed the "Paris of Asia." Most people with stolen plane tickets ended up there. This fact made Uta nervous.

"We should leave," Uta urged. "We'll get caught."

"Relax," Gordon said. "We won't."

Gordon was having fun. He'd lost track of time. He grew a beard and walked around barefoot until the soles of his feet grew tough, like elephant hide. He took mescaline and wrote poetry under the pen name Dubjinsky Barefoot. He haggled at the market and bought a knife inlaid with mother of pearl. He wrote postcards that he never sent—no money for stamps. He picked fights with Uta about nothing in particular. Three weeks had ticked along. It was time to board the plane again. Just as they were heading for the airport, the ground shook. A damaging earthquake. The northern region was in ruins. Air travel was suspended.

Soon after, they flew to India. In their hotel in New Delhi, the phone rang. It was the airline agency. "Madame, you'd better come into the office. There's a problem with your book of tickets."

Uta's voice shook. "I want to leave New Delhi now." Her throat felt tight.

"Yes, Madame, but you must first come into the office." The agent's tone intensified and became threatening.

"They're on to us," Uta told Gordon.

They shredded the first ticket book and headed to the airport. With frantic fingers, Gordon handed Uta the unused tickets. She approached the counter. Behind the desk where the agent stood was a poster that read:

DO NOT ACCEPT ANY STOLEN PLANE TICKETS WRITTEN OUT AT QANTAS IN SAN FRANCISCO ON 10 MAY 1971.

That was exactly what was written on their tickets. Uta willed herself to appear calmer, more regal.

"I'm sorry, Madame," the agent said. "I cannot issue you this ticket. You'll have to go to our office in New Delhi."

"Please, sir," Uta begged. "There's a flight to Bali in one hour. I have some dignitaries I must meet."

The man's face softened. He placed the tickets on the counter.

Uta and my father got through security. At customs, someone tapped Uta on the shoulder. Her heart fell to her knees. "Madame, you forgot your hand luggage," a stranger said.

Phew.

On the flight, as they were celebrating the close encounter over wine, the captain announced: "Ladies and gentlemen, please prepare for landing. We are making an unscheduled stop in Mumbai."

"The plane is landing so they can arrest us," my father said, certain.

They rehearsed what they'd say to the officers. Escape routes mapped in their mind. Each magnified the other's anxiety. They snapped their eyes shut as they landed.

It was just a stop for fuel.

According to my father's journals, they happened to land in Bali on *Kuningan*, a day marked by ancestral spirits descending from the heavens.

Whenever someone would ask his profession, Gordon would say something outlandish with a serious face, like, "I'm a traveling Merkin salesman—a booming business of vaginal wigs." Most of the time, they believed him. By this point, they'd burned through the stacks of stolen tickets the Black Panther had gifted them. His mother wired him a monthly stipend, but he made the bulk of his cash by grifting at the airport bars, selling language pills to people intrigued by how many languages he pretended to speak. "Early stages of a test conducted by the CIA," he'd say. "You see, when God knocked down the Tower of Babel, he divided our tongues. Turns out, all those languages are still encoded in our DNA."

"Where can I—?"

"It's a closed experiment," he'd say. "I shouldn't have told you." And somehow, an extra bottle (of sugar pills) would happen to be in his pocket. A handshake and a few hundred dollars would be exchanged.

Gordon and Uta rented a motorcycle. They bought traditional sarongs. Uta tucked a red hibiscus behind her left ear. They went to trance dances where villagers would stab their bare chests with steel blades and, protected by black magic, remain unscathed. They attended cremations and ceremonies, slaughterings, exorcisms, and weeklong meditations. They fought and made love in the dense jungle that clung to the hillsides, along the serpentine streets, on rice paddies, near ancestral temples, and beneath sacred Banyan trees.

As their spiritual search deepened, their paths diverged. Uta was content to stay in Bali. Gordon was getting antsy; he craved a change of pace. They fought more, about trivial things like the way the other's hair was parted.

"Find yourself a patient Javanese," Uta said to Gordon, her tone bittersweet. "I'm not your girl anymore."

They made love one last time. Sad but resolute, in 1973, he left her in Bali with her new Balinese boyfriend, in the land of Gods. He found a map and let his fingers decide his next steps: *Special Region of Yogyakarta*, an ancient city on the Indonesian island of Java.

In 1974, Gordon found himself in the midst of Indonesia's Independence Day parade in Yogyakarta. He was sur-rounded by thousands of villagers who gaped at him from afar, who inched closer to touch his white skin or else gasped as they watched him eat a chicken skewer with his left hand, the devil's hand.

A group of dancers unfolded their limbs like petals. Gamelan music vibrated. Gongs sounded. Skinny horses and wizened men sat lazily in parked pedicabs, bare and filthy feet peeking out from batik sarongs. Teenagers jammed to Bob Dylan. Sultans were hoisted above the crowd in gilded carriages. People shouted, "*Merdeka!*" Independence!

Gordon heard a laugh, like wind chimes. He followed the sound to a woman with smiling red-stained lips in a hip-hug-ging minidress—a sight far too modern and incongruous in a city renowned as the heart of traditional Javanese culture, where many women, including the one accompanying her, resisted Western influence by continuing to wear classic batik sarongs and lace blouses.

A purple orchid was pinned to the brazenly dressed woman's hair. Her cheekbones were high; she was a ghost of a woman whose force was so overpowering that looking at her turned him on, but also kind of hurt him. She was strolling arm-in-arm with another woman who was carrying a baby in a batik sling.

They walked toward each other, standing inches apart for the few moments their paths intersected. Sweat beads trailed Gordon's brows. His hands shook. She turned her gaze toward him. Their eyes locked. She blushed, but didn't look away. The loquacious and never shy Gordon stood transfixed and mute as they flirted with their eyes for pregnant minutes. All of the pick-up lines he'd ever used, and some he hadn't, flashed through his mind, but none seemed appropriate, especially after translating them into his far-from-fluent Indonesian. When he got up the nerve to introduce himself, he was so tongue-tied he couldn't speak. Instead, he went to buy loose cigarettes at a nearby kiosk. From the corner of his eye, he saw her leaving the parade. He sped after her, elbowing passersby, but she vanished into the crowd.

For the next thirty-four days, Gordon waited where his roommate Jono thought he'd seen her, atop the highest perch of Taman Sari castle, now ruins, his legs and binoculars dangling high above Yogyakarta's bustling bird market.

Word spread about the foreigner in the watchtower looking for love. Curious kids joined him. Others came and brought him daily offerings of magic love potions made of reptile blood and minced ginger, which he drank, happily and hopefully. Several times he thought he saw her, mounted his bike, and peddled off in hot pursuit with his heart thumping a mile a minute, only to find out it was someone else.

Rainy season came and left. It was 1975, and my father had been in Yogyakarta for two years, roughly four years since his trip with Uta had first begun. He walked along a quiet lane during sunset; his head hung low. His thoughts wandered to life in New York City. His parents had offered to pay for the ten-thousand-mile journey home. Penniless and heartbroken, he weighed this option. He had a yen for a hot dog from

Gray's Papaya, a cheesecake from Carnegie Deli, a midnight subway ride.

Gordon looked up. At that moment he spotted a familiar woman. He took out his binoculars. To his astonishment, it was the other woman from the parade who was accompanying his love, with the same baby slung onto her hip—only now doubled in size. He ran up the staircase, panting. The woman gasped; a look of shock struck her lips, which quickly morphed into a smile.

"You're that foreigner from the *Merdeka* parade," she said immediately.

Gordon was surprised she remembered. This gave him a boost.

"We thought you were just passing through, like most white guys, *bules*," she said.

"Please," Gordon begged, lapsing into his unpolished way, "gimme her address."

"I can't," she said. But then she took out a pencil and a pink receipt and began to scribble. "Here."

"NANIES," it read.

"If you love her enough, you'll find her."

He liked this game.

Gordon and Nanies's auspicious wedding date was set by local Javanese mystics.

Uta received word of Gordon's impending marriage and flew from Bali to halt the wedding. She appeared as a tall, blond apparition in a lemon sundress. As soon as Gordon saw her, he felt the deep glow of old friendship. When Uta met his new bride—a princess and dancer from the royal court— she surrendered. She found Nanies's beauty to be poetic and nonthreatening—the rare kind of beauty that made you want to look more like yourself than like her. Uta saw how he guarded Nanies like treasure. He'd grown up, moved on. He'd even cut his hair.

"Nanies centers me in my deepest soul," he told Uta. "She gives balance to my tight-roping spirits way up there in the

rainbow-filled sky of my universal being. She turns my shitty
aspects into gold." Seeing Nanies and Uta together in juxtaposition—contrasting and complementary—was almost a vision-
ary experience for Gordon: two hemispheres of his heart, two
worlds, peacefully colliding.

Nanies, with her Javanese celestial-like peace, seemed a
perfect match to temper Gordon's volatility. What more did
Uta really want for her great love than to wish him well? It
was time for her to leave Indonesia, to close this chapter and
travel home—overland through Asia and Europe—back to
Paris. Visions of them floating hand-in-hand in the Red Sea
looped in her mind. There'd be no more Unzarella. No more
Gordonzolla. Uta exited the scene.

But she never left the scene entirely. When I was a teenager—
motherless—Dad flew me transatlantic to visit her twice a
year. He wanted me to taste mother love. He said Uta was
his gift to me, that without her I probably wouldn't exist.
She taught me how to make gazpacho, how to apply lipstick
expertly, how to retain my mystery. To this day, Uta is still
the person I call when I'm feeling down, because I know she
will console me.

I visited her in 2007 at her home in Ibiza, Spain. Dad had
died six months earlier, on the thirty-second anniversary of
his and Nanies's wedding day.

"I have something for you," I said, reaching into Dad's pale
green attaché case, where he used to keep his ticket books,
long used up, and Dalí's drawings, now lost. "His ashes. I
want you to have some."

Before I said another word, Uta reached across the table,
swiped the baggie from me, and dunked her finger inside.
She lifted her dusty finger to her lips and sucked on it.

"Now he's inside me. He'll never leave me," she said.

I laughed. "Cancer stole his eye, his breast, and his leg.
But he still came to you. Flew here. You were his final
destination."

"He was haunted and charmed," she said. "Destiny can play dirty tricks."

We ate paella and looked out at the Mediterranean Sea twinkling and fading in the evening sky.

"I can't taste the food," Uta said. "I still taste him. He doesn't want to leave."

He'll never have to leave. Even death wouldn't stop my father from traveling. I've now scattered his ashes across thirty-nine countries—and counting. It was his wish, but it has also been my way of immortalizing him, so I could keep him close to me and minimize the grief of losing him. As long as I had his ashes, I felt safe.

But recently I was on a family holiday in Costa Rica with my partner and my seven-month-old baby. My daughter was playing and cooing in her tent under a vast canopy of palm trees. My lover was chanting mantras to a Hindu god. I went for a swim, and there was nobody for as far as the eye could see. As I rose from the water, a dozen horses came out of nowhere, galloping across the sand, zigzagging past us on the deserted beach at dusk. It was a moment so beautiful, I wanted to spread my father's ashes.

Back on the sand, I fumbled in my purse for the tiny jar, but realized I'd left them behind this time. It felt strange to not engage in this ritual, to not be connected with my father at every meaningful moment. All at once, I was overcome by a vast sense of freedom. I looked at my daughter and found him immortalized in the wild twinkle of her eye, in the horizons that loom in mine.

Now, we are his around-the-world plane tickets.

♫ ♫ ♫

Naomi Melati Bishop was born in Indonesia to odd soul mates—a Javanese priyayi *(princess) and a quixotic activist dad from NYC—and moved to NYC when she was eleven. Naomi earned her MFA at NYU's Graduate Creative Writing Program and works as a writer, editor, and teacher. She's currently at work on her first book, a memoir about being a new mother who, stuck at home during a pandemic and grieving the loss of her parents, finds solace in telling her daughter stories about her mysterious origins, her search for love and identity, and her inheritance of worldwide adventures.*

෴ ෴ ෴

Wade in the Water

Following the hidden meanings of spirituals.

*G*azing out over an uneven checkerboard of green marshes and high-tide swells, I feel quiet and grounded. Flecks of Kelly-green wild grasses and golden-brown cattails enliven ribbons of slate-blue water. The tidal wetlands of Blackwater National Wildlife Refuge off Maryland's Chesapeake Bay hold secrets.

Blackwater is still. I glide on a watercolor palette in the setting sun, dipping my paddle into a patchwork sea of peony pinks, magentas, and dusky blues. The bow of my boat cuts through a decrescendo of gold gouache ripples. Everything is moving, yet everything has stopped. It could be 1855.

A great blue heron emits a series of croaking cries. But the past, murkier than the marshland, cries louder. The seasons and tides flow in reverse, past the marches of the 1960s, the Jim Crow laws of the 1920s, the Civil War of the 1860s—all the way back to about 1820, when a baby named Araminta Ross was born with a destiny none could have foreseen.

Wade in the water
Wade in the water, children
Wade in the water
God's gonna trouble the water

As I rock on the water and gaze at the low, late-August sun, my mind wanders the history of this coastal maze. One hundred sixty years ago, Harriet Tubman plied these waters as she led her people to liberty. Born in 1820 as Araminta Ross, enslaved off the Chesapeake Bay in Dorchester County, Maryland, she eventually took her freedom by slipping across the Mason-Dixon line. Known as the "Moses of her people," Tubman returned to the Eastern Shore of Maryland more than fifteen times to lead others to liberation. Now, these waters and woods bear her name.

Perhaps it was a day like this humid summer one that envelops me with a deafening orchestra of cicadas when, with sweat beading on her brow and breath bursting from her lungs, Harriet Tubman parted a curtain of cattails, making her move for freedom. Perhaps the sky was an expansive yet almost-touchable purple-pink when she asserted her humanity and her personhood. Perhaps, like now, a hot red sun hung low in the sky on the day when she escaped slavery forever.

Who's that young girl dressed in red?
Wade in the water
Must be the children that Moses led
God's gonna trouble the water

One-quarter of my own family line comes from St. Mary's County, about twenty miles from here as the crow flies across the warm, muddy-brown Chesapeake Bay. For the past ten years, I have spent considerable time researching my family tree. For all the challenges that normally come from this pursuit, it's doubly difficult because my ancestors were enslaved.

For many, it's a source of joy to read the stories of one's people, to see the heirlooms, to feel the strength of forebears. But while I feel kinship and pride, I am disheartened to see how little information exists. I feel a gnawing in my stomach when I see the birthdates, places, people, and families that were erased, forgotten, or never recorded. Such documentation was deemed unimportant for people who, treated like machinery, powered the economic engine of the early United States.

The little information I have found about my ancestors has led me to an estimated birth year here or a detail there. Enslavement clung to the few recorded details of their lives: Name, Race, Potential cause of death, Post-Civil War job or occupation. In antebellum coastal Maryland, an ancestor of mine was a sharecropper, another an oysterman—industries that re-hung the shadows of slavery for Black Americans.

With little information, it's hard to know what to say about the people who came before us. That's the brilliance of those who benefitted from and perpetrated the trade of enslaved peoples. Enslavement isn't just about the body; it's about attempting to remove control of the mind by subjugating stories, narrative, culture, faith, family.

With little information, we do what we can to honor their lives.

> *See that band all dressed in white?*
> *God's gonna trouble the water*
> *It looks like a band of the Israelites*
> *God's gonna trouble the water*

Spirituals such as "Wade in the Water" are believed to have served as coded instructions to help people navigate the Underground Railroad and safely reach freedom in the North. Another spiritual, "Follow the Drinking Gourd," likens the gourds used by enslaved persons for drinking water to the Big Dipper, and was used as another code to instruct freedom seekers to follow the Big Dipper, which points to the North Star.

The calm wetland waters cradled these freedom seekers—it washed away their tracks, diluted hounds' abilities to catch their scent, and provided them a map as they headed north. The ever-present water was there to cleanse sweat from their brows as they laboriously navigated the coast. In a time of life or death, maybe they looked over the waters as I do—the last of the sunlight dipping below the horizon—and felt a moment of calm. Maybe the coolness of the water kept them awake and alert as they slipped noiselessly through the tides and marsh grasses.

When they needed strength to keep going, this abundant sanctuary was rich with plant and animal life that provided them with nourishment—just as the spirituals of their ancestors gave them wisdom.

Follow the drinkin' gourd
For the old man is comin' just to carry you to freedom
Follow the drinkin' gourd
When the sun comes back, and the first quail calls
Follow the drinkin' gourd

Perhaps it was a warm spring South Carolina night in May 1862 when the water beckoned with the promise of safety and serenity to Robert Smalls, an enslaved man in South Carolina and an ancestor of mine. Perhaps he remembered the lyrics to these spirituals that early morning when the Confederate soldiers took shore leave from the ship *The Planter*, leaving Smalls and several others to consider the unthinkable.

It was a tremendous risk to even consider escape, let alone actually attempt it. If he failed, Smalls would face violent, if not deadly, punishment. But if he succeeded....

Acting quickly, twenty-two-year-old Smalls (a vessels expert wheelman) donned a Confederate uniform, commandeered *The Planter,* and sailed out into the sea, directly toward the Union blockade. Detection and death were probable, but the chance of freedom was palpable to Smalls.

> *Well the riverbank makes a mighty good road*
> *Dead trees will show you the way*
> *Left foot, peg foot, travelin' on*
> *Follow the drinkin' gourd*

Water surrounds. Even the breeze here is heavy with water. Suspended in the thick and humid air, it quenches the verdant coastal forests. Hugging the shoreline, it licks the sandy brink. Here, in this clammy, subtropical climate, it supports life.

On the other side of the world, in what is now modern-day Benin and Nigeria, practitioners of the Yoruba religion believe in Oshun, a goddess of the sweet waters and love, and the benevolent protector of the poor and needy. In West, Central, and Southern Africa, "Mami Wata," or "Mother Water," appears in a variety of roles in an equally wide range of narratives. Her worship is well-documented not only in Africa, but also in the African diaspora, particularly in the Americas and Caribbean. Mentions of her likeness (she is depicted as a mermaid) trace the paths of former slave routes.

> *For the old man is waiting to carry you to freedom*
> *Follow the drinkin' gourd*
> *Well the river ends, between two hills*
> *Follow the drinkin' gourd*

Benin, West Africa: the epicenter of the slave trade. At its heart, the Road of No Return: a dusty, red road that led to the Atlantic Ocean where, chained together by the six hundred, men, women, and children boarded ships, never to be seen again. The last ship set sail in 1860.

The Middle Passage: For every one hundred enslaved people who reached the "New World," around forty died. So many Black Americans' roots are planted in the clay-red soil, including my own.

After capturing their victims in West Africa, Dahomey raiders conducted a forced ceremony for the newly enslaved persons—a ceremony that symbolized the beginning of their forgetting. Seven to nine times, Dahomey raiders directed enslaved men and women to circle around *L'Arbre de L'Oubli*—The Tree of Forgetting. Their enslavement began with the loss of what came before: Their homes. Their culture. Their family. Their roots. Themselves.

> *There's another river on the other side*
> *Follow the drinkin' gourd*
> *For the old man is waiting to carry you to freedom*
> *Follow the drinkin' gourd*

During the raids, there were those who sought safety on the water.

In the small village of Ganvie, a community that still thrives today, thatched homes and businesses mounted on stilts are perched on top of the brown, brackish water. On Lake Nokoué, just outside of Benin's capital of Cotonou, this village has stood and grown since its inception hundreds of years ago. Life runs suspended above the water. Mile-long stretches of intricate netting allow residents to farm fish, while centralized water filtration systems provide potable water fetched daily by families in canoes throughout the village. Schools, places of business, and markets stand alongside people's homes.

The community was the idea of the Tofinu tribe's king. To avoid being captured and sold into slavery to the Portuguese by Dahomey raiders, the king took his people to the water and built a self-sustaining home over the lake. Although the physical barriers keeping them safe were few, Dahomey religious practices and customs held that a people

who lived on the water could not be attacked. And so, water
kept the Tofinu safe.

When Israel was in Egypt's land
Let my people go
Oppress'd so hard they could not stand
Let my people go

Go down, Moses
Way down in Egypt's land
Tell old Pharaoh
Let my people go

By the middle of the eighteenth century, acres upon acres
of land in Georgia and South Carolina Low Country, as well
as the Sea Islands, had been turned into rice fields. Wealthy
plantation owners placed farmers taken from the "Rice
Coast" of Africa onto these islands to cultivate fields in unfa-
vorable conditions. Hacking through cores of tall, scraggly
deciduous trees, mantles of arching and bowing palms, and
bleached, gracefully gnarled driftwood, these expert West
African cultivators transformed the landscape into fertile
rice fields. Through back-breaking labor and hellish living
conditions, they made a fortune for the few people in power:
An enslaved person growing rice could generate more than
six times his or her original purchase price in just one year.

These Gullah communities still live on South Carolina's
coastal plains and Sea Islands. They were the home of
Smalls's mother Lydia, until she was taken at nine years old.
Three of my four family lines also grow from here, in coastal
South Carolina.

Here on the Sea Islands, the water cradled the West African farmers in a sacred semi-isolation. As malaria and yellow
fever spread, non-Africans often left the rice fields (with
maybe one or two people left behind during the spring and

summer months). Despite the heavy toll on the community with many lost to these diseases, the region and the people were culturally freer and able to create and maintain some sense of their collective heritage.

They had the freedom to dictate a portion of how they would live their lives and tell their stories. In defiance of the ceremony of *L'Arbre de L'Oubli*, of their capture, and their separation from their family and home, they joined those around them and created a new culture from many.

Despite being uprooted from their homes, they thrived where they were planted.

> *Well, where the great big river meets the little river*
> *Follow the drinkin' gourd*
> *The old man is waiting to carry you to freedom*
> *Follow the drinkin' gourd*

At two A.M., Smalls put on the straw hat of the vessel's captain, then stopped at a wharf to pick up his wife and children as well as several others.

At 3:25 A.M., *The Planter* surged forward, slicing through Atlantic waters. Passing by other Confederate ships, Smalls flashed the correct naval signals to gain safe passage through the fleet that was tightly protecting Charleston and Sumter. It was just dark enough that he was mistaken several times for the captain of the ship.

It was only once *The Planter* was out of range, as the sun began to rise in the sky, that he dared hoist a bedsheet brought on board by his wife. I imagine that there was barely enough light for Union ships to see the white flag, held high above a ship full of people fleeing slavery.

I imagine how the sense of relief, the weight of what some called a foolhardy escape, and his family's newfound freedom came crashing down on him as the clear blue South Carolina waters surrounded Smalls near the Union blockade. Against all odds, he had found an oasis of security next to a hotbed of hostility. His pulse pounding in his ears must have deafened the commotion around him. The scene unfolding before his eyes must have moved in slow motion, as if he were underwater. He must have felt as if he were watching himself in an undeniably surreal situation. *Is it real? Is it happening? Are we safe?*

For generations, my family has named children after Robert in honor of his bravery, sagacity, and spirit. Although a mere seven miles of turquoise ocean lay between him and life as a free man, it must have felt to him and those on board like the length of the Atlantic.

For the old man is waiting to carry you to freedom
Follow the drinkin' gourd
For the old man is waiting just to carry you to freedom
If you follow the drinkin' gourd

The wisdom of these lyrics urging my people to stay close to the water is rooted in something older and stronger than the thousands of vessels, unimaginable manpower, and unmistakable greed that created and sustained the Transatlantic slave trade. Enslavement was meant to define and overpower my people, but they resisted. Like the water that surrounded them, they carried on with strength, stalwart consistency, and beauty.

I think of Robert Smalls, known as "The Gullah Statesman" for his pride in the heritage of the West African people who thrived on the coastal plains and Sea Islands. Even while under his former masters' command, he wisely learned to navigate these coastal waters. He waited until the clear bright Atlantic was ready to extend the hand of freedom. When the water called, he was ready.

I think of Harriet Tubman. She planned, plotted, laughed, cried, loved, succeeded, failed, and had virtues and vices—she *lived* as a human being. To take her freedom, Harriet, a new Moses, parted the waters not with a rod or staff, but with the deliberate footsteps of a woman bound for the Promised Land on the other side of the Chesapeake Bay.

I think of *L'Arbre de L'Oubli,* the Dahomey raiders, the perilous Middle Passage across the Atlantic, the subjugation of generations of people, the loss, the pain, the fear, and finally—the survival. The remembrance. The wisdom that was passed down, against all odds.

Because of those who came before, I'm here to remember, to share their stories and to proudly live my own.

As I sit in my boat watching the last drops of golden day slip beyond an inky horizon, I follow the people—my people—who came before me, and wade in the water.

> *If you don't believe I've been redeemed*
> *God's gonna trouble the water*
> *Just follow me down to the Jordan's stream*
> *God's gonna trouble the water*

      ❧ ❧ ❧

Alexandria Scott is a writer, educator, and community advocate who helps readers learn about travel, history, language, culture, and policy through the lens of multicultural and anti-bias education. She also enjoys learning and writing about sustainability, parenthood, art, education, and the outdoors. A Baltimore native, she now lives in the Washington, DC area with her husband and three children.

ॐ ॐ ॐ

Headlights

There was danger, even in the presence of angels.

February is not the ideal time for a road trip to northern France, but the moodiness of the sea, wind, and sky appeals to a certain breed of loner like me, drawn to the echoing voids of the off-season. Coastal Normandy is famous for its dramatic weather, and in winter, it grows wilder still, with thrashing winds and squalls of frozen sleet that churn up from the English Channel. The region is a sweep of battlegrounds and fortified castles, stone-cold Norman abbeys, and craggy ports that have hosted centuries of departing and returning soldiers. Here, God and war forge their strange alliance, as they often do, and the backdrop of tempests, tides, and occasional shards of sunlight render it fertile ground for ghosts and their keepers.

I had endeavored to Mont St. Michel to seek some perfect solitude. One night was all I could spare for a brief reconciliation between me and my universe, an instant quelling of the racing brain. I had always wanted to spend a night in

the village beneath the monastery, and the dead of winter
seemed an ideal time to do it—with the theatrical weather
but without swarms of visitors filing into the one narrow
street. I hoped, just for a spell, to experience the abbey as the
pilgrims had, in this place that brings such wonder to the eye
that only heavenly devotion and fear of hell could have con-
ceived it. More than a thousand years ago, men had achieved
the near impossible and built a church atop a granite rock in
the middle of a bay slashed by monster tides and some of the
fiercest currents on earth.

To get there, let alone ferry construction materials on their
backs, meant to brave a racing sea, quicksand, wind, and fog.
Later, pilgrims were obliged to wait for low tide to cross over
to Mont St. Michel, but there was always risk, one the faithful
were willing to take. By the time they arrived to commune
in silence with the resident monks, they had already weeded
themselves out and proven their piety along with their mettle.

I suppose I sought some clue of the divine here, as well. In
France, I often venture into the dusky wombs of cathedrals,
basilicas, and rural parishes. While inside these limestone
temples, I look for proof of the Almighty (signs, anyway) and
the wisdom of saints. In Europe, crosses loom over every village, admonishing me with very little subtlety of what I can
never really abandon. I'm a committed former Catholic, but
the church I was born into and raised in still whispers to me
daily. It is a firm, plaintive voice that offers one truth: *This is
who you are.*

I'm not brave enough to have renounced my religion
outright. Instead, I chucked it aside. Sunday school did an
excellent job of teaching me everything and everyone I was
meant to fear. But not long after my confirmation, I began to
crave adventure with boys—a definite no-no with the nuns.
Soon word sunk in that women were outcasts in the church
and the Pope was O.K. with that. Eventually, I learned that
some of the priests in my native Boston might be criminals.
I slipped away, stopped going to mass. All that I absorbed

from catechism—guilt, sin, purgatory, mercy, the promise of heaven and intense dread of the alternative—still unwittingly shapes my life.

Most of the time when I enter a church, once I cross myself at the holy water font, the outline of faith emerges, as if this ancient gesture tracing out a crucifix on my head and chest offers entry not just to a place of worship but also to comfort and certainty. When I'm in a pew, the sacred space above me intuits my secrets, listens to and forgives them all. For what if not salvation would the ancients construct these elaborate structures, embellish them with statuary and stories told in colored glass? It is safer to believe, and in a church, I do.

And then, it dissipates as soon as I exit from sanctuary to sunlight. These bursts of affinity with something ancient and vast bring not exactly euphoria, but calm. We mortals are not the most important force on earth, so I can get over myself already. Maybe, at Mont St. Michel, with its near miraculous backstory, I'd again find that holy, ethereal sunbeam I never stop chasing. All I needed was a few minutes.

I parked my car and took the bus along the causeway. The last time I had visited, it was July, two decades ago. Then, I wore a tank top, and a water bottle sloshed around my purse. The heat had been severe, and I trekked barefoot across the tidal flats, sun baking my back, flip-flops in hand. It was suffocatingly, grotesquely crowded, and all of us tourists gazed up hopefully at the monastery, as if vying for a gulp of oxygen. And there he was: Archangel Michael, the prince of them all, commander of God's army and Catholicism's literal angel of death. He descends in our final hour to assist the dying and escort us to heaven as long as we proclaim our faith. It was he, during a visitation in 706, who told the local bishop "to build here and build high." His gold figure crowns the spire of Mont St. Michel, and on that sunny day, his wings and raised sword seemed to throw sparks into the sky.

I was surprised when the bus left me a fair distance from the bottom of the hill and the village—it was supposed to stop right at the foot of town. But the stormy February weather had made a mess of things, and the approach was a massive construction zone. Bulldozers and Bobcats were scattered beside the path, as were orange plastic ribbons that formed makeshift do-not-cross fences. It was, I learned, the home stretch for the colossal reclamation project that would return the sea to the Bay of Mont St. Michel, which had been partially silted over by centuries of agricultural development.

The currents, though, were unchanged: still erratic and still deadly. High tide can rise up to forty-five feet, and water sweeps in at an astonishing two hundred feet per minute. Occasionally a video pops up on YouTube of fools who try to beat the sea, fail, and get rescued by helicopter. Also, periodically some deluded danger junkie wanders into the quicksand—there is still quicksand, too—and must be pulled to safety.

The street that strained to accommodate half a million tourists a year was hushed with the absence of people. I climbed to the abbey and walked around the monastery and the Merveille—the church—stopping at the cloister lined with boxwoods and tidy colonnaded *allées*, a green respite on this grim day. From here was a view up the Norman and down the Breton coasts and surrounding it all, the sea. It was gray and thick as wet cement while the sky bore the whites of drifting snow.

I wandered through the chambers and chapels, the vacant assembly rooms and grand halls that bore no reminders of their bustling pasts. I stood at altars and under crosses, friezes and seawater-green stained-glass windows. I gazed up at Gothic choirs, vaults, and across to fireplaces, crucifixes, and the gold-cloaked figure of Notre-Dame-du-Mont-Tombe. But I struggled to feel the presence of a deity in these rooms. The best I could do was reflect on the ingenuity of the men who believed in one so strongly they carried boulders across this godforsaken landscape, hoisted it up, and erected a monument in tribute. I yearned to experience this strength of conviction but all I could do was admire theirs. Here, in the emptiness of this medieval abbey, I felt strangely empty, too. I couldn't even summon a prayer to murmur.

After dinner, darkness crept into the village while the rain dissipated into drizzle, then mist, and at last a cold, clear night. Spotlights replaced daylight, and the building was transformed. From a mottled edifice coated with lichen, tarnish, and rain, it turned pale and fortress-like, stained by shadow from sconces affixed to the façade. The turrets, covered in charcoal slate, had receded into blackness. I descended to the bottom of the village so I could look up at the structure again.

There, perched on the tip of the great spire, was Saint Michael the Archangel, so airborne he seemed to have just touched down. Behind and above him, clouds leaped across the disk of what was now almost a full moon. The light shone on the sword that pierced the sky, and his wings spread in both directions. Warmth seeped honey-like over me. I stared and stared. It—he—was spectacular, so high, so permanent, so patient, and somehow powerful. I could not look away, not until my neck started to ache.

Here, from below, I understood that on this island, faith was proportional to distance. Its power was in the ever-fluid movement of sky over weather over water over stone. The pilgrims must have shared my wonder, exhausted their supply of adjectives and exclamations, even if many met a merciless end on their way here. They ventured to this desolate place with a belief so vast only isolation could accommodate it. Here, now, was the moment I had come for, the elusive crucible of trust and awe and relief. *This is who you are.* And right then I believed. The simplicity of my certitude caught me in the throat.

At four the next morning, I gathered my clothes from the heating rack and woke the desk clerk to confirm with her the special off-hours bus I'd ordered to take me to the parking lot. I had a meeting in Burgundy at two P.M., and it was easily an eight-hour drive. "It is waiting for you," she said.

The rain had returned, hammering, and the structure on the hill that had choked me up hours earlier had slipped behind the gloom. My epiphany about the divine, too, got stuffed back in my travel bag. There was one lonely sound above the wind: my rubber boots clomping on the path down to the landing area. There was no bus. But given that the day before I had to get off and walk a couple hundred yards to the village because of rain and construction, I assumed that today would call for a similar contingency. So I stepped off the road, switched on my iPhone flashlight, and took what I believed was the same parallel walkway toward the place I'd been deposited the prior afternoon.

I walked with speed and purpose, anticipating the relief I would encounter when I reached the bus and then, my car. Grit scraped the wheels of my bag, splashing mud on me as I proceeded. All at once, the trek seemed too far and too long. There was no bus, no turnaround, no clearing. There were no Bobcats or bulldozers. Only wind, sleet, and desolation.

And suddenly, there was a proliferation of warning signs that alarmed me: IT IS **EXTREMELY DANGEROUS** TO VENTURE ALONE INTO THE BAY INCLUDING IMMEDIATELY CLOSE TO MONT SAINT-MICHEL. Passing minutes, then a half hour, leeched my optimism until it hung emptily about me. My parka had absorbed many times its weight in rain and pressed upon my shoulders. The iPhone formed only a wan pool of light before me. I could not discern how close I might be to the water, the tides, blackout. On the bright side, my rubber boots, high and heavy, clutched and warmed everything south of my knees as if they were sentient beings. They seemed to be sacrificing their lives for the integrity of my ankles and feet, and I loved them with all my might.

"Good boots," I cooed, as if they might answer back.

But they were leading me nowhere. I stopped. Mercifully, I still had cell service, so I dialed the hotel. "Where's the bus?" I asked. Panic scraped my windpipe.

"It's right at the bottom," she said.

"But it wasn't there!"

"He probably turned around when he didn't see you."

"I took a wrong turn," I said. The call cut off with an echo of sheer hopelessness.

It seemed absurd to be lost only yards from the third most popular tourist attraction in France. I walked and walked, disconsolate and captive on the road that had no visible beginning or end, composing my obituary. *A mother of two*, it would read, *vanished in the quicksand of Mont St. Michel*. Not embarrassing, exactly. Like a snakebite or a failed rip cord, it was an adventurer's demise. But I was a traveler, not a daredevil. Exploring is great, but danger is for fools.

Fools like me.

It didn't seem appropriate to appeal to the Almighty, whose existence I had pondered and doubted not six hours earlier, so I reluctantly turned to look for Archangel Michael on the spire. But he was invisible, shrouded under the veil of winter and night. Maybe that was a good thing. God's avenger was also the angel of death.

It was so frighteningly dark. I heard the lapping of water and the drone of rainfall. I set forth again. The wind swept around me, forming icy walls that I walked right through, emerging colder and wetter than before. I pictured my husband, my children, our universe that was miniscule compared to this pitiless place. I craved the sanity of my morning routine: coffee, toast. Life.

And then, lights. Small, low ones seeping through the pearly curtain of vapor to form an incandescent glow. They approached me from straight ahead. The car pulled up and someone reached across to open the door.

I never saw him clearly. Blue eyes or brown, pale complexion or ruddy—I haven't a clue. But I remember the grayish spikes of his hair and the sharp contours of his profile, both outlined from the glare of his car's headlights, which froze amidst the wall of rain and bounced back through the windshield with the potency of a ten-watt bulb. His voice was soothing, not quite caffeinated, and very annoyed. It must have been alarming to see my drenched figure shuffling in the inky pre-dawn and then, for this wretched human to take a seat in his car.

"Oh my God," I cried, "I…."

"What in God's name are you doing out here?" he said.

"I'm lost and I…."

"*Au nom de Dieu*," he said. "This is incredibly dangerous!"

"I couldn't find the bus," I sniffed.

"You cannot imagine how crazy this is," he said.

"It was an accident," I said.

"Didn't you see the warning signs?" he asked. He shook his head again and again.

"I did but it was too late," I said.

"You are very lucky, Madame," he said, and as he spoke, his voice shifted from reproachful to kind.

Lucky.

He drove to a well-lit turnaround and stopped the car. I should have passed directly through this clearing an hour earlier, but somehow, inexplicably, I had diverged. The bus was there, idling. "Be careful," he said. "*Soyez sage.*"

"Thank you," I said to his nodding profile. "Thank you."

He brightened with a fraction of a smile, which caused his cheeks to shift upward. The dark swallowed his car instantaneously, as if it had never existed.

I have no idea who he was. I was too cold, distraught, and embarrassed to ask. Maybe he was a worker finishing up the night shift. Perhaps he was an officer on security detail. The site foreman surveying the periphery. I will never know how he found me roaming around this treacherous place in the middle of an ice storm, just when I was ready to call it quits and give myself over to quicksand or dawn, whichever came first.

What is certain is that ten minutes later, I warmed up my car just as daylight glided into place to reveal another soaked winter day in Normandy. As I rounded the highway, I gasped at the distant sight of Mont St. Michel, its jagged black form stark against the soft gray of the sky. How elegant the spire seemed that morning as Archangel Michael emerged, gleaming, from behind the clouds. How worthy of a prayer.

෴ ෴ ෴

Marcia DeSanctis is a former television news producer who worked for Barbara Walters and Peter Jennings at ABC News, and at CBS News 60 Minutes *and NBC News. She is the* New York Times *bestselling author of* 100 Places in France Every Woman Should Go, *and she contributes to* Vogue, Town & Country, Departures, Travel & Leisure, Air Mail, O the Oprah Magazine, BBC Travel, National Geographic Traveler, Tin House, Marie Claire, The New York Times, *and many other publications. Her travel essays have been widely anthologized, including five consecutive years in* The Best Women's Travel Writing *and* The Best Travel Writing. *She is the recipient of five Lowell Thomas Awards for excellence in travel journalism, including one for Travel Journalist of the Year, for her essays from Rwanda, Russia, Haiti, France, and Morocco.*

ANNA VODICKA

✆ ✆ ✆

To the Travelers
Watching Reality TV

Is this the real world?

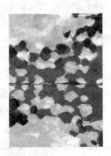

I have forgotten a great deal since 2006, but not the looks on your faces when I entered the hostel common room. In recent years, the memory has resurfaced with frequency. *Haunted* may be too strong a word—though I was fresh from the Mercado de las Brujas, the Witches' Market, that day, bag full of potions, mouth full of coca leaves for the altitude. My pulse throbbed from the steep climbs of La Paz and the heady scents and visions of the market: medicinal herbs, pots of feathers and glassy-eyed frogs, dried llama fetuses tied up with string, and vials of elixirs to ward off illness and debt, to bring love, prosperity, health, fortune.

You circled around the TV in bean bags and a sunken couch, deep in discussion until I walked in and silence fell like a spell cast on the room.

"What's wrong?" I asked.

You turned to me, all eight or ten of you, a local Bolivian desk clerk, a Romanian couple, a few Israelis post-mandatory service, faces from across the globe reflecting disbelief, grief, confusion, disgust, demand for an explanation.

A Polish girl, the other solo female traveler among us, broke the silence.

"Is it true? Is this what it's really like?"

It was Ivanka I saw first, or someone who looked like Ivanka, as rich girls on reality shows did in the early aughts— platinum blondes in designer bikinis with untraceable accents, who were enrolled in private boarding schools or universities, but appeared already to be working professionals, employed in some hazy combination of model-actress-socialite, trailed always by cameras. In 2006, they were all Paris or Nicole or Ivanka to me, though I was an unreliable source on the subject, didn't own a TV, didn't pay attention. I felt a special disorientation before reality shows, a phenomenon critics promised wouldn't last.

In this episode, the rich girls in bikinis were washing cars. Or play-acting washing cars. There were hoses and buckets of soapy water. There was a line of Hummers and Ferraris parked alongside a pool alongside a mansion alongside fountains and manicured hedges. But the girls concentrated primarily on the positions of their bodies before the camera. They sprayed one another, straddled the hoods of their boyfriends' sports cars, held hoses to the sky like so much shook champagne. Occasionally, someone held a hose limply in the direction of a vehicle, laughed when they ruined the leather interior, but—perhaps the biggest spectacle, from the perspective of anyone in land-locked Bolivia—they mostly let the water run.

"This? No, no," I said. "I mean…yes. But…no."

Silence.

"Most Americans are not like this. No one has this much money. This isn't real!"

"It isn't real?" An Israeli guy pointed me again to the screen as if I had missed it. "It's happening."

You nodded in collective agreement. Who could refute the evidence, the scene before our eyes? This image we projected to the world, to Bolivia, land of the Water Wars, of the world's largest salt flat and the highest-from-sea-level city. Bolivia, where foreign gold mines sucked the land dry from below, and the sun baked it close from above, and the earth was cracked and fissured, exposed riverbeds rippling like all the water that wasn't there. It made me thirsty just to look at it.

My throat went dry. I flashed back to high school, Ivanka seductively pouting across the pages of Seventeen, she and Paris and Nicole as much a mystery to me and my rural Midwestern girlfriends as we would have been to them. None of us had ever seen New York.

And yet I simmered in guilt at the memory of long, hot showers, divine steam fogging over my reflection in the mirror.

I felt suddenly like a reluctant and ill-equipped ambassador, naive and fumbling as a babe, though I was a freshly minted college grad, old enough to know...what? *The Real World*? Too-much-tuition's-worth of Latin American literature? I barely felt qualified for my actual job, freelance copywriting for a healthcare marketing firm (a field that sounded suddenly ridiculous in Spanish, in countries where healthcare is a human right), let alone the role of national spokesperson. Alone, abroad, during the War on Terror, I was dodging questions about my President, working hard to mask my easy, credulous smile, my calcium-rich bones, straight from America's Dairyland.

I'd considered pinning a Canadian flag to my backpack—a tip from my fellow Americans. Before I left home, I'd made several trips to the salon to dye my naturally light blond hair a less conspicuous dark brown. The joke of the Fates or the *brujas* was on me: As soon as I hit the high-altitude Andes, the sun bleached every strand a raging bright orange. That's how

I passed through South America: drafting convincing prose about advancements in robotic surgery, birthing centers, and microdermabrasion, with my head on fire.

Is this what it's really like?

A couple of Canadians looked guilty by association. Some of you grew so disgusted you turned to leave, and I couldn't blame you. I myself was searching frantically for a fire escape.

To my relief, one of you reached for the remote. With the click of the power button, the show was over.

I made a fast exit for my three-dollar bunk, though I can't say I slept that night, something gnawing at me beyond the usual discomforts of the shared dorm room. We parted ways the next day, all of us heading, eventually, toward some idea of home.

But I remembered you years later, when a real-life Ivanka breezed past me in an airport, full makeup, hair smoothed professionally in place, as if she'd just wrapped a photo shoot. She retreated to a private lounge, a boxy room of floor-to-ceiling glass. Bored, I settled in to watch with everyone else, suddenly more interested in the manicured life behind the glass than the messy world of connections and departures behind me.

I thought of you in 2010, when Bolivia passed the historic Rights of Mother Earth Law. Built on principles of respect, harmony, multiculturalism, and "the collective good," the legislation defined Mother Earth as "a living dynamic system made up of the undivided community of all living beings," and granted her rights to life, diversity, equilibrium, restoration, air, and water—free from pollution or commercial interests.

And again in 2017, when Bolivia suffered its worst drought in decades—residents allowed to fill two jugs a day, every three-four days—and my country elected a reality TV star to its highest office, a man who boasts of plating his bathroom fixtures in gold.

Is this real? You ask, we ask.

They say that after a rain, a glassy surface of water settles over Bolivia's salt flats, converting the land into the world's largest mirror. I imagine the *brujas*, with their black braids and bowler hats, have something to do with this, holding a looking glass to the world. It takes a courage I didn't have to gaze into it, past the easy mirage of beauty or ugliness, a princess or a hag, to something real, something wounded, wrapped in great complexity and excruciating discomfort. I want to try again, with you. To practice looking in the mirror. To practice staying in the room.

ॐ ॐ ॐ

Anna Vodicka's essays and travel writing have appeared in AFAR, Brevity, Guernica, Harvard Review, McSweeney's Internet Tendency, Longreads, Paste, *Lonely Planet's* An Innocent Abroad, *and* The Best Women's Travel Writing, Volume 11. *She teaches creative writing at Seattle's Hugo House and to women incarcerated at the King County Jail. She thought the reality TV fad would be over by now.*

♫ ♫ ♫

Wingmom

A mother, a daughter, and a
saxophonist walk into a bar...

"Oh no you don't. You're not going to jump off from there,"
Mother called out to me. I stood teetering on the edge
of the schooner, the Aegean Sea below. In the distance, the
white-washed buildings clinging to the caldera's edge looked
like a dusting of snow.

"It's deep enough," I said.

"I forbid it." She put one hand on her hip and pointed at
me with the other.

"Mom, I'm thirty-four."

"Then act like it."

My mother shook her head. I leapt into the sea.

As I climbed the ladder and into the boat, a sandy-haired
stranger smiled at me and winked. I had noticed him as soon
as we'd boarded the sunset cruise. He'd smiled at me then
and, being my mother's daughter, I smiled back. He didn't

look like the usual Santorini tourist—sunburned, tennis-shoe clad, a face tinged with an expression of awe and indigestion.

"What do you think you are, a bloody mermaid?" my mother asked.

"Maybe," I said and looked at the sandy-haired stranger.

My mother caught me. "What are you looking at?" she asked, though she already knew.

After a hiking trip up Nea Kameni volcano and a swim in the cloudy warm springs, the tourists were settled back in the boat, drinks in hand, and the sandy-haired man played the saxophone, serenading the setting sun. My mother and I sipped Greek wine and listened to the breathy music, a sound both sassy and serious.

Mother was scared of most things, which was why she didn't hike the volcano or swim in the sea, but she was also bold and brave in other ways, so it was my mother who introduced herself to the saxophone player. It was my mother who asked Benny—that was his name—to ride the rickety cable car back up to Fira with us and then invited him to dinner. She got away with this behavior because she was a former beauty queen, and even as an older woman, she was still beautiful. Her British accent made her sound charming and funny even when she was being pushy.

It was as if she wanted to make sure somebody was going to have a *Shirley Valentine* experience in Greece. But communication with Benny proved to be an ordeal, since he had a repertoire of about ten English words. He was Albanian but also spoke Greek and Italian. We managed on Benny's Italian and my broken Spanish, understanding about 7 percent of what the other said. We made it through dinner this way, eating take-out gyros on a park bench. My mother shared her cigarettes with him. She pretended she didn't smoke until she had someone to smoke with. "I don't smoke much," she would say, though anytime she deemed it appropriate, she would light up. And then she would blame me, saying, "I only smoke because you make me nervous."

And according to her, her high blood pressure had nothing to do with the cigarettes; that, too, was because of me.

"That Benny sure is nice, isn't he?" Mother said, when he invited us to have drinks later at Enigma, the nightclub where he worked.

"I guess so. It's hard to talk to him," I said. Flirting with him on the boat seemed fun, but I didn't need it to go any further.

"He's handsome."

"Did you see he's missing teeth? In the back?" I asked.

"Don't be so judgmental," she said, which was what she often said when I disagreed with her about something.

We wandered the cobbled streets, past the tourist shops and bougainvillea, and then went for a couple of drinks at an Irish pub called Murphy's. When we thought it was late enough, we headed for Enigma, but still, the bouncer told us we were too early. It was ten P.M. Things wouldn't get started until midnight. Or later.

"Can we just come in for a drink?" my mother asked. "We *know* Benny."

We entered through a neon-lit cave that looked like the tunnel where you wait in line for Disneyland's Space Mountain—low, curved ceilings, the purple neon glowing on the white walls.

We were the only patrons in the club.

We walked to the bar and ordered retsina, which tasted like acetone. I asked the bartender how long the bottle had been open, and he gave me a blank look. My mother told him, "We're *friends* with Benny, you know." Then she turned to me and said, "Why are you always such a wine snob? It's fine." She smiled at the bartender, and he smiled back.

"I used to work in the wine industry," I said. "That's why."

"You have an answer for everything," she said, still smiling at the bartender.

I knew I couldn't have been the first woman to come in looking for Benny after the boat ride, but I may have been the first woman who'd done so accompanied by her mother as wingman.

We sat at one of the white vinyl sofas with our acidic wine, and my mother said, "You're boy crazy, you know that?"

"Me? *You* invited Benny to dinner. What are you talking about?"

"You know what I'm talking about. In high school, you said you wanted to live with that boyfriend of yours."

"I was probably just trying to shock you. Besides, I was a child."

"Of course you were. You're still a child to me. And didn't I find condoms in your purse the night of your prom?"

"You know the answer."

"Do I?" she asked, all innocence. "You know," she added, "I'm only passive-aggressive because if I'm not, you accuse me of being critical of you."

"Being direct doesn't mean you have to be insulting," I said.

"Kill 'em with kindness, that's what I always say."

For my mother, different truths existed in different rooms of the brain. At any given time, she decided which room to live in and whether or not secrets and lies decorated the walls. I'd learned to go along with whatever she wanted. So it didn't seem as strange as it might have when my mother and I danced with Benny on the empty dance floor, the bartender looking on with an amused smile. Or when Benny started calling my mother "Mama," which she tried—unsuccessfully—to discourage because she thought it made her sound old enough to be his mother, which of course she was.

When we returned to the couches, Benny squeezed in next to me. He went in for the kiss, and I gave him my cheek. "Want to see the rooftop terrace?" he asked in Italian. The word "terrace" is the same in Spanish, so I translated for Mother.

"You two go ahead," she said, waving toward the door. "I'll stay here." She took a sip of wine.

"Thanks, Mama," Benny said with a grateful smile.

I followed Benny up to the rooftop terrace.

The lights of Santorini glimmered on the purple Aegean Sea. I breathed in the sea air, and he tried to kiss me again. I squirmed away, but not because of modesty. I liked Benny more from afar; the saxophonist's allure wasn't in the fulfillment of a love affair but in its promise.

"I want to kiss you," he said. These were among his ten English words, and he didn't need them because the way he tried to press his mouth to mine made his intent obvious enough.

"We haven't even had a date," I tried, as if that had ever stopped me before. And admittedly, it would have been easier to kiss him than to converse with him.

"But I love you," he said, trying to kiss me.

"You don't love me. You want to fuck me."

He nodded as if I finally understood. "Yes!" he said. "I want to make fuck, but also I love you."

"Uh-huh."

"You are beautiful, and I want to make fuck," he repeated, now that this option was on the table.

"I'm sure you do," I said. For every backward step I took, Benny took one forward. He nodded and twisted his face into what could pass for sincere. Our bodies projected shadows in the yellow blaze of a nearby streetlamp; we stood at the edge of the terrace against a stone wall, the sea shimmering far below.

"That's fine," I said, "but I don't want to leave my mother for too long. We should go back."

When he looked confused, I said, "Mama," and pointed toward the club.

He nodded. "We will have a date tomorrow," he said in Italian. "I will pick you up on my moto. We will go to the beach."

"Where?" I asked, catching all of it but the last part because the Spanish and Italian words for "beach" are nothing alike.

"To the sea," he said in English.

"What time?" I asked in Spanish.

"Dieci," he said.

"Diez?" I held up all my fingers, and Benny nodded.

I told him the name of our hotel. It was one of those third-drink decisions. And I reasoned that most of us just want to make fuck; at least Benny had been up-front about it. Sometimes the fewer words we're able to exchange with each other, the more honest we become.

Benny smiled and said, "Back to work now."

When I got back to the club, the dance floor was still empty. I didn't really want to go on a date with Benny, but I wasn't sure how to say no. I also knew my mother wanted to be witness to my Greek love affair, and I didn't know how to say no to her, either—it had always been that way with us. She had such a profound influence on me, and in some ways, I wanted to be just like her. But in other ways, I wanted to learn who I was separate from her.

I found her at the bar and said, "Let's go."

"But I just ordered another drink." The club's neon lights strobed across Mother's face.

"It's like vinegar."

"It cost me good money," she said.

"Bring it with you."

"How can I?"

I took the glass off the bar and held it inside my jean jacket. "This is how. Let's go."

"Suzanne!"

"This way it won't be wasted. We can give the glass to Benny tomorrow," I told her as we left the club.

"Tomorrow?"

"I sort of made a date with him."

"That's good," Mother said.

We ended up getting lost on the way back to the hotel, and she asked, "Why are you leading me through the back alleys of Greece?"

"I'm not trying to."

"You're not lost, are you?"

"No," I lied. We walked past a group of stray cats, eating what looked like noodles off sheets of newspaper. Ahead of us, an old woman distributed the food, and cats competed for it, snarling and hissing at one another.

"It smells like urine," my mother whispered. "Oh, why did you bring me into the back alleys?"

"Mom, this is Santorini. There are no back alleys. Stop saying that. Here, have some wine." I handed her the glass. She nodded and drank. A man walked toward us on the path, and she spun around and ran the other way, up the cobbled stairs, spilling wine as she went. I followed her, shouting, "Mom, Mom!"

The next morning, my mother asked if I was going to have a date with Benny. I told her I wasn't. "That's good," she said. "But do give him back the wineglass."

"Last night you were trying to set me up with him."

"I was not. I wouldn't do that. Don't be daft." She rifled through her suitcase and pulled out her bathing suit.

"You did."

"Well, you got us lost in the back alleys with the stray cats," she said. "Luckily, I found the right way to go."

"By running away," I said.

"It got us going in the right direction, didn't it? And away from the hobos."

"Hobos? What hobos?"

"You know what hobos. Why do you ask me things you already know the answer to?"

"Why are you so afraid of everything?" I asked.

"Why are you so mean?"

We stood there looking at each other, neither of us willing to answer the other's questions. I knew the answers would have been too difficult, so I ended the stand-off by apologizing. She nodded and went to the bathroom to change.

I waited in front of the hotel and heard the motor of Benny's moped straining up the hill before I saw him. He wore faded jean cut-offs, a white t-shirt, and sandals made from woven straw. He motioned for me to get on the back of the bike. I tried to explain first in English and then in Spanish that I wasn't coming, but Benny just half-smiled, patting the vinyl seat behind him.

"I changed my mind," I said.

And when Benny still didn't seem to understand, I said in Spanish, "I change my mind," mixing up verb tenses so it came out in the present tense, making it seem more right than before.

"You don't like the beach? We'll have coffee instead," Benny said, patting the seat again.

"No, it's not that. It's just that I don't want to leave my mother. She's sick," I lied. "Mama sick. Mama *enferma*," I said, hoping the Italian word for "sick" resembled the Spanish.

It doesn't, so Benny stared at me, pressing his lips together. Then he exhaled and asked, "So we are finished?"

Because I didn't have the words to explain, I said, "Yes."

Benny shook his head, not trying to conceal his disappointment. "But I like you too much." He crossed his arms over his chest.

I nodded. He started his moped and sped back down the hill. I stood there holding the empty wineglass. I couldn't figure out how to explain and give it to him, so I left it at the hotel bar on my way back up to the room.

I know it would have made a better story had I gone with Benny to the sea. Sometimes my literature students wonder what a character in a novel might have done in another circumstance. Or what might have happened if a character had acted differently, chosen another path. What if Edna Pontellier could have divorced her husband? Would she still have walked into the sea? The point, I tell them, is not what didn't happen but what did; anything else is off the page.

That evening, my mother and I went for appetizers at a balcony restaurant under the windmill in Oia. The sun dropped like a stone into the water; the sunset cruise sailed by below the white-washed buildings, the blue-domed roofs, and the rocky caldera. An older gentleman at the next table smiled at my mother. She smiled back and whispered to me, "See! I can still get an old codger."

"Or a young one," I said, and we laughed.

Saxophone music rode the wind. "Do you hear that?" Mother asked. "I wonder if it's Benny?"

"How many saxophone players are in Santorini?" I asked, and we both laughed again.

My body felt full of *what ifs* and *why nots*. I'd liked Benny from afar—the smile, the wink, the boundary of desire. I wondered what would have happened if I had gone with him on the back of his bike, winding paths to the sea.

But that's off the page.

The ending of my Greek story was right there, sitting in the salty, pink sunlight, laughing with my beautiful mother, listening to the far-off notes of a saxophone.

♫ ♫ ♫

Suzanne Roberts is the author of the travel essay collection Bad Tourist: Misadventures in Love and Travel *and the memoir* Almost Somewhere: Twenty-Eight Days on the John Muir Trail *(winner of the National Outdoor Book Award), as well as four books of poems. Her work has appeared in* The New York Times, CNN, Creative Nonfiction, Brevity, The Rumpus, Hippocampus, The Normal School, River Teeth, *and elsewhere. She holds a doctorate in literature and the environment from the University of Nevada-Reno and teaches for the low residency MFA program in Creative Writing at Sierra Nevada University. She lives in South Lake Tahoe, California. More information may be found on her website: www.suzanneroberts.net.*

JILL K. ROBINSON

❧ ❧ ❧

Tracking a Ghost

It was the very stuff of human longing.

The urgent shout comes from outside my tent somewhere. I'm half asleep, half dressed, and cradling a cup of chai to warm half-frozen hands in the chilly Himalayan morning, but the voice gets my whole attention.

Hoping I really heard the word I've been waiting for, I scramble: Chai sloshes across my pants as I shove feet into socks, pull a sweater over my head, cram gloves and hat into pockets, unzip my tent with one hand, and grab my camera and boots with another. I sprint in my socks to where Sonam, the tracker who shouted the alert, stands, head down, seemingly merged with the telescope. After a quick *"jullay"* (an all-purpose Ladakhi word for hello, goodbye, and thank you), he steps aside to let me look.

Up to this point on my trekking expedition into the spectacularly jagged Ladakh region of India, high in the Himalayas at the northern corner of the country, the creature we've been tracking has lived up to its reputation for extreme elusiveness. Venturing halfway around the world on assignment for a newspaper travel article, I've wondered if perhaps my dreams of seeking out the most mysterious big cat on earth have overshadowed my very slim chance of seeing one.

But among these snow-draped mountains is where the cat lives, quietly and stealthily. It's what brought author Peter Matthiessen to the same mountain range in Nepal in 1973, and it's what brings me here, nearly fifty years later. The allure of spying the animal "whose terrible beauty is the very stuff of human longing," Matthiessen wrote, can make it difficult to live with potential disappointment.

It's a thought that's hard to escape, even as I lean in to Sonam's telescope. My expectations rise and fall like the landscape, with the constant awareness that in the end, tracking a snow leopard might be tracking a ghost.

Just yesterday, with our duffel bags and camping supplies tied to the backs of sturdy mountain ponies, we hiked up the trail to our campground in Hemis High Altitude National Park. The more than two-thousand-square-mile park in the northernmost district of Ladakh is home to perhaps sixty snow leopards, said Khendrup, a camera trap specialist who has worked with the local forest department and the Snow Leopard Conservancy. About nine of those reside in the Husing Valley, the deep canyon at 12,500 feet, where our camp was based. Thankfully, our local trackers—Sonam, Chitta, and Morup—are experts in this territory and the wildlife that inhabits it.

More than merely a reporter, I'd dreamt of this opportunity since childhood, likely from the moment I first learned about the snow leopard—an animal difficult to study due to its remote territory and preference to avoid humans. But that very quality could jeopardize my article. Despite the belief that the best stories emerge from things going wrong, there was a significant chance that I wouldn't catch sight of a snow leopard at all.

As we walked, herds of bharal climbed the steep cliffs of slate-blue shale on either side of the canyon. Also known as blue sheep, they're one of the snow leopard's main prey and are sometimes hard to spot, so well does their coloring blend with the stone.

We reached camp and settled in, organizing, hanging prayer flags, and fetching water from the river through a hole cut in the thick ice. Before our tents were pitched, a large black yak with intimidating twisted horns wandered through our site, finally choosing to hang out near the kitchen tent, where scraps were plentiful. Realizing it was safe to approach him as long as I was wary of those horns, I scratched his nose and he leaned into my hand like a Labrador.

Meanwhile, we all scanned the horizon with eyes, camera lenses, and telescopes. Before the light disappeared behind the Zanskar range, we took short hikes to acclimate to the higher elevation and view wildlife. Along the way, we spied more bharals, lammergeiers (bearded vultures), chukar partridges, and wooly hares. No snow leopards.

But after we crossed the frozen river, Chitta pointed: leopard tracks from the previous night. He showed us their rounded shape and lack of nail impressions. As he spoke, I felt my attention floating away. A snow leopard had walked here, this close to camp. I swiveled my head, hoping to see one peacefully perched on a nearby rock.

I had a seven-year-old daughter back home in California, and I'd clearly watched too many Disney movies in which the heroine convened with animals and discovered she could converse with them. In reality, it would be extraordinary to catch sight of a leopard at even the distance where I could see it through a telescope.

"Do you want to smell a scent marking?" Chitta asked. "There's one on this rock."

I had never been so excited to smell cat pee. I'm not a urine connoisseur and certainly couldn't distinguish between animals' individual marks, but when else in my life would I have the opportunity to know what *this* animal smelled like? Imagining the boulder as a cat communications center where snow leopards regularly paused to check the status of one another's travels, I leaned close to the rock and took a deep whiff. It stank, like musky housecat pee left to age for weeks. It was unpleasant and rank and made me even more eager to continue on the quest.

A photographer friend who'd visited this same region a couple months ago was lucky enough to see a mother and her two cubs. I wasn't a counter of things like passport stamps, countries visited, or social media followers, but what if all I saw of the legendary animals were tracks and scent markings?

Before coming on this trip, I'd watched hours of film on snow leopards, familiarizing myself with their appearance, behavior, and habitat. I told myself it was just study, something I'd also done as an animal-obsessed child. Back then, it was as if I had a folder in my brain where I stored the data I gleaned from obsessively reading books and watching Mutual of Omaha's *Wild Kingdom*.

Silver-haired zoologist Marlin Perkins may have been the host of that TV series, but my hero was his assistant, naturalist Jim Fowler. It always seemed that Perkins relied on Fowler to tackle the dangerous tasks, while Perkins stood at a safe distance and watched through binoculars. Though I mentally logged all the animal facts Perkins rattled off in each show (and repeated them to anyone who would listen), I had no interest in safe distances. I wanted to be out in the field like Fowler. I scoured my back yard for wild animals I could study on my own.

When I got an assignment to go into the field and track one of the world's most enigmatic wild animals, I reminded myself that even Matthiessen, author of the classic memoir *The Snow Leopard*, never succeeded in seeing one in the wild. Ultimately, the animal's elusiveness became a lesson in the Buddhist concept of nonattachment. I attempted to channel Matthiessen and detach my expectations from outcome. I added an unofficial mantra in discussing the upcoming trip. "I'm going to search for snow leopards," I'd say. "I probably won't see any, but that's O.K."

I tried to convince myself I truly meant it.

When dinner was over and everyone had settled into their sleeping bags with two hot water bottles each, I bundled up against the freezing temperature and walked quietly in the dark across the trail to gaze at the night sky in the clear air. Breathing in had an evaporative, cooling effect, like inhaling menthol. Staring straight up at the brilliance of stars, I heard the *whoosh* of an animal running past me. In the beam of my flashlight, I found it—not a snow leopard, but a red fox.

Like another light, a passage from *The Snow Leopard* flicked on in my memory: "If the snow leopard should manifest itself, then I am ready to see the snow leopard…. That the snow leopard is, that it is there, that its frosty eyes watch us from the mountain—that is enough."

Would it be enough for me, too, just being here in the home of the beast often referred to as the Gray Ghost? By this time, it was becoming apparent that unlike Matthiessen, I could not release all expectation. I knew if I didn't see at least one leopard, I'd be crushed.

However, with an estimated number of only two hundred to three hundred snow leopards in the entire Ladakh region— at best, an average of one per seventy-six miles—I also knew it wouldn't be easy. And it's not just numbers that make snow leopards a challenge to spot. In the rugged mountains, between the fields of bright snow and the rust- and amber-colored rocky outcrops, the snow leopard's thick, frosty gray fur, patterned with darker gray open rosettes, is a chameleon-grade camouflage.

Still, this almost supernatural landscape—in a former Buddhist kingdom with picturesque gompas, whitewashed stupas, and mani walls, amidst some of the planet's harshest conditions—felt like the appropriate place to search for a creature whose mystique seemed rivaled only by yeti and unicorns.

But now, gazing into Sonam's telescope in the morning, having run from my tent after hearing his shout of "Leopard! Leopard! Leopard!" I see nothing but rock and cliff face. No movement, no magnificent leopard. If it's there, it's invisible. I look harder, trying to force my tired eyes awake.

And then, I see it, stalking across a ridge—pale gold eyes fixed on something beyond my view. Its fur has a hint of topaz, and the thick tail that measures as long as the animal's body sways in the air, like the twitching tail of a house cat. Broad paws tread slowly on the edges of the cliff, and the leopard, like moonlight on snow, flows low to the ground in a crouch.

Suddenly, it leaps down the cliff face, twice diving into the dirt to cloak its scent, before charging in the direction of a small herd of bharal. They scatter, jumping in all directions across crumbling rock and patches of snow, like a handful of dust in the air—*poof*. Thwarted, the leopard stops and looks down the mountain in the direction of the small collection of trackers and photographers that have been silently and excitedly gathering since Sonam's call.

Every time I lean in to the telescope, I forget to breathe. Time slows down. Anything aside from the leopard is forgotten. We continue to watch the snow-cloud-colored cat for five hours, while it naps on a sunbeam-warmed rock, stalks more bharal (but doesn't catch one), and sniffs the air. I hardly notice that I'm still clutching my now-empty cup in my hands, never tied my boot laces, and haven't yet eaten.

I have seen what I came for, but the trip isn't over yet. Is it greedy to hope I'll see more snow leopards?

Days later, a second sighting. Deeper into the valley, we stand in the snow and take turns watching one of the cats stalking along a ridgeline. We wonder if it's the same one as before, but still count it as number two.

Nobody has an exact count of the majestic *shan*, as it's called in Ladakh, not only because the animal is so elusive but also because it inhabits a challenging and remote habitat of desert, mountains, glaciers, high passes, and plateaus. Researchers estimate there are 3,500 to 7,000 left in the wild, and though that number may initially seem large, the animals are scattered in remote regions across Afghanistan, Bhutan, China, India, Kazakhstan, Kyrgyz Republic, Mongolia, Nepal, Pakistan, Russia, Tajikistan, and Uzbekistan. The cats have already disappeared from some areas where they formerly lived, such as parts of Mongolia.

Historically, snow leopards have been poached for their fur, or killed by ranchers, whose sheep or cattle are their prey. As is the case with most endangered species, human encroachment and environmental threats negatively affect their habitat, but in recent years, locals in some regions have seen the value of leopard-related tourism and are working to preserve them. Still, is animal-based tourism just another form of human consumption, causing more damage than good? While resources and attention from visitors around the world assist conservation efforts and lend awareness to dwindling animal habitat, humankind's appetite for remote places and attempted dominion over the animal kingdom contributes to the problem.

With all the challenges for the snow leopard, that we have seen two thus far seems like a miracle.

Still, we move on.

The village of Ulley lies north of the Indus River, in the Ulley Chhu Valley, at an altitude of thirteen-thousand feet. The village holds maybe seven houses, one of which is the Snow Leopard Lodge, where we drop our bags quickly before following the local trackers to a small rise where we can scan nearby mountain ridges for wildlife.

Our trio of trackers is among the best in Ladakh—they've contributed to BBC coverage of the cats in the past and are well-known among filmmakers and photographers. Other small groups in Ulley make note of where and when Sonam, Chitta, and Morup are about, because their intuition may lead to a sighting. The resulting scrum looks like a Hollywood-style phalanx of paparazzi.

Instead of the bharal from Husing, this region is populated by goat-like ibex and urial, horned sheep with long legs. We immediately spy examples of each, but there's no sign of a snow leopard.

The animals' rarity doesn't completely explain why photographers and wildlife buffs are so compelled to trek into thin air to find them. Likely it's also due to the popularity of Matthiessen's book and its focus on the glory of a good quest. For me, the thrill of seeing animals in their own habitat seems like the natural progression of my childhood craze. Study first, maybe a little field trip to a zoo or natural history museum, then venture out into the world like a wildlife explorer.

The cycle continues with my daughter, a fellow critter freak. I photograph and film animals I encounter while on assignment and share them with her, fueling her own passion to read and learn more. Though she gravitates to the fuzzy and cute, she's just as happy finding hermit crabs at the beach or stalking bugs in the back yard. When she's older, I hope to bring her along into the larger wild kingdom.

For now, on my ninth day in Ladakh, I stand in the cold on a ridge in Ulley with a small group of snow leopard enthusiasts, the light snowfall causing concerns about limited visibility. On one side of the valley, a pack of Tibetan wolves plays hide-and-seek with our telescopes—coming out into the open when they see our attention is divided and hiding behind a ridge when we focus on them.

On the other side, proving that patience sometimes wins out, a lone snow leopard stalks a group of urial. It's my third sighting, a number that will always be connected to this trip. Outdoors in the grandeur of the Himalayas, humans stop for a moment, whisper, trade places at telescopes, share chai, and wonder at the magic of a ghost turned real.

The leopard is too far away for my big Nikon lens to capture it well, so I take a photo by lining up my phone lens with Morup's telescope, the way he taught me on my first day in Ladakh. It's not the most spectacular wildlife shot, but perhaps my daughter won't mind. Maybe the miracle of the moment, the extraordinary possibility of being in nature and seeing a wild animal live its life, will be enough for her. I know it is for me.

ॐ ॐ ॐ

Jill K. Robinson is a writer and photographer. Her work has appeared in AFAR, National Geographic, Outside, Sierra, Travel + Leisure, San Francisco Chronicle*, Travelers' Tales books (*The Best Travel Writing *and* The Best Women's Travel Writing*) and more. She still collects bizarre animal facts. Follow her on Instagram and Twitter @dangerjr.*

ALISON SINGH GEE

❧ ❧ ❧

Half Dome

It was a place that accepted them for who they were.

There's a 1950s photograph stuck into a dusty album in my childhood home that always reveals to me who my father once was. In it, he is looking out into a glorious August sky, handsome in the way only a twenty-three-year-old can be, with a thick black swath of hair swept back, and Hawaiian shirt and slacks on his slim, muscular frame. He sits next to my mother, then seventeen—his new bride, plucked from a chicken farming family in Sacramento, and before that, fresh off the boat from Hong Kong. She's wearing a hand-sewn skirt with a twenty-two-inch waistband and a white eyelet blouse, her home-permed hair styled into a wave. They pose in front of a redwood, the sunlight dappling their perfect faces.

"Yosemite," my mother told me when I was about six. "Our honeymoon. We drove up from Chinatown in the morning, stayed overnight, and drove back the next day." When I asked her where they lodged, she said, "Someplace with a funny name." As it turns out, my father's father, then the mayor of Los Angeles's Chinatown, had splashed out for one night at the Ahwahnee for his beloved son and new teenage daughter-in-law. They dined in the grand hotel's candlelit hall, and my mother still remembers what they ate: roast chicken and potatoes for her, and filet mignon—served rare—for my dad. He rhapsodized about that meal for years afterward. With its sprigs of rosemary, slick of melted butter, and its earthy umami, that dinner was California on a plate for him.

But what truly reveals my father is the emotion beaming from his face. It's pure, rare happiness, uncomplicated by the failed dreams or the eight mouths he would eventually have to feed—the struggles that would later define his life. Here, among the granite gods of the valley, he was an amateur geologist let loose in nature's playground, a homegrown botanist sleuthing down giant sequoias and monkey flowers, a proud American, no other qualifier needed. Away from L.A.'s inner city, my father experienced none of the racial taunts—*China Boy! Go back to where you came from!*—he had grown to expect. Here, he could move freely among the shimmering lakes and towering pines, communing with what he loved most: California shaped by magical hands.

By the time his six kids came along, my father seemed to know everything there was to know about the world's greatest national park. Every summer, or as often as we could afford it, my father—Ba, as we called him—rented a rickety cabin near the valley floor, and as soon as we arrived, our education would begin. In the morning, we set out to conquer waterfalls and trails, visit the ranger station for bear talks and date-nut bread made by the ranger's wife, and ride our bikes in the shadow of Half Dome. Ba drove us past the monuments and asked us each to claim one—mine was El Capitan, my lifelong spirit rock. I chose it not just for its sparkling beauty, but because it was more impressive than my brother's, Half Dome.

Of course, we weren't the first Chinese Americans to discover Yosemite. A few years back, Yosemite National Park ranger Yenyen Chan stumbled across a 19th-century photograph of Cantonese laborers. The workmen had been drawn to the West—Gold Mountain, they called it in Canton Province—by the promise of mineral riches. In this often-hostile new land, some two hundred fifty of them had found arduous work building roads to Yosemite during the winter, when blizzards pummeled the mountains.

But it was Ba who built my road to Yosemite.

In the days before Google Maps, my father knew enough to drive us all the way to Tuolumne Meadows. Our mission was to find Soda Springs, where naturally carbonated water bubbled from the earth. Once there, we broke out a pitcher, a family-sized sachet of raspberry Kool-Aid, and eight glasses: "Homemade soda!" my father proclaimed, filling the vessel with the spring's fizzy water and passing out sips (I remember it tasting like fruity rust). Throughout our hikes in the park, my father regaled us with stories of the Sierra adventures of John Muir, the Donner Party, and Ansel Adams, pausing only long enough to inhale the mountain air and take in the vistas.

After all day bounding about in our outdoor classroom, we'd return to the cabin and gather around a wooden picnic table while my father threw chicken legs slathered in hoisin sauce and *lopcheng*, Chinese sausage, onto the grill. We never had to say it aloud, but it was something we all felt in our bones: Yosemite was a place that accepted us for who we were. With our banged-up station wagon, our strange-smelling grill foods, we were a raggedy clan of Chinese Americans claiming this Californian dreamland as our own. I believe my father found his truest self in the valley. In fact, until he died in 1999, he kept a black-and-white portrait of Half Dome in a drugstore frame on the wall—a reminder, perhaps, that a perfect world really did exist, only a six-hour drive away.

One day we putted over to a Yosemite country store and waited in line for fishing licenses. Then we hit the Merced, wading in our swimsuits, bucket hats, and fishing poles. I pulled a trout straight out of the cold, rippling river, its body flipping back and forth in protest, the summer sun glinting off its shiny scales. That night we grilled my river prize in a frying pan, its moist meat made even more savory with a browned butter jus. The fish was so small, we could have only one bite each. We would surely have gone out foraging through the pine forests for mushrooms before dinner, but my father had recently read a newspaper article about a Laotian family who had done the same thing. They scooped up what they thought was a cache of chanterelles, savory with the tang of mountain earth, but ended up eating toxic Jack O' Lanterns instead. The whole clan wound up at the Yosemite Valley Hospital, curled into balls of pain, the poison slowly passing through their system.

It was during these trips that I began to understand the power of *terroir*—not that my nine-year-old self would have known such a fancy word. But I began to connect that the landscape from which our meal was collected, and where it was simmered and devoured, created its distinct flavors, its history, its soul. The meals we made in Yosemite, branded as our own with the spices and sauces of our Chinese-American household, transformed into cellular memories of this sage-scented terrain. I would never forget the meals I ate in the glow of El Capitan and Half Dome.

Those memories of family and food shimmered in my mind throughout my life, carrying me through my chaotic teen years, when our household imploded—when my father disappeared into a fog of delusions, returning to the family table only to lambaste us with the crimes of the moral and academic failures we had so clearly committed. "Nobody loves Ba!" he would wail, emerging from his bedroom in his striped flannel pajamas and thick black-framed glasses. "I work so hard for you people, and what do I get in return?"

It was the recollections of Yosemite summers that also got me through my sister's wayward years as a groupie, my brother's youthful forays into punk rock culture, and the fire sale of my father's dream house in the San Fernando Valley, after his bi-polar disorder had spiraled so out of control he could no longer work.

My gleaming memories of towering rock saviors and meadow picnics kept me reaching for the sun, until the day that I could finally take my own family to the valley floor and bicycle with them past Yosemite Falls and around Mirror Lake. Just before the trip, I told my four-year-old daughter, Anais, that we would hike up to Vernal Falls.

What Anais didn't know was that I had a secret reason for wanting to hike to the falls. She also didn't know that not all of my Yosemite memories were positive. In fact, Vernal and Nevada Falls had taunted me since I was little.

One morning when I was about eight, Ba had led us to the falls. "We are here to conquer the trail, kids!" he'd bellowed to us under a canopy of ancient oaks and sugar pines. But within minutes of setting out, he'd sent me back down to my mother, waiting on the footbridge below. "You're not strong enough for this," he said.

Hours after scrambling up the small, steep path, my siblings had returned, all flushed cheeks and beaming accomplishment. "It was great!" my little brother shouted. "Too bad you couldn't come." My mother consoled me with a store-bought hotdog and Drumstick ice cream, but even those treats hadn't healed my new wound. From that day forward, the trail lived on in my mind as the granite behemoth I would one day conquer.

Now, as Anais and I looked at internet photographs of the trail up Vernal Falls, my decades-long nemesis, she shook her head: "I don't think so, Mommy."

"You can do this!" I cheered.

But of course, I was also convincing myself.

Three weeks later, on the morning of our scheduled hike, I carefully arranged curried chicken salad sandwiches, paneer tikka and naan, a thermos of lemonade, and an entire blueberry pie into a daypack for the long trek upward. My Indian husband, Ajay, his backpack stuffed with water bottles and mosquito repellent, bounded up the trail's slick steps with Anais. As I heaved our sack of lunch, I felt like an earthbound pack mule, to their lithe mountain goats.

Halfway up, my knees started to ache, and I had to rest. "Go on without me," I said, shame flushing my cheeks as I lowered myself onto the mossy steps. "I'll see you back down the mountain, at the footbridge. Just go."

"Are you sure?" Ajay asked. I nodded.

My family disappeared into the mist and up the mountain, and I sat there shaking away the tears. Some thirty years later, the trail had beaten me again.

But after a few minutes of rest, a thought flashed through my brain. My daughter would forever remember this day: she and Papa at the top, and Mommy too weak to make it, stumbling back to the footbridge. Rubbing my knees one last time, I willed myself to stand and get back on the trail. "Not this time, Vernal Falls," I muttered, practically shaking my fist at the mountain walls.

An hour later, I found my husband and daughter cooling their feet in the sparkling pool between Vernal Falls and Nevada Falls. The total hike had been three long hours of climbing, and every sweaty cell within me knew it. Dropping the food sack—at last!—I ripped off my sneakers and splashed myself with cool water. Then, drenched, I spread a woven Indian blanket on the earth and collapsed on top, gazing up into the sky.

My father would have loved the mist from the falls and the eternal pines that swayed around us, but most of all, he would have loved the promise of that blueberry pie.

I whispered, "This one's for you, Ba."

The clouds above me shifted.

❧ ❧ ❧

Despite her resounding love for Yosemite, Alison, as a six-year-old, almost drowned in the Merced, when her fun-loving siblings put her on a log and let her float downstream. She overcame that watery near-death experience to write about her complicated relationship with her family, throughout her career as a journalist and essayist. Her Hong Kong-India St. Martin's Press memoir, Where the Peacocks Sing: A Palace, a Prince and the Search for Home, *chronicles her discovery that her Indian-journalist fiancé grew up in a 19th-century palace outside Old Delhi; it is currently being translated for the screen. Alison lives with her husband Ajay, daughter Anais, and two dachshunds in Los Angeles, where she teaches creative nonfiction and literary travel writing at UCLA Extension. Alison is working on a sequel memoir,* Cooking for the Maharani: Four Continents, Five Chefs, and One Tall Glass of Revenge, *in which she learns to cook from iconic chefs around the world, including her Cantonese mother, and then makes seven nights of feast for her royal Indian mother-in-law. Please say hello to her at facebook.com/AlisonSinghGee.*

ANITA CABRERA

❧ ❧ ❧

Casi Loco

He ordered her into the car. She obeyed.

*L*oaded into the back of the family station wagon, en route to the annual vacation week at a rented cottage on the Cape or a cabin in Maine, we children wrangled for spots near the windows. When the highway finally narrowed to a road, and the road to a lane, and the lane to a dirt path closed in enough that tree branches and leaves were within reach, we free-reining passengers of an era unfettered by seatbelts pushed and shoved in the vastness of the back seat, jockeying for position to grab at any foliage our fingers could snatch as the car drove on, our arms yanked backwards until we let go or tore the greenery free. The victors would hold up the spoils—torn leaves and twigs clutched in child-sized fists. "Proof," we called it. Not in the evidence sense of the word, but a name native to the family lexicon, assigned by children labeling the world around them.

I have not shared this childhood detail with my teenage sons. It is of no consequence; they would not be interested.

To them, their father and I are potential embarrassments, tottering toward old in failing bodies and comfortable shoes, grounded by apathetic aspirations—an early evening in, an occasional dinner out, a predictable furnished monotony punctuated by a concert or play, maybe even a once-in-a-lifetime eco-safari on the Serengeti or a trek to Patagonia in a last-ditch attempt at adventure. Our offspring humor us, as if we are the youngsters who must prevail in game after game of Sorry or Go Fish, lest we break out in a fit of poor sportsmanship. They chuckle at jokes they don't find funny, endure near-miss witticisms. They try to protect us, the way we want to protect them.

And so my sons have no knowledge of Casi Loco. I hold what happened in my closed hand as if clutching a fistful of dead and crumpled leaves. I want—no, *need*—to record it before I forget it. I must remind myself, because from this vantage point, already it seems impossible. Proof pulled from trees I passed close to, while wending my way before them.

Casi Loco belonged to Cartagena, Colombia, a beautiful city back then, even when Medellin, the country's second largest city, was the reputed murder capital of the world. It was 1989, and I had been following a parallel route with two women I'd met in Costa Rica, Katrina and Carlotta, an Aussie and a Brit, respectively, in their late twenties like me, who had paired up as traveling buddies. We'd made one another's acquaintance at a clapboard hostel in the Caribbean beach town of Cahuita, and they invited me along while our loose itineraries coincided. Of the two redheads, Katrina had more freckles and charm, a contagious, bawdy enthusiasm accentuated by a Queensland drawl. Carlotta was less spontaneous, meticulously planning the day's activities down to "having a shower" at the same time each afternoon. Both were equipped with the requisite guidebooks that mapped out the Gringo Trail through South America.

I followed along with them to an economy *pensión* in Cartagena. The lone American, I didn't want to seem too

persnickety. Though I had been staying in cheap accommo-
dations all along, the one they'd found was the dingiest and
darkest I'd considered up to that point. But I was tired of
traveling on my own and appreciated the company, even if
their pragmatism and resolutely outsider observations often
burst the romantic bubble I moved in, the one in which I
imagined myself a local wherever I went, with my Ecuador-
ean lineage and almost fluent Spanish. I took my own room
and they shared one, but the bugs bothered me. I could not
unsee the little black spots that darted about the sheets. I convinced myself they were lifeless specks, forcing myself to lie
on them each night.

Yet, I *knew* what I had seen from the little balcony off my
room above the unlit alley: the van into which two policemen
shoved a dark-skinned, short-skirted, cursing young woman.
And despite the cries and shouts coming from the shaking
van, nobody else appeared on the balconies above the alley,
even as her shrieks rattled the night. The residents whose
windows faced the dark passage must have known not to get
involved. Was I less or more safe as a foreigner who spoke
with an accent? The distance between me and the woman
whose muffled cries the van could not contain, and those
people behind closed curtains, was no longer disputable. That
distance, like a fleshy hand over my mouth, silenced me into
shameful complicity, forced me to inhabit my tourist status,
my outsider's bubble.

Perhaps it's this distance that provides a thin layer of
protection, allows a tourist in a strange place to take in what
is brilliant, acts as a sheer film distorting or blurring the
more unsightly. Because Cartagena was beautiful—the white-
washed buildings glistening in the sun, or deep blue or yellow
stucco houses with terracotta roofs and bursts of purple and red
bougainvillea vines winding up the walls, the towering royal
palms in the hot breezes, ferrying the salted breath of a warm
Caribbean sea. The plazas and cathedrals, the *malecón*—it
was hard to not think of Cartagena as one of the most striking

cities in the world, even with its egregious abuses, perhaps more flagrantly committed than in other places.

Oddly enough, in the heart of a country renowned for its quality coffee, we were served Nescafé instant in the local cafes we visited. One day, we were having a breakfast of toast and coffee granules in hot water when I mentioned I needed to exchange money. Carlotta and Katrina reminded me that the guidebooks warned against changing money on the streets, as con men were known to pull quick, sleight-of-hand switcheroos to swindle unknowing tourists. But changing money on the black market always yielded a higher rate than banks and other legitimate venues.

Carlotta pursed her lips. Mind you, she told me, *all* of the guidebooks advise against it; even the American ones. She nodded as if agreeing with herself.

Thanks, I said. But I've been trading on the street almost exclusively for two months.

I tried not to sound cocky, but the difference in exchange rates, though small to someone with a more generous travel budget, was considerable if you were counting every bus ticket and coffee (instant or otherwise). I had limited funds and was determined to scrape by on as little as possible to make them last.

I left Carlotta and Katrina mapping out a day of museums and churches, and set off for the district with the most exchange houses, where storied entrepreneurial *coyotes* offered competitive rates. I hadn't made it a hundred yards from the door of the first exchange house when a trim, mustached fellow in a yellow-and-white striped dress shirt and cream-colored pants sidled up to me and spoke, head bent down, in lowered tones. *Amiga. ¿Buscas el mejor precio? Compro dolares, libras, francos suizos.... ¿Que tienes?*

He was calling me "friend," asking if I was looking for the best deal. It was too easy, as if he were reading a script from the guidebooks' warning about exchange scams, offering to buy any kind of currency I might be carrying. I told

him I wasn't interested and continued on to the exchange
house with a bright red awning, perturbed by the stranger's
accurate appraisal of me, as if I had a sign suspended above
me that read TOURIST with an arrow pointing straight down
at my head. I had checked the daily exchange rate listed at
the national banks, so I knew I'd suffer a slight financial loss
by cashing dollars at an exchange house. But the banks had
long lines, and the transaction could take a whole afternoon,
another reason I preferred to do business on the black market. Still, this *casa de cambio* was going to make money, and I
would lose money at the rate posted. I turned away from the
door; the fellow was still watching me from nearby.

I went up to him, looked him in the eyes. How do I know
you won't rip me off?

No, *amiga*, no. Everyone changes money on the street.
Those ones there; they are the thieves, he said, jutting his chin
in the direction of the exchange house. The street was busy
with people moving around us, and he led me to a doorway
where we had more privacy. He offered a rate not much
better than the exchange house gave; forget it, I said. He complained he would be losing money.

I turned and started down the steps of the alcove. Wait,
he said, and came back with a better rate. Not good enough,
I insisted, pointing out that the banks would buy the dollars
for more. But I need to make *some* profit, he reasoned. We
went back and forth, both of us calling the other's bluff until
we reached an agreement. I said I'd change US$100 with him,
and he counted out the Colombian pesos, with the larger bills
on top. The transaction completed, we parted ways.

I had walked only a few blocks when something made
me stop and pull out the bills he'd given me. It was half the
amount he'd counted out. I checked again, hoping I was
mistaken. But no, I was missing US$50 worth of pesos. My
stomach sank; my whole body felt the blush of gullibility.
How had he pulled it off right in front of me? I had watched

him intently, with my own eyes, as he counted out the bills, his hands in plain view.

I went back to the exchange houses and looked around. This time, people on the street I hadn't noticed before seemed to be looking at me. Two cabbies leaning against their cars at the taxi stand stopped talking as I approached. Hey, have you seen a small guy with a mustache and yellow-and-white striped shirt?

They knew exactly who I was talking about. You mean Casi Loco?

Casi Loco? The stranger with whom I had entrusted my currency exchange was known as Almost Crazy? Maybe they didn't understand. I held up my hand to show his height, described the white pants and shoes, the yellow-and-white striped shirt. He was hanging around here a little while ago, I explained.

Si, Es Casi Loco. One of the cabbies jerked a thumb toward the exchange house, the smoldering end of a cigar jammed between his index and middle fingers, leaving a faint trail of smoke. *El anda por allá.* How quickly they gave him up, telling me his name and confirming his corridor of commerce.

I blew off my plan to meet back up with Carlotta and Katrina and hung around in the recess of a doorway as I had seen detectives do in old movies, missing only a fedora and trench coat. I waited, fueled by adrenaline, emboldened by indignation. The only way to alleviate my self-reproach would be to get my money back. Finally, he came sauntering down the street with the gait of a man who owned the sidewalk. I ran up to him, close to his face. *Casi Loco, me robaste. Dame lo que me debes.* I kept my voice from quivering as best I could, accusing him of ripping me off, demanding he pay me back, even in another language.

He stepped back slightly and looked around, as if checking that I wasn't speaking to someone else. What are you talking about? He acted as if he'd never seen me. He moved around me and continued on his way.

I trailed after him. Give me the rest of my money.

Déjame, he snapped, and kept walking. He couldn't get rid of me that easily. I ran ahead and stood in his way. I was slightly taller than him. We could have been related, with our slight builds, black hair, and dark features, standing only inches apart. Onlookers took notice and stopped conversations, turning to watch the street drama unfold.

I could smell a saccharine citrus scent of aftershave. Give me my money, I repeated. He began yelling now for me to stop bothering him.

A police car screeched onto the curb, blocking the small street, and stopped right where Casi Loco and I stood face-to-face, surrounded by a small crowd taking in the afternoon show. An older uniformed officer came between us, while a younger one pulled out his club and stood to the side. What's going on?

He robbed me, I insisted, just as Casi Loco held up his hands in innocent protest.

She's lying. I don't know what she's talking about.

Get in the car, they commanded. I didn't have time to process the directive. Even as I moved toward the squad car, my mind and body diverged, startled out of sync, my physical self obeying in an act of self-preservation, ignoring a deeper internal alarm. What else could I do? It made no sense to get in a car with these people, so I rationalized away the unnamed fear: *Of course, we'll go to the station and straighten this whole thing out.*

The younger policeman pushed Casi Loco into the back seat, motioned for me to follow, and then climbed in after. The officers said nothing as we drove away from the picturesque colonial section of town, through a more rundown area. *¿A donde vamos?* In the silence that followed, my voice sounded childlike. Casi Loco sat scowling, quieted in this state of captivity. Even if my gringa status might have conferred some deference with the law, this was not the time to talk.

The patrol car entered a roundabout, then a freeway ramp. His thigh pressing against my leg in the back of the car, the younger cop put his arm around me and squeezed my shoulder. I kept my eyes focused on the windshield in front, not daring to glance anywhere but straight ahead, sensing him looking at me intently. He leaned in and planted a kiss on my cheek. My face stung where he had pecked it. My shoulder, the officer's hand still cupped over it, stiffened, as if it belonged to a mannequin. I did not know how long we'd been driving; it seemed only minutes before they pulled off the highway.

And then there was nothing—no buildings, no people—just a dry, garbage-strewn landscape with bare, bent shrubbery.

The driver stopped the car. He and the younger officer got out and ordered Casi Loco to do the same. Every new action presented a different potential scenario. Despite his having ripped me off unceremoniously, I was afraid for Casi Loco. Any bravado or swagger he brandished in the streets didn't follow him here, in the company of these hefty, uniformed men who barely deigned to look at him. In this isolated setting, the officers' silence was more menacing, as they moved together in a choreographed sequence. They must have acted out the scenario before. If I kept quiet, they might forget I was there.

The younger, taller policeman held Casi Loco's thin arms behind his back, right outside the car where I sat with the windows open. I flinched inside, dreading what they would do next. Casi Loco and I shared a recent past, the short time before we were both at the mercy of two cops at a deserted highway turn-off. I wanted justice, not revenge. Did not want to be the cause, or the recipient, of violence. But nobody threw a punch. Instead, the older one rifled through Casi Loco's pockets, pulling out two fat wads of bills. He held them up, as if presenting the evidence.

Then he bent down and poked his head through the window. How much did he take from you?

Seventy-five US dollars, I answered, adding a bit more to the amount Casi Loco had ripped me off.

Liar! Bitch! Whore! Fuck you! I didn't take that much from her! Casi Loco strained against his captor's grasp. The younger cop spun Casi Loco around, grabbed him by the collar, yanked him closer. *¡Callate!*

The senior officer was busy shuffling through the worn, flimsy bills in pale hues of green, blue, red, and yellow, counting to himself before passing me a handful. Then he counted out more, and gave what looked like half to his partner before shoving the diminished wad back at Casi Loco. The *coyote* shot a glance right through me and spit into the dust. He didn't say a word. None of us did. It felt over, the score settled, the men in charge satisfied. The pesos were in my pocket.

The three men climbed back in the car, the younger policeman paying less attention to me now. But as long as we were still in the car, moving, I was not yet free. They had control; I was at their mercy. I focused on breathing soundlessly, imperceptibly. I willed myself to believe that remaining still and quiet would keep them from taking any other detours.

At last, they dropped us off where they'd picked us up. I said thank you. I didn't add "for my life." Casi Loco straightened his shirt collar and walked away, in a hurry to get anywhere else. We avoided each other's eyes like embarrassed strangers after a one-night stand.

I headed back to meet up with Carlotta and Katrina, spying on myself from afar as I walked through the shaded, narrow streets of Cartagena, over uneven cobblestones wedged between stucco buildings, numbed by the energy charging every cell, shuddering with each twinge of survival. I thought about what I would tell my companions, how they might react. It didn't matter if they believed me. I couldn't imagine they'd understand. Telling them would change nothing; I'd be asking only for them to bear witness, something I didn't deserve. I had not stepped up as witness to the woman in the van. And unlike her, I'd emerged from my encounter unharmed. There was no justice in it, any of it.

Nonetheless, as I neared the *pensión*, my heart expanded with relief and resumed a deliberate, regular beating, reaffirming its purpose: to pump the blood through my body.

Carlotta and Katrina would surely be done with the museums by now. After Carlotta had her shower, I would join them for an evening meal. But first I would sit on the balcony outside my room, smoke a cigarette, and take it all in.

I felt so tired.

Not the way I am tired these days. From routine and abundance, family and friends, a job, clean sheets, and all of the blessings and pain and suffering, the world's and our own. The nights when my sons return home short of breath, eyes bright as if holding a vision of their own lives almost extinguished, a secret suppressed in a shrug of the shoulders, a mumbled "nothing" in response to my asking what they've been up to—those nights are the reason I have not shared my story of Casi Loco. It would give them more license than they already take. Besides, I have no handful of torn shrubbery or ripped leaves to hold aloft, no remnants of that trip, that day, that car ride, that lie.

🐦 🐦 🐦

Anita Cabrera is a writer, teacher, and parent in San Francisco whose work frequently explores the themes of addiction, mental illness, and the complexities in parent-child relationships. Her fiction has been nominated for a Pushcart and, more recently, adapted for the stage by Word for Word Performing Arts Company. When not writing or teaching, she spends time dancing and volunteering in the recovery community both at home and abroad.

EVA HOLLAND

✺ ✺ ✺

A Strange Ambition

She had come intending to suffer.

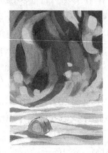

*B*efore she climbed on her snowmobile and drove away, leaving us to the ice, Sarah had a few parting words. "Don't burn the tent down," she said, hugging all of us hard. "Don't lose each other."

She pulled away and headed to her machine. Soon its red tail light receded in the distance, veering right and left as she steered along the ocean's rough, frozen skin. A cold wind blew at our backs as we watched her go; the hum of the machine vanished almost immediately. We three people—who had met just a few days earlier—were alone on the sea ice of Frobisher Bay, on the east coast of Canada's Baffin Island, two and a half degrees south of the Arctic Circle.

Eirliani, a chatty, high-energy ex-diplomat from Singapore who went by Lin, broke the quiet. "This is weird, no?"

Jonatan, a ponytailed Dane who could have been cast as one of the rugged men of Rohan in *Lord of the Rings*, was stoic. "Not really," he said.

I didn't say anything at all, just watched the snowmobile shrink to a dark blur before finally vanishing into the white. Until this moment, I hadn't quite believed Sarah would really leave us out here—we weren't ready, I'd figured she would say. We weren't strong enough. My excitement arm-wrestled with fear and dread. For the past three days, Sarah had led us out across the ice from her home in Iqaluit, the capital of Nunavut, the largest and northernmost territory in Canada. For a week before that, she and her mother, Matty, had attempted to cram our brains full of information about how to travel in the polar regions under our own steam, and survive.

Now Jonatan, Lin, and I had seventy-two hours to find our way back to town. To get there, we'd have to ski across the ice in harnesses, towing heavy pulks—fancy sleds, basically—loaded with all the gear we needed to stay alive in extreme cold. We'd have to navigate using all the tools at our disposal. We'd melt snow for water, pitch our tent in gale-force gusts, eat and sleep and ski and piss and shit in temperatures as low as minus forty Fahrenheit. And we'd do it all while dodging dehydration, frostbite, hypothermia, injury, navigational error, loss of critical gear, fuel spills, a tent fire, and a good old-fashioned societal breakdown in our civilization of three.

This was the final test.

We were students in the two-week Extreme Polar Training course offered each year by Northwinds Expeditions, the Iqaluit-based guiding outfit that Matty McNair founded and ran for more than twenty-five years. Her daughter, Sarah McNair-Landry, had recently taken over the business. Between the two of them, they knew everything there was to know about traveling over ice in both the Arctic and Antarctic. We had come to Iqaluit to soak up wisdom from the best, and now we would find out how well we had learned.

I'd arrived at the waterfront headquarters of Northwinds Expeditions on a dark, cold March night. Iqaluit, home to about eight thousand people, wraps itself around an inlet of Frobisher Bay—the town's bungalows and low-rise office buildings begin at water level and march up a series of benches before the open, rolling tundra of Baffin Island takes over. In summer, the land is brown and bare, but in winter the area is a patchwork of white: snow-packed roads, snow-covered hills curving down to the sea ice that locks the ocean in place. The bay is frozen over for at least half the year, and the area becomes a snowy jumble of parked snow-mobiles, grounded boats, and the sea cans and shacks used for storage. The McNair house was right on the beach, where the line between land and sea is marked only by broken ice piled up along the shore.

I was two days late, thanks to an Arctic blizzard and a long flight delay, and the other three students were already settled into tents pitched on sea ice in front of the house. I had shown up in jeans and a t-shirt, and I didn't feel psy-chically prepared to sleep outside on a night that dropped to minus fifteen. I changed into long johns and snow pants in a gear room, and pulled on a big down jacket and clunky expedition-grade winter boots. The elation I felt on the plane had twisted into fear.

For the past several years, I had hovered on the fringes of the McNairs' world. I read voraciously about polar explo-ration, wrote stories about other people's adventures at the frozen ends of the planet, and lived within a day's drive of the Arctic Circle. I joked with friends that the beauty of journal-ism was precisely that I didn't have to ski to the North Pole myself; I could just interview someone who had. Deep down, I wanted to be out there on the ice, not just asking questions. But here, now, I finally had my chance, and I was terrified.

I'd winter-camped in extreme cold before: A year earlier, I spent my thirty-fourth birthday on a frozen lake, on a night that plunged to minus twenty-nine, part of a fat-biking expe-dition meant to simulate conditions at the South Pole. So I knew what it felt like to lie awake, shivering in an inadequate sleeping bag, too cold to sleep and almost too afraid to try. Now, as I slogged through deep snow and deeper darkness toward my tent, tripping and scraping my shins on chunks of broken ice concealed by fresh powder, I reminded myself that I had come here intending to suffer.

The history of polar exploration, after all, is a story of pain. White men, many of them British, battered their way through or across the ice that covers the top and bottom of the world in a parade of frostbite and scurvy. They froze. They starved. For the most part, they ignored the accumulated knowledge of the indigenous peoples they met in the Arctic. Instead, they ate their dogs, their shoes, and sometimes each other.

Perversely, the hardships endured by the earlier expeditions inspired those who came later. Roald Amundsen, the great Norwegian explorer, wrote in a memoir that his polar dreams were cemented when he read a chronicle of an earlier Arctic attempt. The element that most caught his imagination, Amundsen said of his teenage self, was the suffering the men endured. "A strange ambition burned within me to endure those same sufferings," he wrote.

This urge to fling yourself into a sufferfest and come out the other side still animates plenty of people. But my expectation upon arrival in Iqaluit—that I was about to endure two weeks of relentless discomfort—was misplaced. It turns out the McNairs don't traffic in suffering for its own sake.

I first met Sarah at a writing residency in Banff, Alberta, a couple years ago. If you were to come across her in a city or town, she wouldn't seem extraordinary at first. Pale and brown-haired, quick to smile, she's taller than average, and fit-looking, but you wouldn't see her at a coffee shop and think, *that woman is ripped*. She doesn't brag about her achievements—you'd never know, from her laid-back exterior, that she has coolly stared down the barrel of a shotgun at a polar bear that pounced on her tent in the night, fired a warning shot just above its head, and let it walk away.

Now thirty-one, Sarah is one of the world's most accomplished young polar explorers. She's been to the South Pole three times and the North Pole twice, and in 2011, with her brother Eric, she completed the first transit by kite-ski of the Northwest Passage. In 2015, she and her boyfriend, kayaker-turned-polar explorer Erik Boomer, became only the second team to complete a full circumnavigation of Baffin Island by dogsled. (Her mother, Matty, and her father, Paul Landry, were the first.)

Matty was a pioneer of the modern polar guiding industry; she led the first commercial guided trip to the North Pole and has been to the South Pole five times. At sixty-six, she still held the record for the fastest expedition to the North Pole with dogs—thirty-six days, twenty-two hours, and eleven minutes—a mark set in 2005 on a classic route that starts off the northern coast of Ellesmere Island.

The McNairs' secret, oddly enough, is to have fun. To thrive, Matty believes, you have to find the beauty and wonder in polar travel instead of dwelling on the obstacles and suffering. She and Sarah teach a sequence of interlocking systems intended to prevent any enduring-of-hardships or eating-of-boots. Just one of a dozen examples: Matty designed and sews her own Velcro-sealed snack packs for use during a day's travel, with wide openings and beefy pull tabs. That means you can shove your ration of frozen bacon and cheese and chocolate into your mouth without removing your bulky overgloves and exposing your hands to near-instant frostnip.

That first night on the ice, once I made it into my layered sleeping bags, I was shocked to feel cozy and warm. As I settled in for sleep, I felt hope for the first time that there might be more to polar travel than fear and misery. But the night still seemed deadly: The tent thrashed around in a heavy wind, the huskies chained nearby howled, and the ice creaked and boomed as it shifted in the grip of the tide.

———

The next morning I was up early, and wired. Lin was still REM-cycling in our shared tent, so I quietly pulled on my outer layers, packed up my sleep system—two bags, a liner, and two pads—and slogged through deep snow to the house. It was not yet six, but as the spring equinox approached, the Arctic days were stretching longer: The day was bright and sunny. I let myself into Matty's workshop and waited anxiously for the household to stir.

A handful of people sign up for Extreme Polar Training each year, paying $5,200 Canadian (around US$4,125) plus the hefty price of flights to and from Iqaluit, for the privilege of soaking up the McNairs' know-how. In an intensive, jam-packed, two-week boot camp, they learn about moisture and calorie management, about weather and navigation, about polar bear deterrence and crevasse rescue. They learn how to solve problems they never even knew existed—like how to melt snow in a pot without burning it (a real thing that happens). Some want to lead polar expeditions of their own, while for others it's a sort of mutual audition: They might be interested in hiring Sarah as their guide, and the training program offers them a chance to give her leadership a test. Likewise, the training lets her get a sense of students' attitudes and abilities, and whether she'd like to share a tent with them for eighty-odd days.

The four of us students were here for a mix of reasons. Eddie was a local guy who was keen to know more about surviving in the Arctic backcountry and had been helping with the McNairs' sled dogs for weeks. He would only be around for the first week of classroom sessions, and I knew from day one that I'd miss his cannibalism jokes and his laughter when we were out on our own. Jonatan had trained for the military, hoping to be deployed to Greenland as a member of Denmark's prestigious Sirius Patrol. He was already experienced and extremely fit; Sarah would load his pulk with two forty-four-pound bags of dog food in an effort to slow him down every time we went out for a practice ski. Lin was working toward a South Pole expedition, with Sarah as her potential guide. She'd been training hard and had the necessary cardio bandwidth, but she'd only just learned how to cross-country ski and struggled at times. In good conditions, Lin would leave me in her frozen wake. In rougher terrain or with poor visibility, my experience with the climate helped make up for my lack of conditioning.

After breakfast, the other three sped me through one of the lessons I'd missed—a PowerPoint on preventing, identifying, and treating cold-weather injuries. (I have now seen a photo of a blackened, frostbitten penis. There is no turning back.) Then Matty sat us down at the dining room table for a session on the art and science of polar navigation.

"To be a good navigator, you have to use everything," she told us. That meant the whole array, from GPS units, maps, and compasses to the sun, wind, landmarks (if any), and the sastrugi, lines carved into the snowpack by the prevailing northwest winds. We tossed out a list of potential tools while Matty scribbled on a whiteboard. "Stars," someone suggested. She wrote it down. But, she reminded us, the North Star—that old navigational standby—is worthless in the Arctic, where it sits directly overhead.

She added "dead reckoning" to the list, a term I'd seen but had never heard defined. "Dead reckoning is a good guess," Matty explained. "It's a guesstimate. But a lot of people discount their gut." Our intuition could be more valuable than we realized, she said. I scribbled notes, already feeling overwhelmed.

That afternoon, we layered up, strapped ourselves into harnesses, and headed out to the sea ice on skinny cross-country skis with half-skins attached, towing pulks loaded with dog food and the short list of essentials Sarah had told us never to be without: goggles, our heaviest mitts, big down jackets, insulated down pants, an insulated water bottle, headlamp, lighter, compass, and map. It was minus ten, clear and sunny, but a sharp breeze dropped the windchill to minus forty. We traveled in a convoy, single file, taking turns breaking trail. We practiced throwing on our heaviest layers the moment we stopped skiing, watering and feeding ourselves, and then delayering and skiing on.

I worried about the icy wind on my face—I was still working out the best combination of balaclava, buff, goggles, face mask, and nose guard to keep me safe while letting me breathe freely—but otherwise the excursion was glorious. I leaned into my harness, throwing my body weight forward to lift my pulk over and through the soft mounds of snow. Sometimes, in deeper drifts, I braced my feet, turned, and hauled it past an obstacle hand over hand. The sun sank toward the frozen horizon ahead of us, turning the snowscape pink and orange.

Then we headed for home. It was my turn to lead, and I faced a cold, hard wind. My legs began to go numb, and I felt sweat running down my back and belly in alarming quantities. The fleece neck gaiter I had pulled up to protect myself clogged with frozen breath, and I couldn't seem to suck enough air through it. The Arctic night came on quickly as I struggled along, and when I stopped to pull out my headlamp, I couldn't find it right away. I stripped off my big mitts to feel for it in my sled bag, and my fingers began to ache in the cold.

That morning, when they'd gotten me caught up, Jonatan, Lin, and Eddie had passed along the five iron rules of polar travel: Eat before you're hungry. Drink before you're thirsty. Remove layers before you sweat. Put them back on before you get cold. And stop before you're exhausted. By my count, I had broken at least three, and I could feel myself unraveling. It was shocking how quickly I'd gotten myself into a potentially dangerous situation—and on just my first short ski, within sight of town.

Silently, Jonatan relieved my sled of its forty-four pounds of dog food, and Sarah's boyfriend, Boomer, loaned me his headlamp. I staggered the rest of the way back on shaky legs, trying to hang on to the elation I'd felt during the outbound trip and push away the fear that found me on our way home.

After a week of lessons and training, it was time for our full-blown mini-expedition. We left Iqaluit at midmorning, skiing out of Koojesse Inlet and into Frobisher Bay proper. Our plan was to head west along the bay's jagged northern shore, then cut south through a maze of islands before slanting east and then north again, completing a weeklong forty-mile loop. Our halfway point was a polynya, an area where strong, churning currents keep the water from freezing. That was where Sarah and Boomer would leave us on the ice to get home on our own.

We managed to cover just three and a half miles on our first day. The next morning, I took the initial lead. A haze had rolled in, and the day was gray, the light flat. There was no reference to tell ice from air. Deep, fresh snow compounded the problem, and we struggled along slowly, stumbling through unexpected valleys of powder between hard crusts of wind slab, our pulks catching in every drift.

The tough going was worse for Lin, who wore glasses and struggled to keep them from fogging. I stopped periodically to let her catch up; sometimes I'd hear her words drift forward on the wind. "I'm sick of this shit." "I can't see for fuck!"

I tried to focus inward, tried to channel Matty and see each valley of powder I blundered through, or each wind-carved wave of sastrugi, as a beautiful little challenge. I tried to think of the journey not as a struggle but as a game, and to find joy in each tiny victory.

Late that afternoon, we had our first major disagreement. A fierce wind had whipped up, and during our brief hourly break, we huddled under a tarp to debate what to do. Lin voted to stop for the day, while Jonatan and I wanted to push on for another hour and then stop to reassess. I hoped to put more mileage behind us. Visibility could be even worse tomorrow, I said.

"How could it be worse?" Lin asked.

Sarah had stayed out of the discussion so far, letting us hash it out ourselves. But now she laughed. "It can always get worse."

We carried on. It was Lin's turn to lead and break trail, but Jonatan stepped in for her. He rarely said much, but I sensed this wouldn't be the last conflict he resolved by simply taking on a larger share of the work. I was grateful. I didn't have a drop of strength to spare.

Sarah and Boomer left us on the afternoon of the fourth day. They had tried not to babysit us for the first half of the trip, forcing us to make our own decisions. But still, we'd always known they were there: calm, experienced, blessed with seemingly limitless energy.

It was Sunday, and we had until Wednesday at noon to find our way back to town. Retreating the way we'd come would mean failing the course. We had to complete the loop. And on Tuesday, our second-to-last day, we were required to cover at least eleven and a half miles—a fair bit more than we'd managed so far.

It had been a sunny day, but on cue, the sky darkened with thick clouds, and the wind picked up. The weather reports promised an incoming blizzard, with winds gusting up to forty mph and visibility below a mile. As we started skiing, I tried to focus on the harsh beauty of the ice walls lining the frozen channel we were moving through. I was determined to bury my fears in sheer wonder and suffocate them.

The next morning, Jonatan took the first lead. The island where we'd camped vanished behind us, and that was it— there was nothing to orient us in the world. Frozen ground merged with frozen sky. I squinted hard at my skis, trying to discern the snowpack's ups and downs, staggering through each unseen valley, each unexpected drift of soft snow. Every so often, in a lull in the wind, I could hear the squeak of my skis and my pulk on the surface, or the occasional "Fuck!" drifting up from Lin, behind me.

It was hard, slow going. After an hour, it was my turn to lead. I shuffled to the front and checked our compass bearing. Our desired direction had me facing almost directly into the wind—it struck the point of my left shoulder first, before smacking me in the face. My skis lined up nearly perpendicular to the sastrugi carved into the snowpack. These would be my only navigational tools: I tried to memorize the angle of my skis against the lines in the snow and the feeling of the wind hitting my shoulder.

At first, I stopped to check the compass every hundred yards or so, and each time I did, we were still bang on course. It was working! I got more confident, halting the group less often. Despite the wind and the cold and the headache settling in behind my forehead, I grinned. I felt like I'd acquired a superpower.

Still, the travel was brutal. The wind gusted strong enough to send me sliding backwards. It pushed my hood off and forced my jacket zipper open. Eventually I gave up on standing straight and started to move in an awkward lunging crouch, squatting and pushing one ski forward, then the other, making myself small.

I glanced behind me sometimes and noticed Jonatan and Lin were partially obscured in the haze. Sarah had told us not to move if we couldn't see each other—advice that had seemed obvious at the time, although we were now coming close to violating it. Jonatan had the stove and fuel, the tent, and satellite phone—plus all that dog food—in his heavily laden pulk. I had an InReach—a satellite texting device—plus two sleep systems and our shovel. Lin had a sleep system to keep her warm but no way to contact anybody.

If we got into real trouble, Sarah was just a sat-phone call and short ride away. But, I reminded myself, it wasn't that simple in practice. The phone or the InReach, both frozen solid, would need nearly an hour to warm up against a human body or inside a warm tent, and there was no saying whether a rescuer on a snowmobile would be able to find us—or even safely look—until the storm weakened.

I pushed on. As my hour wound down, patches of blue appeared high above us. The faint shadows of islands and coastline peeked through the gray. The wind began to ease up slightly. We carried on for three more hour-long rotations, then called a halt in midafternoon, still a few hours short of sunset. We were in position for our final stretch: exactly 11.51 miles from Monument Island, our goal for the next day. I was proud of our progress, but we had averaged only a little more than a half-mile per hour. If tomorrow brought flat light, winds, and whiteout or a soft snow surface, it would be a very long day.

We were on skis and ready to go by 6:20 A.M. The lights of Iqaluit were visible on the horizon, fifteen miles away, glowing through the gray dawn. I was excited, nervous, antsy to start—I had the same flutters in my stomach I used to feel when I played rugby, bouncing on my toes and shoving my mouthguard into place in the very last moments before kickoff.

The night before, we had figured the day's required mileage would likely take us twelve to fourteen hours of skiing. We planned to try a strategy Matty and Sarah called "rolling the clock"—after several hours of pushing hard, we would set up the tent for a quick two- or three-hour rest and attempt to trick our bodies into feeling like they'd had a full night's sleep. With the sun vanishing around seven P.M., it would mean night skiing, finishing our long day a few hours after sunset. But we hoped the gain in our strength and efficiency would be worth the trade-off.

We set out with Lin in the lead, and everything went better than expected. We skied across a hard, smooth surface;

the light was good, visibility clear. In our first two hour-long pushes, we covered nearly four miles.

By my second lead of the day, our fifth hour-long push, I was giddy. A whiteout had rolled in far ahead of us, and so, though we traveled under blue skies, we could no longer see where we needed to go. But with the sun behind me, I navigated by the feel of the wind on my right backside, the angle of my shadow falling ahead and to the left of my skis: the Incredible Human Sundial! I kept twisting in my skis to turn back to Jonatan, in line behind me, trying to transmit my delight.

That push ended at noon, and as we clustered together, we realized we had only three miles to go. We stopped to snooze for a couple hours in the sun-warmed tent before carrying on to the finish.

We made camp that night, just ten and a half hours after we'd set out. We had passed the test and would be back at the McNair house in time for lunch the following day. If skiing for hours across a frozen ocean while towing a loaded sled can ever be described as "a breeze," this was the time. In the tent, Jonatan passed around our last stash of cookies in low-key celebration.

We were in bed early, but I woke around eleven P.M. I had to pee. I lay on my back in my layers, staring into the darkness. I wondered if I could ignore the urge and fall back asleep. Aside from my insistent bladder, I was warm and comfortable.

Finally, I felt around in the dark for my mitts and head-lamp, unzipped the two sleeping bags, shimmied out of my liner bag, and staggered into the night, my down booties squeaking quietly on the snow.

I was still grumbling to myself when I looked up at the sky. The usual dark bowl filled with stars greeted me, but this time it was ribboned with the vivid green of the north-ern lights, each stripe undulating from horizon to horizon. I craned my neck back and stared, and I forgot about the cold, or the risk of my mitts blowing away while I fumbled with zippers, or the hassle it would be to get my sleeping bags aligned just right again.

Here was that same lesson I had learned and relearned over these two weeks. Joy and awe would always win out, if I let them. The Arctic had an alchemical ability to transform my fears and suffering into raw wonder. If I kept coming back, kept flinging myself onto the ice, moments like these were the rewards. It was a lesson no interviewee could ever have taught me over the phone. I had to be here, on the ice, to learn it for myself.

I watched the sky ripple and burn for a few more moments. Then I crawled into the tent and zipped myself in, warm and happy and safe.

ॐ ॐ ॐ

Eva Holland is a freelance writer based in Canada's Yukon Territory. She is a correspondent for Outside *magazine, and the author of* Nerve: Adventures in the Science of Fear. *She's still plotting her next Arctic adventure.*

ANNE P. BEATTY

ஃ ஃ ஃ

You Don't Have to Be Here

Too much safety poses its own dangers.

abin knew I was afraid to light the kerosene stove. His patient instructions accompanied open-mouthed delight at my ineptitude. This ten-year-old Nepali, wearing only limp cotton shorts, loved being my teacher in the tiny village where my Peace Corps training took place. My homework was to practice lighting the stove so when I set off to my post in Biratnagar a month later, I could boil water and not die of giardia (or so I said; one doesn't die of giardia, it turns out). Rabin knelt by the smudged brass canister, pointing. *Here you pump. Here you adjust the flow of gas. Here you hold the match, until poof! A ball of fire.* His elegant hands exploded in my face to make sure I understood. That explosion was what I feared.

After several pantomimes, Rabin asked if I was ready. I nodded. Rabin's aunt, watching, serenely threaded the buds of decapitated marigolds onto mala necklaces. Other family members gathered to watch, too. I smelled acrid kerosene.

"Now," Rabin said, "where are those matches?"

We looked. His two-year-old cousin sat nearby, playing with the box labeled Safety Matches.

I often wondered, during my time in Nepal, why more injuries did not happen in a place so riddled with danger. American children were admonished not to play with fire; preteen Nepali girls used it to prepare meals for the whole family. Six-year-olds in the United States were not allowed to walk to school alone; here, they were charged with carrying younger siblings through dense rickshaw traffic in the bazaar. A preschool-aged boy, who back in my homeland might be responsible for a sippy cup, shepherded the family's one-thousand-pound water buffalo in from the fields in Nepal. Out bus windows, I often saw such a boy reclined along the animal's spine, a switch dangling unused over the beast's massive flank. Perhaps we Americans were obsessed with safety.

I joined the Peace Corps as a way out of my safe white middle-class existence, one that, at the age of twenty-one, struck me as so insulated as to be numbing. I had taken French, painting, Native American anthropology, and literature courses in college, but I still felt exiled in a hostile world of big box stores, other people's happiness, and keg parties to which I was not invited. Few people my age seemed to feel this sense of peril, and by the end of my senior year, I felt utterly cut off from my Frisbee-toting peers. Moving abroad was an antidote to anesthetization.

Knowing almost nothing about Nepal except what information the Peace Corps had provided in a slim folder, I didn't pack well. My governing principle was not to be a stereotypical Peace Corps volunteer, whom I pictured as an earnest do-gooder with hairy armpits and worn Birkenstocks or, worse, Tevas. This dogma led me to pack things like a faux suede bomber jacket with synthetic fur, which I'd bought at Goodwill for five dollars, and a pair of baby blue Adidas. I'd expected to live in the Himalayas but was posted sixty miles south in the Terai—the tropical strip of land in southern Nepal that runs like a lush hem across the bottom of the country. The jacket was so heavy and cumbersome my Peace Corps friends dubbed it "the pet," and the shoes immediately began sprouting mold in the swampy heat. After a few humbling weeks, I asked my mother to please buy and ship me a pair of Teva sandals. They arrived in Biratnagar, via diplomatic pouch.

Nearly every day, I visited a little shop two blocks from my apartment that I called the *doodh pasal*, or "milk shop," because they occasionally sold cartons of refrigerated water-buffalo milk. Two brothers in their twenties, Kumar and Guru, ran the shop. Guru was older, slightly rougher, and more handsome. His shorts and white tank top, combined with two days' worth of stubble, gave him the air of a frat brother who had just finished a round of beer pong. Kumar, gawky and taller, wore a pressed button-down shirt and was clean-shaven except for a carefully trimmed mustache. Only his bare feet, protruding from gray slacks, suggested how hot it was—115 degrees—in the wooden shack where he sat.

They adopted me, insisting I not stand outside the counter but set the kickstand on my bicycle and come inside their shack. They lounged on a pallet under shelves with neatly stacked packets of dried noodles, laundry powder, and cookies. Cloudy plastic jars housed hard candies that Kumar promised I'd like, only to laugh at the faces I made when I tasted the flavors: spicy candy, pepper candy, and the particularly stomach-turning *dal bhat* candy, which was supposed to taste like the national rice and lentil dish but seemed a blend of fermented cabbage and tomato paste.

They asked me simple questions in Nepali, and by flailing through answers, I learned to say more than the basic phrases I'd learned in training: *It's hot* or *I like fruit*.

"Who lives in your house?"

"My mother, father, and brother."

"Where do your grandparents live?"

"In a different building. A building full of other old people."

"Why?"

"In America, old people live in buildings full of other old people."

"Why?"

Here I didn't know what to say. Because old people would rather be around other old people? Because Americans like their old people out of sight? Because a little distance makes everyone more comfortable? None of my answers seemed right, or I didn't have the vocabulary to articulate them. I shrugged.

I liked both brothers, but Kumar was my special friend, patient and guileless. Guru spoke too quickly, sometimes wedging in a side comment to make Kumar laugh.

"What'd he say?" I'd demand.

"Oh, nothing, nothing." Kumar would grin. "Come, Annieji, sit down. *Basnu na.*"

They insisted I stop every time I passed by, if only to inspect my purchases ("How much did you pay for those oranges?"). One day, they stopped me on my way to the bazaar.

"Annieji! How are you?" Kumar yelled.

"Not so good," I said, straddling my bike. "My new stereo broke!" I pulled the tiny cassette player out of my backpack and passed it to Guru, who already had his hand out.

"Of course it broke!" he said, turning it over.

"But I just bought it. It cost eight hundred rupees!"

"This," Guru said, "was made in China."

"This is use-and-throw," Kumar said, inserting the English phrase to mean "disposable." In Nepali: *Yo use-and-throw cha.*

They passed it around to several of their buddies lounging in the shop. Everyone agreed it was use-and-throw.

"Well, I'm going to take it back where I bought it," I said.

"And they will tell you"—Guru paused dramatically—"that this is use-and-throw. Whatever you do, don't buy a new one from China. Get one made in Nepal."

"Nepal doesn't make stereos," Kumar scoffed.

"*Ke garne.* Get one that is made in India!" Guru called.

Ke garne is one of the first Nepali expressions foreigners learn. Literally translated as "what to do?" the meaning feels closer to "what can you do?"

You're mad about your new stereo breaking?

Ke garne.

You don't like my joking?

Ke garne.

Its refrain carries the implicit fatalism of a nation notorious for poverty and corruption, a textbook case of development gone wrong. The expression also suggests the acceptance of suffering, advocated by the Buddha, whose birthplace is Lumbini, in southern Nepal. This acceptance is both what frustrates outsiders in Nepal—"Nothing ever gets done around here!"—and what appeals to us—"If only I could be so content with the way life is."

First, I noticed how few injuries occurred in Nepal; months in, I noticed how rarely people expressed outrage or indignation when things went wrong. *Ke garne*, Nepalis said when the power went out in the evenings. *Ke garne*, Nepalis said when I complained about teaching *The Great Gatsby* to twelfth graders who didn't understand English. *Ke garne*, they said when I discovered a locked room in my school with a new donated computer disassembled in various cardboard boxes. *We cannot let the students use. They will break.*

Most foreigners in Nepal appropriate this phrase, first with irony, then wholeheartedly. I found it then, as now, an enviable way to live, as did the others in my cohort. It was a relief, after an American childhood, to take everything—even our own safety—less seriously. Risk was everywhere, but this did not make life precious. It made it thrilling.

How worldly it made us feel to toss around the names of parasites we knew intimately. Cyclospora? Roundworm? Hookworm? *Ke garne!* How cavalierly we set out with our medical kit, as if a plastic briefcase packed with throat lozenges, dental floss, ciprofloxacin, and rehydration salts would save us. Peace Corps forbade us from riding on top of buses, as was the local custom, though nearly everyone did it at least once if only to say she had. A seasoned volunteer warned us greenhorns during training, "Only fly Buddha Air. They use instruments; the others all use dead reckoning. It's called 'dead' for a reason." His words were serious, but his tone blasé. We all nodded as if we knew that already. Duh.

Maoist rebels, who modeled their insurgency on the terrifying rhetoric of Peru's Shining Path, lurked in the hills and often called for strikes to close stores and schools. Occasionally, we saw busloads of them careen down into the flatlands, where most Peace Corps volunteers lived. Though newspaper photos showed them in uniform, all of the rebels I saw were seemingly nineteen years old, in red t-shirts and with scraps of red fabric tied around their foreheads, as if they were in a B-grade movie about a Maoist insurgency. Radio Nepal's morning report included a body count from battles the day before. Over 32-ounce Kingfisher beers, volunteers discussed the latest statistics, the merits and drawbacks of the Maoists, the rumors we'd heard of how kindly they treated villagers, their use of child soldiers, and the impossibility of their campaign. Such talk lent our capers gravitas. Everyone knew if things got really bad, Peace Corps would send us home.

Bravado led us to mock other volunteers who were sent home for mental health reasons, i.e. "wack-evacked." We expressed grudging admiration for those willing to eat things that made others blanch: goat meat, sometimes with tufts of wiry hair still attached, or pigeon. ("What? Lots of cultures eat it! In England, it's called squab.")

What we took most seriously were our attempts to bridge the distance between our culture and Nepal's. We set up all kinds of measurements to mark how much we had absorbed. We all knew the Nepali word for "rice," but the volunteer who could also say "rice" in Limbu and Newari won. It was a point of pride to distinguish between the Hindu gods Saraswathi and Parvati, or to know that proselytizing is strongly discouraged in Hinduism, or to identify a rare type of citrus and casually mention in which month it ripens. People on the outside often view a Peace Corps stint as service, but everyone who has done it knows it involves more taking than giving. We had enough sense to know we were there to be schooled.

Nepalis' genuine goodwill disarmed our jaded irony. *You don't have to be here*, they told us, *but you came*. They accepted our sudden presence in their lives without question, opening their homes to us and protecting us from whatever they deemed dangerous: unscrupulous marketplace vendors, dirty water, eating citrus when you had a cold. "The guest is god," my students often recited. Nepalis' kindness and curiosity toward Americans made us want to sit through seven-hour weddings or visit a dozen families on a holiday. We complained about this privilege. We delighted in the burden.

On April 25, 2015, thirteen years after I finished my service in Nepal, the Indian subcontinent thrust its way farther under the Tibetan plateau's overbite. The glass beads hanging in thick strands in the stalls of Rakhi Bazaar in Kathmandu rattled against each other, blue colliding into green, green into yellow, yellow into orange, orange into red. The wooden stalls began to collapse. People honked their horns until they realized what had happened, and then the sounds disintegrated into shouts of terror. Afterwards, great silence.

Or so I imagine. April 25th was a rainy day in North Carolina, where I lived with my husband, Adam, a fellow volunteer I met in Nepal. We let our kids watch cartoons in the next room while we scrolled through image after image on the internet: buildings reduced to brick heaps; Nepalis holding cell phone cameras above three-foot fissures in the

asphalt; the nineteenth-century, nine-story Dharahara Tower
brought down to a mere mound, like a sand castle smoothed
by a wave; bright saris spread to dry over rooftop walls that
lunged at forty-five-degree angles. Women in shawls and
men in woven *topis* peered over bodies on the sidewalk. Mari-
gold malas encircled the feet of orange-shrouded corpses.
Survivors pulled from the wreckage and caked with dust and
debris looked like ghosts, and children, haunted-looking,
huddled with their families. I recognized the golden hoops
bent crookedly through the earlobes of toddler girls and
boys alike. I recognized their eyes, ringed with the kohl their
mothers had smeared on to protect them from evil spirits.
And when I read that all the Peace Corps volunteers were
safe in the US Embassy, I felt a twinge of envy that they were
there and I was home. Safe. I had an urge, absurd and mis-
guided, to jump on a plane.

My five-year-old son wandered in. "What's that?" he asked.

"An earthquake hit Nepal. The ground started shaking,
and buildings collapsed. A lot of people were hurt. See?" I
showed him. "Daddy and I used to live there. Remember?—
we told you."

He studied the pictures then asked, "That couldn't happen
here, right?"

Eventually, we closed the laptop and took the children
to Safari Nation, a room of bounce houses, where machines
light up and blare and beep and occasionally dispense prizes.
Friendly inflatable snakes and gorillas perch above the slides
and tunnels. There are nachos. There are Slush Puppies.
Almost all surfaces are padded. My children bounced as I
made a mental list of all we try to protect them from: mosquitoes, bullying, peanut and egg products, sunburn, traffic, low
self-esteem, splinters, strange dogs....

We spent thirty dollars in two hours—my monthly rent
while in Nepal. Surveying the crushed chips underfoot, the
parents peering into screens, the children amped up on play
without imagination, I asked Adam, "Is it morally bankrupt

of us to be here today?" Nepal had never felt so distant, or so close.

For a week, I was weepy. I checked the news every fifteen minutes and gave Adam constant death toll updates, which he politely tolerated. He is a mathematician, so when I said, "Seven thousand," he said, "You know, over two hundred thousand died in the Haiti earthquake." I conceded his point. But I've never been to Haiti.

At the same time, my unchecked melodrama embarrassed me. I'm not Nepali. I am hardly in contact with any Nepalis these days. My life was virtually untouched by the disaster. It was puzzling, almost shameful, how when the few people in my current life who remember my connection to Nepal asked about it, my eyes welled up. As if the earthquake was something that had happened to me. As if my own life had been in danger.

On September 12, 2001, I was a year into my Peace Corps service in Nepal when I saw the U.S. Twin Towers on the cover of the *Kathmandu Post*: three grainy photographs depicting the slow-motion sequence of the second plane hitting the south tower. I first heard of the attacks when my post mate, an American from New York City, called to say, "Something's happened at home." Now the news was everywhere: in newspapers passed around my school's office, on restaurant TVs, in the mouths of Nepalis who called out to us on the street. (Adam learned of it when a Nepali student on a dirt path shouted to him, "An airplane just hit the world's biggest house!"). This was my country, my homeland, under attack. And yet, through the filter of Nepal, the attacks felt far, far away.

On the streets in Biratnagar, people saw me as America and offered their condolences. Strangers flagged me down to say I could come in anytime to watch BBC on their televisions. A few days after the attacks, my host mother said, "Your parents and brother can come here. We'll love them like we do you."

It didn't surprise me that our country had created such enemies. Adam, quoting Malcolm X's comment on President Kennedy's assassination, said, "Chickens coming home to roost." But not everyone saw the same connections.

In October, a volunteer passing through met me for morning rice and lentils. He spread open a newspaper and thumped the headline: The United States had begun bombing Afghanistan.

"Let's bomb the shit out of them," he said with satisfaction. Here was an American abroad, a supposed champion of peace, who couldn't wait to start the war. If this was what a Peace Corps volunteer thought, what were people saying back in the United States?

I kept thinking how much the pictures of Afghans reminded me of Nepalis—in their eyes, their dress, their familiarity. Feeling morose, on my way home, I stopped by the *doodh pasal*.

"You need to call George Bush," Guru told me right away.

"O.K." I played along. They joked about everything. Of course, a terrorist attack wouldn't be any different. "Why?"

"You need to call and tell him not to bomb Nepal."

"Nepal is very close to Afghanistan," Kumar added.

"He might get mixed up," Guru said. "And we're scared."

"Very scared! We don't want to be bombed."

"Who knows? America might bomb anybody," I said slowly, trying to get the verbs right.

"Exactly." Guru smiled. "So give him a call. Please. Do it for us." His tone was light, but we all knew how dangerous my wounded country was.

Many Americans expected me to come home that year following the attacks. To them, the foreign world seemed newly dangerous, an indistinguishable hostile mass. But going home never occurred to me. If anything, 9/11 and the subsequent bombing campaigns gave me another reason to stay away for thirteen more months, no matter how clumsy an ambassador I was. Nepal wasn't dangerous. Nepal went on exactly the same as it had before, Auden's horse scratching its behind against a tree—only it was a water buffalo wallowing in the mud. Whereas before, I might have read Auden's poem as a critique of the world's indifference to suffering, I now saw compassionate pragmatism in the rest of the world's determination to keep going. *Ke garne?* What else can you do?

My service with the Peace Corps ended in October 2002. When I first got home, people kept saying what a brave and admirable thing I had done. This praise seemed ludicrous. All I'd done was learn how sheltered and privileged I was. I had been willing to sit with that discomfort, and now I was back in the land of safe drinking water and free public schools. I spent a few months grading standardized tests at a temp job and staring down from my childhood bedroom window at the still, silent street below. Then, to heighten our culture shock, Adam and I moved to Los Angeles, where we set about converting the price of everything into rupees. This did not make us very fun to hang out with.

After being home in the U.S. for eighteen months, which felt like an unbearably long time away from Nepal, we went back for a visit. On the taxi ride from Tribhuvan airport, I remembered how life is lived in the open there. Already I had forgotten. A man had created a barbershop by nailing a mirror to a tree. In a chair propped in front of the mirror, men tilted their necks to the sky, trusting a straight razor, its edge meeting lather. A boy walked along the roadside with cucumbers as big as clubs, the vegetables quartered and displayed under a dusty glass case that looked as if it should instead house antique watches. A girl brushed her teeth as she eyed the traffic. Maintaining eye contact with me, she spit a white beam of Neem toothpaste foam into a patch of dirt. A young boy, bare-bottomed, squatted just beside the road, a golden pile of shit forming beneath him. But he was not the spectacle. I was. He watched my blurred white face, protected behind glass.

In Biratnagar, at the *doodh pasal*, I was disappointed to learn Kumar was visiting his uncle in Kathmandu.

"You're going back to K'du, right?" Guru asked. "Maybe you'll see him."

I pointed out that Kathmandu was a city of almost a million people and without street signs.

Guru shrugged. "Maybe you'll run into him." He wrote down the name of his uncle's neighborhood.

A week later, on our last night in Kathmandu, Adam and I went to the Buddhist stupa Swayambhunath. Its huge white dome is decorated with Buddha's elaborately lined eyes and a golden-topped tower. Strings of prayer flags stretch from the dome to the surrounding shops in the pavilion, like the spokes of a wheel. At sunset, you can sit at the base of the stupa and survey the hazy city as young Buddhist monks in burgundy robes stroll past. Swayambhunath is somewhat near Kumar's uncle's neighborhood—but this is where my memory and Adam's memory differ. Did we go looking for the uncle's house? Did we even know Swayambhunath was near his neighborhood at the time? We cannot remember how it happened, only that it did.

At twilight in Nepal, everyone is on the streets, coming home from work or hurrying out, plaid plastic shopping bags in hand, to buy pumpkin vines for curry. The evening settles like a benediction. You let go of whatever has or hasn't happened that day—*ke garne*, go home, have some rice—and are content until morning. In this turmeric-scented hustle, on a crowded street, Kumar appeared just ahead of me. I was sure it was him.

"Kumar!" I called.

He turned around.

"Annieji!" He greeted me as if we'd last met yesterday and he'd been expecting me here around now. Time folded neatly, like a hanky.

"I can't believe it!" I kept saying. "I can't believe I just ran into you like this!"

Kumar was as unfazed as I was incredulous. His nonchalant acceptance of the improbable was characteristically Nepali, perhaps borne out of living with fewer illusions of control. For two years, I had witnessed how people could rest easily alongside chance and contradiction, but I am still an American. Knee-jerk astonishment and indignation is my birthright. After many handshakes, Kumar strode off. I watched his dark head recede until I was no longer certain I saw him anymore. It's as if he is still moving away from me, all these years later.

I meant to return to Nepal, but life intervened. A year in South America. Then grad school. Babies. A mortgage. Somehow, in eleven years, we hadn't gone back. The earthquake reminded me that to know another country well is both a gain and a loss—for the rest of your life, there is always somewhere you could be but are not.

In Thamel, Kathmandu's tourist district, you can buy souvenirs: Maithili paintings of elephants; incense pellets; bootleg CDs of the ever-present chant *Om Mani Padme Hum*; a nose ring; sustainably made purses from women's collectives; a smoothie that may or may not give you giardia, which, in any case, won't kill you; Tibetan singing bowls; thangka paintings of intricate mandalas limned in gold; wrapping paper stamped with water buffalo; postcards of Mt. Everest; lapis lazuli rings; pashmina shawls; knockoff North Face jackets and Mountain Hardwear tents; Gurkha *kukri* knives; and quilts made from vintage saris.

I shipped some of these things home because I could not bring home the angular hindquarters of cows that stand at dawn with their heads inside storefronts, waiting to be fed from nosebags. I could not take the tiny glasses of *chiya*, sweet milk tea, sold at roadside stands with a torn piece of newsprint covering the glass and sealed by steam. I could not take the mangy monkey on a chain, his earring glinting in the sun. Or the lane of tailor shops, tiny hovels where men operate their ancient foot-pedal sewing machines. Or the bus park in Kathmandu where ticket sellers grind tobacco in their palms with betel leaf and slaked lime.

I have a trekking map of Nepal on my living room wall and a green glass Buddha in my bedroom, but most of the things I brought home are folded in closets or boxed in the basement. More than any souvenir, Nepal gave me an idea of how big the world is and how small my own place in it. My years there gave me some distance from my own culture, which seems obsessively, often to its detriment, focused on protection, whether for our children or for our borders.

When I remember Nepal, I realize that earthquakes and fires and illnesses happen all over the world, including in my country, and that it may be better for kids to be brave and happy than safe and bored. We balance the risks of the physical world—malaria, plane crashes—with the risks of an insular life, lived underground, in fear. Too much safety creates its own dangers. I'm still an American mother with hand sanitizer in the diaper bag, but when I remember that learning requires exposure, I'm happier and calmer. I'm a better parent and wife and teacher. I laugh more. It's hard, joyless work being so damn afraid all the time. This is what I want to teach my kids.

While I'm kneeling on the tile to give my infant son a bath, the memory of a water tap in Nepal might well up unbidden, the shouts of girls bathing together, no thought given to the baby cobras gliding through the fields beyond. These memories arrive like an expanding breath: the scope of the world working on me from within, as a stent widens an airway, creating the space to make me feel safe. Or safe enough.

꒰ꋜ꒱ ꒰ꋜ꒱ ꒰ꋜ꒱

Anne P. Beatty is a writer and teacher who lives in Greensboro, North Carolina. Her nonfiction has been published in The Atlantic, The American Scholar, Creative Nonfiction, *and elsewhere. Her essay "Rich Country" was published in* The Best Women's Travel Writing, Volume 11.

Diane LeBow

❧ ❧ ❧

A Bedtime Story

Things heat up on an Italian train.

othing was moving; everyone seemed stunned. The Berlin Wall had recently come down, and Eastern Europe was like a sea between two tides. It was July 4, 2000, in the midst of World Cup frenzy. Earlier that day I'd left Prague on a train bound for Rome and then to see friends who lived south of Pompeii. It had taken two days of waiting in long lines to get a plane or train ticket out of Prague.

Now that I was finally on my way, weariness seeped into me, the kind that comes from being on the road, a rather bumpy one, for quite a while. I was returning to Italy. *Bella Italia*. I sighed and relaxed. No more warm milk over boiled potatoes and cabbage. My head was spinning with accounts from Party members who feared they would lose their jobs and so many who longed for some abstract of freedom. My notebook held all their tales, and I looked forward to sorting them out into stories. After the asceticism of Eastern Europe, soon I would be pampered with Italian food, joviality, and gentle landscapes. Comforts awaited me.

The only other person in my train compartment, a burly fellow in a pale blue cotton shirt, pulled off his well-worn cap, exposing thinning, light-brown hair, and pumped my hand up and down. His vigor was a healthy contrast to our stuffy quarters. "Andrej, *mi piacere*," he said. "I am heading down to the soccer matches. I am coach for the Czechoslovakian team."

So here was a bit of Eastern Europe beginning to spill out from behind the wilted Iron Curtain. Andrej's slightly dazed and pale demeanor reminded me of someone venturing into sunlight after a long illness in a darkened room. Using German as our common language, we discussed bits of our lives. He told me about his work at a small university just outside of Prague. I taught in a college, too, near San Francisco, so we compared our students, discussing our enjoyment of seeing them succeed, sympathizing about how frustrating the lazy ones were. I had never thought about physical education teachers at communist universities. Small, glum groups discussing Marxist theory had been my Western propagandized mental imagery, not fatherly looking coaches laughing with their students.

"*Ja*, what a hot night!" I agreed, and we each settled into our bunks on opposite sides of the otherwise unoccupied space.

With each passing moment, the unventilated car became ever more sizzling. I dozed fitfully, and at four A.M., I finally realized a radiator adjacent to my couchette was on, blasting just beside my right ear. Sweat poured off my body, and I had a terrible headache.

I decided to go against a major commandment when traveling the Italian rails. "Thou shalt keep your door locked, particularly while asleep." *I'm such a light sleeper*, I thought. *If I just slide the door open a bit, I'll get some air. With my purse under my head and my arm resting on my suitcase, I'll be fine.*

Andrej was snoring softly as I quietly unlocked and opened our compartment door, then slipped back onto my bunk.

The next thing I knew I was having one of those dreams in which you try to move but are paralyzed. I managed to raise my heavy eyelids ever so slightly. A nightmarish mirage stunned me.

An angular man backed out of our space, past the sleeping soccer coach, smirking while at the same time nodding reassuringly at me. His glance and raised hand warned: "Don't get up. Don't move. Just lie there." The man's reddish-hued, elongated face and lean body had the cast of the devil. Disheveled hair, the color of watery blood, stood up on both sides of his sweaty skull, like two horns. I strained to raise my arms, to move my legs. Nothing. Though I was only partially conscious, some reflexive part of my brain told me I had to force myself to grab for my purse. Weakly, I moved my right hand behind my head.

My purse was gone. Just a few moments earlier, my black leather traveling purse had cushioned my head and neck. Securely nested inside the purse—in addition to my wallet, money, credit cards, address book, favorite jewelry, and return ticket to the States—was my notebook from the last four weeks of travel. Stretching my arm and hand back behind my head, I probed again, harder and deeper. Everything had vanished.

Like the Cheshire Cat, the vermilion northern Italian had evaporated along with all my valuables, leaving behind, sizzled into my memory, only his malevolent smirk.

The torridity of the night oozed into every part of my body. "Something really terrible has just happened to me," I murmured to myself. I shook my head, trying to clear my brain. Drugged, had I been drugged? How?

Andrej had slept through everything. Struggling to reach a standing, if wobbly, position, I shouted, hoping he could help me. "I've been robbed!" I tried saying this in English, French, and German. He got the idea and sat up on his bunk, rubbing his eyes with his large fingers.

On trembling knees, balancing myself against the compartment walls as the train jolted along, I tottered out into the train aisle and shouted: "Help, I've been robbed."

"So have we," replied Australian voices. Several young men in jeans were stumbling around in the train aisle. "Someone's got everything. Our musical instruments. We were to give a concert in Firenze. We're earning our way by playing as we go." Three men in their early twenties stood there, looking helpless. One sobbed: "My only pair of eyeglasses were in my cello case. I can't see without them. All our money's gone."

As we commiserated, we realized we were having a classic Italian train experience, one I'd been warned about: During brief stops at stations, in this case Ferrara en route to Florence, professional thieves board the train and shoot an aerosol chloroform preparation into the compartments, which temporarily paralyzes the occupants. The thieves then grab valuables and jump off the train as it leaves the station, too late for the stunned victims to do anything except wail and get off at the next stop to report their losses to indifferent authorities who hear the same stories every day.

The conductor, who was slinking about, smirked at me. "You have insurance, no? All Americans have insurance. You'll be O.K." It dawned on me that he was involved in the theft.

"Who do you think put the heat on in the train, on such a beastly hot night?" I said to the Australians.

"Righto," said the calmest of the Australians, "and we unsuspecting foreigners opened our compartment doors for a little breath of air."

My adrenaline-fueled blood pressure made my head want to explode. I needed to act. I insisted the conductor go with me, and we inspected the trash in every toilet on the train.

Although I was pretty sure my purse was long gone, I wanted to annoy him as much as possible.

As the train pulled into the Rome station, Andrej turned to me. "I would like to help you out and give you some money," he said, "but you know we don't have credit cards yet in Eastern Europe, and my foreign currency is really limited, but here's what I can spare. It's not much." He handed me ten thousand lire, enough for a sandwich and drink. I had another six hours of travel ahead of me. He was meeting his team in Italy and kept only a few thousand lire for himself. The conductor was holding my passport and ticket, which would get me to my friends in the South.

That was it. As we said goodbye, I choked back tears, reluctant to leave this small connection with a kinder world.

"You must take me to the police station," I told the conductor, who was looking sheepish. I tried to make my five-feet-two inches as tall and my voice as assertive as possible. I was afraid that if the conductor didn't accompany me to the police office in the cavernous Rome train station, I'd lose my way and miss my connection to southern Italy. If that happened, I had no money to buy an additional ticket. Also, I was still floating in the ether of illusion that often helps us puny humans through crummy experiences. Somehow, I thought reporting the theft might magically cause my personal belongings, especially my notebook, to be returned to me.

Inside the humid, rancid-smelling police office, about one hundred angry people pushed and shouted, trying to get the attention of a bald, sweating man with a badge. The mob seemed, like me, to be foreigners who had been robbed. We all filled out forms and pressed toward the front where the man was stamping papers.

The officer looked at my papers and up at me. Then he scrunched up his dripping face and started winking at me. For a moment, I was caught up in this bit of good spirits in the midst of an otherwise gloomy day, wanting to bet on the basic goodness of human nature. *He will help me,* I thought.

Then he leered at me. "It's almost my break," he said. "Come into the back room with me and I'll go over your papers." The crowd pressed against me, and I looked down to avoid tripping over someone's foot. I noticed his scuffed brown shoes were down at the heels. Not the shoes of a savior at all. Worse yet, as I raised my eyes, I saw that his poorly fitting, faded gray polyester trousers had stains in inappropriate places and an obvious and unprofessional bulge at the crotch.

"Come, come, into the back room with me," he urged. It was about one hundred degrees in the Rome train station. I hadn't slept in forty-eight hours. I had lost many of my immediate worldly possessions, and the policeman in charge of taking my report concerning my theft was urging me into the back room of the station with him.

I snapped. Suddenly, I was waving my arms and shouting Italian slang I hadn't even been aware I knew: "*Diavolo! Va all'inferno!*" It may or may not have been grammatically correct or made any sense. He stamped my forms.

Finally my train pulled out of the Rome station. Once again, I was moving south.

This time it was daylight. The compartment was breezy but warm, and I was feeling numb from shock, lack of sleep, and the heat. Across from me sat an Italian man, around thirty, handsome, mustachioed—and watching me intently. Speaking Italian, he introduced himself: "I have to travel a lot for my work. We live in Battipaglia." He slid the doors shut and closed the curtains to the aisle. "I've been married just one month. It's difficult being away from my wife so much." I knew he wasn't thinking about thieves.

After a few minutes, he began blowing me little kisses. "*Amore, amore,*" he chanted like a mantra.

A few years before, while eating *cozze con orecchiette* followed by glasses of *grappa* at a friend's house in Rome, my Italian women friends had revealed a secret to me. "Many Italian men," they said, "feel responsible for maintaining the international Italian image of macho virility, by attempting to seduce every foreign woman they can. But you know what? Most of them really aren't interested. And many of them aren't such good lovers anyway. They just feel obligated to pretend to seduce. They are counting on you to turn them down."

I looked at the young man across the compartment from me. "*Non, non*," I said firmly, and opened my book. I was on "The Fifth Day" of Boccaccio's *Decameron*. In this section, all the tales were about lovers who won happiness after grief or misfortune. A good omen, it seemed. Outside the window, green fields, ancient apartment houses with red shutters, and old women walking with their donkeys flew by. *It's Italy*, I thought. *I'm still alive, and soon I'll be with my friends.* I grinned. In the end, we're all just making our way along as best we can.

My fellow traveler had quietly reopened the curtains and door to the aisle. Like a reprimanded school child, he slid away from me as far as he could on the bench, knees tightly pressed together, and stared into space. Then, glancing at me from the corner of his lovely dark eye, he noticed my book.

"*Ecco*. Boccaccio. I like very much. Would you like I read to you *un poco*?"

Eagerly, he took my bi-lingual text and read. The sonorous tones of medieval Italian soothed me as we sailed south, into the heart of Italy. Drowsily, I heard him read: "In these tales will be seen the gay and sad adventures of lovers and other happenings both of ancient and modern times."

I closed my eyes and fell into a deep, delicious sleep.

∽ ∽ ∽

In addition to being chloroformed and robbed on an Italian train, Diane has worked for women's rights in Afghanistan, ridden a camel through locust swarms on the Libyan Sahara, and searched for Amazon women's descendants among Mongolian horsewomen. Her work has appeared in anthologies and other publications, including Salon, Via, Image, Cleis, Seal, *and* Travelers' Tales *presses, and has won many awards, including eleven Solas Awards and a Lifetime Achievement Award from Douglass College (Rutgers University) for her writing, photojournalism, women's rights work all over the world, and as a pioneer of women's studies and innovative college teaching in Paris, Holland, and the USA. She earned one of the first Ph.D's in Women's Studies, University of California. Her travel memoir will be published soon. www. dianelebow.com*

స్తు స్తు స్తు

In the Presence of Boys

Sometimes you get something you didn't expect.

The boys arrive carrying mismatched gifts: potato chips, chocolate chip cookies, and an orange drink. They have come to fix my shoji doors.

It is the last Saturday in January, the only Saturday students have off from junior high school. The boys heard about my doors last week. I don't remember how it came up, but once I mentioned it—that my doors were torn in a dozen different places; that I wanted to fix them but didn't know how—the boys shouted out they would be happy to help.

"We know how to do it," they said.

They're boasting, I thought. Showing off for the rest of the class. But they persisted.

"When can we come?" they asked, rushing up to me after class.

We agreed Saturday would be a good day to work.

Suteki, they say, standing in my entranceway, peeking around the corner to my small kitchen, *honto ni suteki,* meaning the place looks really nice. I thank them for coming and politely they thank me in return. They have traveled an hour on two buses to get here. Now, standing in front of me in grown-up clothes instead of their school uniforms, they have taken off their boots, their coats, given me their presents. Then we all become quiet, tongue-tied in a way we've never been at school.

Shu and Horiuchi and I met two and a half years ago on the first field trip I took with students at Meizen Junior High. I had been in Japan for only a few weeks. We were visiting a small art museum, then going to a *wasabi* farm afterward where we all ate horseradish ice cream that surprised me by tasting very good. The director of the museum, a well-meaning middle-aged woman, saw a blond-haired Westerner walk in the door and proceeded to blast me with questions, firing off one after another in Japanese, a language I didn't understand beyond essentials: *Hello. Goodbye. Beer please. Where's the toilet? Where's the train?*

Shu and Horiuchi tried to help. Shu repeated the woman's questions s-l-o-w-l-y, but still in Japanese, thinking perhaps she had simply spoken too fast. Horiuchi, realizing language, not speed, was the central problem, took a different approach. He translated bits and pieces of the woman's questions into what English he knew: "Where...from? Here...Japan... what doing?" After just a couple of questions, all three of us started to laugh. We walked away from the woman in the museum but kept talking.

For more than two years now, we have conversed, Shu and Horiuchi and I and all the other students, too, all of us sliding in and out of model sentences, using patterns learned from our textbooks at school.

Do you like tea? they ask. *Do you like Japan? Do you like Meizen?*

"Yes," I answer. "Yes, I do." "Yes, of course. Meizen is my favorite school."

On Saturday, they come prepared, Shu with a tube of glue in his backpack, Horiuchi a roll of white paper, six inches wide. They examine the doors. Six strips of rice paper hang behind the two wooden frames. We don't know it yet but we have about seven hours of work ahead, starting with figuring out how to maneuver the doors off their hinges. The shoji doors hide sliding glass doors, which in turn cover two screens. All three layers lead to a small balcony where I hang my laundry out to dry. The paper doors filter out light, but just barely. At night, streetlight bathes the room in a wash of soft white. But sometimes on Saturday mornings when I want to sleep late, the glare of sun hurts my head. I cover the doors with tall bamboo shades that most people in Japan use only outdoors—one more layer to keep out and make muted the harsh morning light.

We work through the morning and into the afternoon, peeling off old paper, scrubbing hard glue from the wooden frames, and talking.

With the sliding doors open and torn rice paper fluttering in the wind, I tell them the tenant before me, an American woman like me, lived here. Her Japanese boyfriend, a black-belt in karate, practiced kicks and punches in this room. Damage was done, I say. It wasn't me who ruined the doors. I want them to know I wouldn't be so careless. They laugh. They tell me they've seen doors much worse than these.

They whisper to each other, then motion to me. Shu pulls fists to his face, then punches his right hand through my paper door. Horiuchi goes next. Both boys motion for me to try too. I poke a fist through a paper square, surprised at how loud the crackle sounds. I'm tentative at first but soon we are all punching and jabbing, sparring with rice paper, pretending to punch one another, too.

———

We work all morning and into the afternoon. Horiuchi holds a damp rag in his right hand, a dictionary in the other, as he asks me questions in English. "Do you think," he asks, "Japanese people nervous?"

I laugh. "Some are. Some aren't. Look at 3-1 class," I say. "No one in *that* class is nervous or shy!"

This is their homeroom, 3-1. In seventh grade it was 1-1 and in eighth grade 2-1. In Japan, students progress through junior high accompanied by the same classmates and the same homeroom teacher year after year. Students stay put in the same room for years at a time. Teachers, instead, rotate, traveling from room to room, packing portable lessons in history or English or math or science, meeting students on the students' home turf. As a foreign English teacher, I travel between three schools, spending two weeks at each place, visiting each class at those schools maybe once or twice a month at most. It is 3-1 class I look forward to seeing, 3-1 I miss most when away, and 3-1 that has become, over time, the closest thing to a homeroom I will have while teaching in Japan.

No matter the classroom and no matter the season, boys at school drape their arms around each other and sit on one another's laps. When I first arrived in Japan, all that touching left me unnerved. Girls held hands in the hallways and students massaged the necks of their teachers during breaks between classes, no one commenting on or even raising an eyebrow to all that touching. At first I was surprised, but then, after a few months, the gestures seemed commonplace, as ordinary as eating rice every day. Still, I felt pangs of jealousy and thought how strange it was that no one ever touched me.

In my apartment, we stick to safe topics, never lingering too long over any particular one. We talk about sports. The Chicago Bulls. The Phoenix Suns. The Raiders, Shu's favorite team. Horiuchi tells me in a whisper that, really, he is Michael

Jordan. ("But don't tell the others," he says.) Shu says that, really, he is Charles Barkley. ("A secret," he warns.) "I am honored to have such fine guests," I tell them, and I mean what I say.

We talk, too, about school. They say Miss Kiryu's class is boring, that she never varies her style of teaching, her lessons are always the same. I tell them Miss Kiryu is young and needs time and they need to learn patience. They tell me how much they like *my* visits to the classroom, the Bob Marley songs I bring to class, the Bingo games I insist we play, and the prizes I give to students bold enough to practice their English by speaking out loud. I am flattered, of course, and they know it. So now, with the sliding doors open and torn rice paper fluttering in the afternoon wind, it's clear: we're more than a little smitten.

On the way to school, boys walk in pairs and in packs but rarely alone. Riding bikes to school is against the rules. For all their energy, these boys are accustomed to following rules. In spring, when one boy gets caught playing *pachinko* downtown, his whole soccer team gets punished for his mistake. For a week, soccer is canceled and every boy on the team has to clean up the school grounds after class instead.

No one will say which boy was to blame. No one tattles or complains.

Small details and fragments of stories come out, unfolding over time. What I know about the boys is a jumbled mix, part hearsay, part fact, part fiction, perhaps—stories I have made up or constructed or imagined or observed.

These are the stories I give myself, a present because I am a woman alone.

I watch them, the boys and the girls, but only the boys dare to watch me back. Shu is stocky, built like a wrestler. Horiuchi is thin and wiry, all angles and sharp planes. In ninth grade Horiuchi got new glasses, tortoise shell frames that make him look like Waldo, the cartoon character known here as Wally, a kid wearing a red-and-white striped shirt, always lost in a crowd of look-alike boys. The two are opposites: Shu physical but prone to illness; Horiuchi academic but healthy and good at sports. Shu breaks the rules. Horiuchi tends to follow. In seventh grade, Shu hung out with the older boys, chewing gum between classes, wearing purple socks, drinking Coke in the hallways—all infractions in a Japanese school. By ninth grade, the fighting began.

Once Shu came to school with a face so bruised and mis-shapen that all I could think of was the Japanese word for eggplant, that his face looked like *nasu*. Miss Kiryu said what happened was this: Two boys from another school provoked Shu, along with another of Shu's friends, also a Meizen boy. Two other boys, also from Meizen but not from 3-1 class, watched but did not help. Miss Kiryu said what bothered teachers most is that the Meizen boys did not try to stop the fight or help out in any way. In fact, there was reason to believe the Meizen boys had arranged the fight, orchestrating things so two bullies from a nearby school would get a chance to beat on Shu.

"Why?" I asked. Why would these unnamed boys want to hurt Shu? For all his faults, his restlessness in class, his defiance of most rules, his faltering grades, and a temper that sometimes flared, Shu is a kind young man. That was the word Miss Kiryu used. Kind and gentle. *Yasashii.*

"Because they envy him," Miss Kiryu told me. "Because Shu does what he wants."

Earlier this year, Shu was rumored to have pulled a knife on the chief English teacher at Meizen, Mr. Iguchi. Mr. Iguchi would not tell me about the incident. Neither would Miss Kiryu. In fact, no one ever mentioned the incident again, which left me wondering what I really knew of Shu.

What we talk about now are girls. We roll out rice paper, preparing to glue the final strip to the door. It's cold outside.

The boys are in t-shirts and jeans. I want to tell them to put on their coats but somehow, it doesn't seem my place.

We've been working on the shoji doors all day without a break. I forgot to offer the boys something to eat, some potato chips, perhaps, or the store-bought chocolate chip cookies they so graciously brought to me. I forgot to offer them something to drink, orange punch or Coke or tea.

Junior high school girls are babies, Shu says. He smirks in case I fail to catch his aim to shock. I give him my best poker face and think about how Shu may have a baby himself one day soon—sooner than me. Horiuchi likes girls, too, but not the same way as Shu. "Only friends," he says when Shu and I ask him to count up his girlfriends. Even in the face of teasing, he remains resolute. "Only friends," he repeats.

I wonder what these boys will be like when they grow up. What we don't know yet is that Shu will fail the high school entrance exam and go to work for his parents' ramen shop full time. Horiuchi will pass the exam with decent scores and go to one of Matsumoto's middle-range schools, confirming what Miss Kiryu has said: that Horiuchi is clever but lazy. He could have gone to Fukashi, Matsumoto's top high school, she told me, the one that sends its graduates on to Tokyo University, the Harvard of Japan, but Horiuchi will fail to study hard enough along the way. But that, perhaps, is part of why I like him. Because he likes so many other things: basketball (especially the Chicago Bulls); reggae music (Bob Marley); running (he's one of the fastest at his school). He also likes Shu, and Shu likes him, each of them declaring the other his No. 1 *ichiban*, best friend in the world, each of them using the kind of sweeping authority that accompanies youth.

When it turns dark outside, the mood becomes subdued. We have one more strip to apply. It would be easy to become careless. Shu cuts the paper with a knife, reminds us to go slow, take care, and do the last of this job just right.

Finally the doors are finished. The boys fit them back into the sliding rods on the floor. Tired of English, they talk quickly now in Japanese. Something about the essence of shoji doors. Something to do with peace and quiet. Something about honor, too, which I don't fully understand until Horiuchi explains that they've been talking about how the best fight among men involves a conflict over winning the affections of a woman, and I'm reminded of a day at school not too long ago.

I had brought a photo album to 3-1 class. In it were pictures of Meizen students that I'd taken. Good for conversation, Miss Kiryu had said. And I agreed. All went well or as well as one can expect from the rambunctious 3-1 class. After class, the students gathered round the teacher's desk to scan the pictures, hoping, no doubt, to spot themselves. A boy with a shaved head pointed to one of me and called me an *o-ba-san* and *baka* to boot. An *old woman?* And *foolish?* I may not be young, but I'm not *that* dumb, I thought. I had half a mind to teach this boy certain idioms in English, beginning with "Watch me knock your block off, kid!" But Shu stepped in, said sternly in English, "No, no, no." He pointed to my picture and without looking at me, announced as if it were fact, "Bee-yoo-tee-full." Then before I could thank him, he walked away, his words hanging in the air like a paper crane come alive, the intricacies of the folds invisible now, an imaginary bird—and this beautiful outspoken boy—now soaring mid-flight.

They look around my apartment for a clock. It is after six o'clock. By 6:30 Horiuchi's mother will be waiting for the boys at Jusco, a shopping mall near my house. They should go, they say. I try to imagine what Horiuchi's mother looks like. I wonder if she is tall and thin and smart like him. I have heard Shu's mother is young and beautiful, thirty-two, two years older than I am now. I try to imagine how the boys will describe what happened today, what they will say to their mothers, what they will leave in, what will get left out. I try to imagine mothering boys like this, what it would feel like, if it would be anything close to this.

Two months later, on Graduation Day, Shu will storm up to my desk to give me a present, a silver skull necklace he has worn under his uniform, in secret, against the school's rules. It's a necklace I'll hold onto for many years and many moves to come, though I'll never wear it—a reminder, I will think, that you can love something, even cherish it, without the object ever touching your skin. Horiuchi, by contrast, will hang back when he comes to say goodbye, looking nervous, saying he is sorry for not studying harder, for failing to speak English so well. He will do his best in high school, he says; the next time we meet, we will speak English, he says, with ease. I will study Japanese, too, I will tell him, but the truth is, we will both get busy, caught up in the still-fuzzy future, interested in other things.

Gambare, Horiuchi will say.

Hai, gambare. Do your best.

Take care, we all say. *Take care. Take care.*

We will say goodbye, the three of us, awkwardly, like every other parting I have had with men. "Take care," I add one last time, repeating the word in Japanese just to be safe. I will want to thank them, Shu and Horiuchi, and all the others, too, but thank them for what?

I want to tell them I am a woman alone, someone who wanted children of her own. Sometimes things don't work out the way you want. Sometimes you get something you didn't expect, something you didn't know you wanted. That something surprises you by how much it means.

In my apartment after a long day of repairs, Shu and Horiuchi pull cameras out of their backpacks.

Pictures? they ask.

Awkwardly we take turns standing in pairs, each of us posing in front of the now-perfect shoji doors. Language, culture, age, and gender—these things ought to separate us like veils thick as velvet curtains. Parting now, I am struck by the intensity, though, of what we share: a curiosity about one another, a longing that feels like love, and, in the end, a desire for a simple souvenir. A picture. A reminder of a very fine day.

I am shorter than both boys. As we pose, I begin to reach up to touch them, to wrap an arm around a shoulder. But I stop myself, stand stiffly, arms dangling. In the photos, I stand close to these boys, arms barely touching, and we are smiling.

℘ ℘ ℘

Marilyn Abildskov is the author of The Men in My Country, *a memoir set in Japan. She is the recipient of a Rona Jaffe Writers' Award, a Glenna Luschei* Prairie Schooner *Award, and honors from the Corporation of Yaddo and the Djerassi Writing Residency. Her short stories and essays have appeared recently in* Sewanee Review, Southern Review, StoryQuarterly, Epoch, *and* Best American Essays. *She lives in the San Francisco Bay Area and teaches creative nonfiction in the MFA Program at Saint Mary's College of California.*

༄ ༄ ༄

Traveling Queer and Far

Suddenly, every interaction mattered.

The time to stop hiding came as we sat in the back of a van somewhere along the road between Ranthambore National Park and Udaipur. Not that we'd ever been trying to hide, exactly. But we knew the moment would come.

Packing for our trip to India, I had brought it up. Sarah and I were taking our daughter, Willa, four years old at that point, to Delhi for her godmother's wedding, after which we were going to explore the country for a few weeks. We wouldn't advertise that we were two moms traveling with a kid—I wasn't going to get t-shirts printed or anything—but if we were asked directly? Willa was old enough. If we hedged, or seemed uncomfortable, or worse, lied and said yeah, we were just friends or sisters, she would know. She would understand. She'd get the message that her family was something shameful, something less than. We knew it wasn't, but we also knew that too much of the world still believed it was.

It's a thing queer people sometimes do when we travel to less-than-queer-friendly places. Not so much play straight as just blend, letting people's assumptions wash over us like just another facet of cultural immersion. I eat with my hands or wear long sleeves or politely chuckle when a stranger asks if I have a husband as I'm standing, right there, next to my girl-friend. You could call it something between fear and coward-ice, but it's rooted in a genuine respect for other people and what they might feel about such issues. Some battles are not worth picking. This is a vacation, not a crusade.

I actually don't remember having to address it before we had Willa. I've always felt obviously gay, at least walking around in New York City, and when I was in far-off places like Iowa or Indonesia, I knew I was gay, and that felt like enough. Plus, there's an existential question here: If you're traveling alone, without a partner, are you just theoretically gay? If a lesbian falls in a forest, but there isn't another woman there to hear her, does she nonetheless make a pride-ful squelch?

When Sarah and I started traveling together, there were times we could have been considered only theoretically gay, too. Even that time on a deserted beach in Vieques, Puerto Rico, just a few months after we started dating, when Sarah persuaded me to sunbathe topless for the first time—to an observer, we could've been friends. Thankfully, there was no one else around. Then again, it would have been nice if some-one other than Sarah had been there to remind me to reapply sunscreen. But let's face it, most of the time, Sarah and I were too obsessed with each other to pay attention to what anyone else was noticing.

A child changes everything. Eventually. When Willa was a little over a year old, we took her to Tulum in Mexico. When we checked in and asked for a king-size bed, I have some vague memory about the receptionist asking if we were sisters and me mumbling some unspecific response. It didn't matter. Whatever would get me to my beach chair and margarita faster. What I remember much more specifically was realizing that a beach vacation suddenly isn't a vacation when you are chasing a toddler around trying to keep her from eating sand and/or drowning. I also remember the moment I realized the quaint rustling sound in the roof of our casita at night was actually scurrying rodents. When I was demanding a refund at two in the morning, I'm not sure if the hotel manager thought I was an angry lesbian or an angry straight woman or an angry, homely sister to my much hotter, femmeier sister, and honestly, I'm not sure either of us cared. Angry moms transcend all categories of gender and sexuality. As do margaritas, which are an excellent coping mechanism after discovering the roof of your hotel is crawling with rodents.

India was different. Now that Willa was older, it wasn't about us. It was about her—her sense of belonging and equality, in the world and in her own skin. Part of traveling is what you learn about the rest of the world, but part of it is what you learn about yourself. What would we be teaching Willa?

Which brings us to the February morning when the man driving us across Rajasthan—Gopal, who asked us to call him Gopalji—asked if Sarah and I were sisters. (That's always weird, by the way. We look nothing alike. Though I guess when you're with someone for an eternity, you might both take on some similar characteristics. But still.)

No, I said, shaking my head. We're partners. Which is what we usually say, though that also feels weird, like we run a business together. Maybe a struggling law firm. Understandably, Gopalji seemed confused.

Wives, I tried. Though we're not, because I still think marriage is a patriarchal institution, so saying we were wives, in its way, was a lie. Would Willa notice? That I wasn't actively demeaning gay families but that I was implicitly elevating married ones?

I shook my head again, like it was an Etch A Sketch, to make a new attempt. Two moms, I said. Both moms. Which was accurate and clear and made sense to Gopalji, who tilted his head, then seemed to shrug in his mind and move on. Perhaps he added this newly discovered difference between us to the tapestry of differences that already included nationality and race and religion and class, but perhaps being honest, making myself vulnerable, made us more connected, too.

Later in the ride, the dirt roads pockmarked with potholes took my usual carsickness to monumental new levels, so I moved to the front seat. To all appearances, I could have been Gopal's partner or wife. Maybe we were now a new family, a subset of the human family in which we all belong, making our way through a beautiful and complicated and messy world, the injustices against queer families blowing through our hair along with the injustices against poor Indian men who drive tourists around their country, all of us bumping up and down.

Gopalji drove us to a boat dock in Udaipur for our venture to the Taj Lake Palace hotel, which is exactly what it sounds like, a floating palace in the middle of Lake Pichola that Sarah had kept a picture of since she was a bit older than Willa was now. As we exited the boat that brought us across the lake, then walked up the marble staircase while rose petals descended gently on our heads, tossed by an unseen attendant perched on the roof, we were completely gobsmacked—I think that's the only word for it—by the grandeur around us. As Sarah and I were picking our jaws up off the floor, Willa wandered away and found what looked like an ancient—and very expensive—stone urn filled with water and more rose petals, standing on a pedestal.

She accidentally knocked it over.

Water and petals and pieces of urn flew everywhere, Sarah and I screamed, Willa cried, and I remember thinking that this—this?—was the impression of gay families we were making. We hadn't told anyone at the hotel that we were a gay family in advance, and suddenly we were making a big splash. Literally.

As one gracious hotel staff person started mopping up, another bent down to comfort Willa and handed her a stuffed animal, a toy peacock. Suddenly I felt like a bad parent not because my child had broken a priceless heirloom but because I'd yelled at her for it. Is that the bigger lesson? That all of us are broken, all of us are a mess?

You can't necessarily make life less messy, but you can make it a tiny bit less confusing. Now, when we travel, I'm more explicit up front. Before we set foot wherever we're going, I make sure the hotel or restaurant or tour guide knows we're two moms and our kid. Of course, before that happens, they usually ask my husband's name during our email exchange. I find it funny. That's not their fault, that's just the world we all live in. And my family has the privilege of helping change it.

ꙮ ꙮ ꙮ

Sally Kohn is one of the leading progressive voices in America today. She is a frequent guest on CNN, MSNBC, and Fox News. Her first book, The Opposite of Hate: A Field Guide to Repairing Our Humanity, *was published in 2018, and her writing has appeared in* The Washington Post, The New York Times, New York Magazine, Time, *and many other outlets. She is on the Board of Contributors for* USA Today *and a contributing editor to* AFAR *magazine. She is also a TED Curator, and her three hit TED Talks have been viewed more than 6 million times. Sally is a popular keynote speaker, talking about political division, hate, otherizing, diversity, and identity—and how we can solve the deep problems of our past and present. Her work has been highlighted by outlets ranging from the Colbert Report to the National Review.*

JENNIFER BALJKO

🙟 🙟 🙟

Meeting Joy

Two continents, ten thousand miles,
finding coins, grapes, and kindness.

Another day on this treeless road. Another day inching
toward 110-degree temperatures. With a dirty sleeve,
I wipe away the sweat burning my eyes. The act of this slows
my already slow pace. I stumble over my feet, catching myself
before I tip sideways and am strangled by the straps of my
50-pound backpack.

Twenty months of walking, and I'm still haunted by heat.
It snuck up on me the first morning we walked out of Bangkok, that fateful day in January 2016, when my life partner,
Lluís, and I set out joyfully, innocently, to discover kindness
in the world at a pace of three kilometers per hour. I collapsed
under the weight of that heat months later in Burma and
Uzbekistan. Now, despite all this newly acquired life-learn-
ing experience, hellish hotness continues to torment me in
Azerbaijan.

I crave a cold glass of something, anything. I fantasize about ice. It's a wasted wish. All I have is a homemade, sun-brewed concoction of water, basil seeds, and a packet of sugar I swiped from a cafe. The Iranians we met a few weeks ago told us the basil seeds, which expand like chia seeds and look like drowning ants, would help keep me hydrated, would help my body hold water longer. I need more than basil seeds. I swish the warm water around my dry mouth, wondering how much time has passed since I last peed.

What I really need is a coin. That would cheer me up, I think. Heat makes me cranky. Coins make me happy. They have proven time and again to pull me out of uncomfortable slumps and redirect my thoughts to our relatively unique adventure of retracing human footsteps in a world that seems, at the turtle's pace we go, more connected than divided.

Soon after Lluís and I started our almost-ten thousand-mile walk across Asia and Europe, coins found on the side of roads transformed into good luck tokens. I equate their magical appearances to cosmic breadcrumbs steering our courage homeward to Barcelona.

Today, though, the unforgiving heat may break me... again. Bitterness runs like tar, oozing out of my throat. "What is the joy in this?" I ask Lluís. "This is not fun. This is *hell!*" Frustration spits from my cracked lips. "Why are we walking in *August?* We should be somewhere else. You know, even the cows here go home this time of day." I conjure up the memory of an extraordinary event we witnessed a few days ago: a herd of cows leaving their golden, sun-scorched pasture around solar noon, crossing the road behind us, clearly heading in the direction of the shade of their stable. Cows calling it a day before dusk? We stopped and gaped, and I joked about feeling the same way and wanting to follow them.

Now I throw in, for the good measure of needing to be right, "We are smart people who make dumb decisions. Why do we keep doing that?"

As much as this foot journey fills me with reverence and humility, it empties me each time Lluís and I squabble about the hundred little decisions we have to make every day. Before this walk, we rarely argued; ten years of cohabitation were good to us. But now, the unusual situation of living together twenty-four hours a day for years has us physically and psychologically maxed out. We clash on how many kilometers we should walk each day, when we can take a day off, and how long we'll sit in a sliver of shade provided by the occasional signpost on a treeless backcountry road in the middle of nowhere Azerbaijan during the worst days of summer.

"Dying from heat exhaustion was never part of the plan," I add. I don't have the satisfaction of yelling. My throat is too dry.

Lluís has heard my rant before. "You know why we are doing this," he says, and then repeats what he always says when he sees me wobbling emotionally. "We are *walking* from Bangkok to Barcelona. We have a visa that limits how many days we can be here. We have to cover a certain distance every day to make it to the next border."

I flash him my look, the one with the exaggerated eye roll and drawn-out sigh that suggests he's irritating me. He gives me his look, the one where he stares at me quizzically over his glasses and says, "What? You know it's true."

This guy. Lluís the Brave, I've started calling him. He is a source of strength in trying moments, my lionhearted warrior, a person with an endless and admirable well of determination and persistence. His enthusiastic willingness to be in a constant state of discomfort as we steadfastly move toward completing our goal baffles me.

This guy. Lluís the Stubborn, I have also called him. He is my biggest opposition, a person I sometimes wish I could walk away from (or choke, depending on the day's battle), and whom I know, in the deepest part of my heart, is right. I hate him for being right this time.

Lluís the Optimist pivots the conversation.

"What about all these wonderful people we meet? These people who help us, share their lives with us? What about these experiences we're having? Don't they give you joy?" He's trying to squash my grouchiness. He might have succeeded if chocolate were part of the equation, but all he has is his homemade concoction of never-give-up mottos.

I take a breath, close my eyes for three seconds (the amount of time I can walk without falling), and exhale. I flip through the string of faces and names popping to mind: Ahmad. Alex. Azadeh. Azita. BeeBee. Mahrokh. Majid. Mehmet. Namrita. Sam. Sushma. Vahid. Yousef. Yun. Zahra. Just a few of the strangers-turned friends we've met along the way. "Those moments when we stop and spend time with people—are my best moments. I know this walk is a gift; I am grateful. But for so many hours, I can't breathe."

I leave it there. He knows the rest: I'm tired. I'm overheated. I'm hungry. I'm thirsty. I smell bad. Our walking clothes are grimy with about a week's worth of dust layered into the frayed edges we can no longer sew. My back and hips hurt. My shoulders and ankles ache. I didn't expect walking the world to be easy. But neither did I expect it to feel so incessantly demanding, like a wailing infant with a fever who can't tell his parents what he needs.

We continue in silence. Not on purpose. It's just what we do. It takes too much energy to talk and walk during our ten-hour days on foot. Silence is a comfortable space for us. It's a sound we covet and seldom hear on the roads that forge our westward route linking cultures and languages, differences and similarities—our own and others'.

The distance between us widens. Our steps fall out of sync and into their own rhythms. My guidepost is Lluís's hunched-over form about three-hundred meters ahead with his turtle shell, an oversized, faded navy-blue backpack. My eyes drift from the white painted line marking the road's boundary to the flat green landscape. Pastures have turned into vineyards.

Vineyards remind me of home, of Catalonia, and how far we are from there.

"*Salam,*" I say to the farmers selling grapes on the narrow shoulder. They return the greeting. It's nice to smile, even if mine feels fake.

It's harvest time. I love harvest time.

Back home, for many years, we volunteered to help our vineyard-owning friend and his team of workers pick grapes. In small groups, we made our way up and down rows of old vines—those too narrow for machines—clipping bunches of *macabeo, parellada* and *xarel·lo*, the local varieties, and gently placing them in buckets sticky with juice. Listening to Bulgarian and Moroccan pop songs from someone's mobile phone, Lluís and I moved in appreciation, honoring the place where sun and soil sprout sweetness.

Tears come. Harvest. My privileged life, before and today. This never-ending challenge I keep showing up for day in, day out. Does it matter? Does any of it matter? It's too much sometimes, all this attachment I carry. Joy feels far away, far out of view.

I scold myself for being sentimental. "Stop! You're losing salt and water," I mumble out loud, getting control of my voice. I pull a crumpled, snot-filled tissue out of my pants pocket and wipe away my self-pity. "You've walked in heat before. Just keep going. One step at a time."

As I wrap myself in feel-good affirmations, a white 4×4 comes to a sudden stop across the road. A thirty-something-year-old man sporting a thick, trimmed hipster beard and a crisp, button-down white shirt jumps out and dashes around the car to the makeshift thatched grape-selling stall a few steps in front of me.

"Hi. What are you doing here?" the man asks me in perfect English. He is surprised to find me here, wherever here is, decked out in a long-sleeve shirt, long pants, a sun hat, a bandana around my neck, and an enormous backpack. His eyes squint slightly. He is running scenarios in his head of how I got here, and how I can endure summer dressed this way. We notice other people's dismay dozens of times a day. He correctly assesses my thirst and hunger. "I'll buy you grapes. Which color do you want—black or white?"

"Thanks, but I can buy grapes," I say, unconvincingly. "We are walking Azerbaijan."

"No, you are our guest. Which ones do you want?" He talks to the farmer in Azeri. "You're walking Azerbaijan? Walking?! Why are you doing that? Where are you going next?"

"O.K., thank you. The white grapes look good."

My whole body resets, relaxes, and his kindness brings memories of other kindnesses. They spin like a movie sequence in my mind: The Thai man who jumped off his moped to hand us plastic bags filled with soymilk for breakfast. The family in Bangladesh who taught us the best way to ball up and eat rice with our fingers. The Indian gentleman who insisted we sit with other guests of honor at his nephew's wedding. The Pamiris who took us in night after night, stacking up thin mattresses so we could sleep comfortably. The Uzbeks who propped us up on their teabed pillows and filled us with bread and sweets. The Iranians, with their endless invitations to attend family picnics and stay as guests in their homes.

"Yeah, it's a pretty crazy thing to do," I say, "especially on a hot day like today. We're on a multi-year walking journey from Bangkok to Barcelona. We're heading toward Georgia."

"Wow, that's amazing," the man hands me the plastic bag with the white grapes, and keeps the one with red grapes. He waves to his wife, who is in the driver's seat, and their son to join us.

"You have to hear this," he says to his wife. She shakes my hand and then kisses each of my cheeks, Azerbaijani style. Her playful brown eyes seem to invite me into her life. Her welcoming smile comforts me, refreshes me.

I share the highlights of our walk. It's a habitually repeated thirty-second pitch of where we've been (Thailand,

Burma, Bangladesh, India, the Pamir mountains, Tajikistan, Uzbekistan, and Iran), where we are going (Georgia, Turkey, Greece, the Balkans and westward through Europe), and the choice to watch the world reveal itself in slow motion, in such a challenging, intimate way. They tell me about their weekend escape to the nearby lake and mountains, far enough away from the heatwave engulfing Baku, the capital city. Like with the cows, I want to follow them into their cooler circumstances.

"We travel often, and would love to do it more," the husband says, laying his arm on his son's shoulders.

"But not by foot!" his wife teases. "With wheels would be better." Her laughter sounds to my ears like a bird celebrating sunrise.

He takes out a card, and she writes their phone numbers on it and hands it to me, and I give them our website address. Finally, we introduce ourselves.

"I'm Vusal," he says. "This is my son, Mehdi." The teen offers a handshake, which I accept with a smile, a real one this time. More names I'll store in my mental memory bank.

"I'm Sevinj," Vusal's wife adds cheerfully, "but you can call me Joy. Sevinj means joy in English."

And, there it is.

Joy has come into my life. I just met Joy.

She is standing right in front of me.

"It is so nice to meet you," I sputter, soaking in the irony. Maybe Joy is always standing there in front of me. I don't always remember to notice.

I hug Joy goodbye. My crankiness and self-righteousness—the way I obstinately wanted to define this day up until this moment—melt into her sisterly embrace. Joy kisses my cheeks. I kiss hers.

I wave to Vusal and Mehdi. I blow a kiss into the air as they drive off and pop some grapes into my mouth.

Tears come again. This time, I let them. Saltiness. Sweetness. Hardship. Harmony. Tribulations. Tenderness. Anger.

Altruism. Frustration. Friendship. All these flavors mingle. They season my life, my very privileged life.

I catch up to Lluís, who is sitting on a rickety metal chair partially shaded by a half-thatched roof of another grape stand farther up the road. He stands, offering me a rest. I scooch to the edge of the chair, finding the balance point that prevents my backpack from tipping me too far in any direction.

"Guess what? I just met a woman named Joy! JOY…as in what I was just talking about, as in how I was missing joy! They bought us grapes. Have a few." I so want this roadside rendezvous to be a good sign. "Of all the names that exist on the planet, hers is Sevinj, Joy! Strange, huh?"

"Yes, it is. Do you feel better now?" Lluís plucks a handful of grapes. His eyes and smile send another wave of gratitude to the 4x4 slipping out of view on the far side of the horizon.

I mull over my response. I'm better—in this moment. Tickled with joy. Yes, that would be true. But, is it enough to keep me going today, tomorrow, next month, next year?

We walk on. We always walk on.

"Look!" Lluís points to the ground.

It's a coin!

Of course it's a coin. Joy wasn't enough. There had to be a coin, too. I wonder if the universe is cheering us on or laughing at us.

Lluís picks up the twenty qəpik, worth about twelve U.S. cents, and hands it to me. I stare at the drawing of a spiral staircase. Its helix shape, jutting lines, and random mathematical symbols give me pause. The etchings say to me that we are all, one way or another, climbing life's staircase, calculating the next step, and reaching for deeper connections to ourselves—and to others.

Meeting Joy and this coin are today's cosmic breadcrumbs. They give me courage to keep walking home. They are the morsels that make me believe it's all worthwhile.

ℬ ℬ ℬ

Jennifer Baljko, a journalist and freelance writer for 27 years, and her partner, Lluís, finished their 9,972-mile walk in June 2019. Having survived around-the-clock coupleness for 3.5 years, they continue to share their story at public events around Catalonia as they gradually adjust to a quieter life surrounded by vineyards, an hour south of Barcelona. Jennifer is shaping an encore career for her fifties, encouraging men and women to rev up their resilience, tap into their inner resourcefulness, and design their "next big thing." She still dreams of the rosewater and saffron ice cream from Iran. To read more about the walk, visit bangkokbarcelonaonfoot. com. To find out what Jennifer's up to, visit alwaysonmyway.com.

Martha McCully

⁂

Save the Date

The very special joy of traveling the world to
witness the matrimonial bliss of others.

*T*hree little words many women love to hear are enough
to make my scalp tingle with dread. They toss together a
lively mix of aversion, embarrassment, and guilt, with a dash
of unspeakable envy. They are "Save the Date."

Some Save the Dates are easy to wriggle out of. Baby
shower? Sorry, I'm away that weekend. Others are more tol-
erable: Fiftieth birthday party in the private room at Mozza?
Sure! I can Uber there and be home by ten, all while celebrating someone else aging. But the motherlode of STDs (not
to be confused with anything sexual—at all, in fact), cannot
be dismissed with a flimsy excuse, and it's one that summons
trunks upon trunks of baggage: The Destination Wedding.

For happy, rich couples—or singles unencumbered by
mortgages—a destination wedding can present a wonderful
opportunity to travel to a new place without having to plan

anything (because your time won't be your own anyway). But once you're past the wedding-every-weekend age and, like me, still flying solo, it's an invite akin to a jury duty summons, except I'm on trial.

For me, a destination wedding will involve packing my lonely toothbrush in a Ziploc bag, trying to smuggle all my healthy routines in a carry-on (is my Chinese herb broth over 3.4 ounces? Do I bring my own celery for my morning juice in Mexico?) and soul-searching from my aisle seat about why my past relationships have landed me as a permanent wedding guest, not host.

Of course, I adore my friends and am thrilled for their heartfelt expressions of love, and I want to be present for their eternal pledges to each other and all that. But the far-flung country is really the bride's and groom's fantasy, not the guests', and I have personally confirmed this by traveling to witness nuptials nineteen times. Think Venice, Paris, Florence, Torino, Portofino, Oaxaca, Portugal, Cape Cod (four times), Martha's Vineyard, Colorado Springs, Santa Fe, Santa Barbara. Sounds glamorous, I'm sure! I could write a guidebook. The truth is, attending a destination wedding solo is lonelier than a Lonely Planet vacation and more self-confrontational than an Instagram bikini selfie. One *could* consider it a big group vacation, but there's no mistaking the main event. This is a journey to celebrate people falling in love and getting married, neither of which I have done recently.

Not long ago, when I received a lovely Save The Date—a bundle of postcards wrapped in hand-stitched fabric from the market in Barcelona—I was thrilled for the happy couple. Then I put down the cards and went back to watching "Ozark" on Netflix, assured that even this series about cartels, rednecks, and human survival was less anxiety-provoking.

But after abandoning hope of any other travel that year, and watching a drug lord's head get blown off, I RSVP'd.

After all, I loved the bride and wanted to support her. Yes, I would attend. Yes, by myself.

Don't get me wrong: there *are* certain plusses to not having a plus-one. For example, I often have deep relationships with the betrothed because, undistracted by a relationship of my own, I've spent quality time with them while they were forming their unit. So, I tend to get booked into the prime hotel, where the couple is staying and where the reception is held. I can also partake in activities like bungee jumping (not that I actually would) without worrying about my brood being left to an orphanage. And when friends complain about FedExing car seats to their in-laws, I'm happy I have neither.

Before the wedding in Barcelona, I was excited to hang out with one of the bride's friends I'd heard was also single. But when I arrived, I found her at the hotel pool chirping happily to a last-minute plus-one: the new date she'd met on Hinge. I chatted with a nice couple instead, and they invited me to join them for a yoga class the next day. When it came time to practice, though, I found them sitting together, holding hands, deeply ensconced in a guru's spiritual talk about an ancient Catalonian mating ritual. I backed out of their space. And so, the weekend began.

I've developed a few strategies for surviving these three- or four- or five- or six-day events, without too much disdain.

First, find your own thing. For example, after the mating couple abandoned me, I hired a yoga instructor, Pablo, who came to my hotel to give me private lessons. He was adorable. I spent almost two hours a day with him and learned how to do a *perro hacia abajo*. The bride suggested I bring him to the reception. "Great idea!" I said. She was kidding. I wasn't.

Secondly, don't drink too much. It's a gateway to despair. I bring tissues to the ceremony and sure, I'm shedding tears of joy for the couple. But let's be honest, they're mostly for me. Drinking can turn a perfectly good cry into a downpour, and no one wants rain, or a drunk friend attempting a toast in Spanish, at their wedding.

Third, don't think about the money. Why focus on how the couple's idea of a perfect vacation is replacing your idea of a perfect vacation, for at least the next year? This is not about you, it's about them. Just like the vows, the costs are what they are—unnegotiable.

At one of the many group meals in Barcelona, there was a kind of competition for the worst destination-wedding story. (I may or may not have started that conversation.) A woman told us she was on a flight to Maine once when serious turbulence struck. The passenger next to her hadn't quite fastened his seatbelt so when the plane dropped a thousand feet, he was hurled to the ceiling, breaking his neck instantly. She had to fly the remaining ninety minutes with a dead body next to her. She won.

Leading up to the reception, the dinner seating plan was hanging over me like a chuppah, even though the bride had assured me I'd be sitting between two men, Marco and Billy, who were there alone. Do not, however, confuse "alone" with "eligible." Marco's wife was home with a newborn, and Billy would have been more interested in Pablo, had he actually been invited.

"They're good dancers," the bride had told me, optimistically.

When Marco repeatedly asked me if I had really traveled there alone (yes, on the plane and everything!) I became suspicious. When he asked if he could "tuck me in," I became repulsed. And that night, after I locked my hotel room door behind me, I listened to a faint but persistent knocking and watched the door handle move in expectation. So much for weddings being the perfect place to meet a mate.

Mind you, I haven't always attended weddings alone, and I've had plenty of boyfriends; they just didn't turn into husbands. I took one to Paris for my best friend's wedding. He was a

personal trainer who insisted he had clients there. (*Really!?*) I
waited for him after a "session" in a French bar and ordered
a Lillet. The bartender brought me a glass of milk. This
seemed fitting, as across town, my bestie from babyhood was
clinking champagne flutes with her new husband, and I was
reduced to longing for my mom.

To Portofino I brought a sweet date whose three-year-old
had just contracted Coxsackievirus, also known as hand, foot,
and mouth disease. By the time we arrived at the gorgeous
Italian feast, I had a raging fever and open blisters on my
palms and feet and in my mouth.

For my cousin's wedding on Cape Cod, I invited the
live-in boyfriend I'd just broken up with, because I was in a
fragile state, and because it was easier to invite the Harvard
lawyer than explain to my great aunt why I wasn't engaged
to the Harvard lawyer. But being a narcissist, the Harvard
lawyer positioned himself in every family portrait. No one
has ever seen the photos.

My most bad-ass move, though, was to bring along not just
one, but two guests who truly love me: my parents. When I
couldn't bear yet another wedding alone on the Cape in the
darkest time of year, Thanksgiving (note to engaged couples:
holiday-weekend weddings are especially soul-crushing for
singles), my parents had the brilliant idea of tagging along.
"We'll rent a condo! We'll see our friends!" And so, we drove
together and stayed together. Mom and Dad were even graciously invited to the Sunday brunch, and no one felt left out.

There's no denying the stigma of the never-married at a
wedding, no matter how independent women have become.
But I don't want to justify my singledom. The walk down the
aisle is just one trip I haven't yet taken.

In the Madrid airport on the return from Barcelona, I ran into
a friend from New York, another intrepid traveler and single
woman, Paola. The last time I'd seen her was at the Portofino
wedding where I had the hand, foot, and mouth blisters, so

I was excited to tell her about the ceremony in Barcelona, a happier event (for me, anyway).

Paola was returning from a weekend in Bilbao. She told me of her new crush, and how much she loved her job, and she introduced me to her pals on our flight. I spent the first half of the six-hour flight hoping these adventurous, free-spirited women wouldn't see my airplane read—a book called *The One: Finding and Keeping Soulmate Love*—at the top of my carry-on, next to my Chinese herb broth.

But after a while I stopped worrying and began to appreciate their unfettered joy. I was reminded of how much fun it can be to be single—even if that comes in the form of someone else's fabulous wedding. And how traveling to any new city or country, with paella lessons and drunk dancing and Cava at every meal including breakfast, is an experience and luxury I'm grateful for. And I remembered that the best part of traveling alone—even to a destination wedding—is the unwavering hope that my forever guy will be seated right there in the middle seat next to me.

჻ ჻ ჻

Martha McCully is a brand consultant and contributor to various publications including ELLE, Harper's Bazaar, *and* the Los Angeles Times. *In her pre-economic-downturn life, Martha was an editor at* In Style *and* Allure. *These days, she is impatiently waiting for the Covid-19 vaccine so she can resume travel to more weddings, now of her friends' children. To complicate her mate search, Martha lives in Venice, California, and East Hampton, New York, which you can follow on Instagram @marthamccully.*

ERIN BYRNE

❧ ❧ ❧

Our Ravaged Lady

A cathedral and a life catch fire.

S he had lived many lives, and here was the burnt offering of another.

Notre Dame's lace spire sizzled, crumbled, and fell, and the gigantic hole it created became a cauldron. Flames, golden to orange to red, assaulted Paris's lavender-tinged sky, and smoke billowed in gray explosions. Silhouetted against glowing cinders, her bell towers stood dignified but unprotected.

My friends and I watched from the edge of Île Saint Louis, mouths agape, tears stinging our eyes, joining in a collective, horror-filled gasp as the cathedral battled for her very existence. The hollow, meandering roar of the conflagration was punctuated by the thunder of falling wood and stone and the screeching of twisting iron.

Firefighters wrestled with the blaze as the stone edifice trapped flames and smoke, rendering the burning "forest" of ceiling beams unreachable. The 850-year-old wood had flared up like kindling, and by the time the firefighters arrived, it was out of control. Fierce heat scorched them as they ran in to rescue precious relics from the inferno. Victor Hugo's "vast symphony of stone" had Stravinskied.

As she burned, my gut echoed the sentiment. Over the past few years, it seemed my own life had caught fire.

I'd gone through a divorce after a thirty-two-year marriage, and although a long separation had fooled me into feeling prepared, sorrow tore through me.

I'd ushered my two sons into the world of adulthood, a letting go reminiscent of their first day of Kindergarten, when I'd held them tightly, buried my face in their hair, and inhaled sweet, little-boy scents. They'd held me too, their mouths quivering as they adjusted their backpacks and swaggered off.

I'd placed cherished items from my old life around the California house where I was starting over, all the while pining for the home I left behind in Washington state.

And I'd lost my father: my funny, beloved father who'd taken me sailing, taught me to worship jazz, and always, upon seeing me, called out my name with gusto. His death hurt in a place that seemed unreachable.

I'd also broken my shoulder, endured four concussions, suffered a stroke, and had a heart recorder inserted surgically.

At times, my brain was toast. Daily tasks like pressing garlic or doing dishes caused my head to explode into migraines. I forgot appointments, struggled to find words, and mixed up numbers. My energy plummeted. Depression and anxiety crumbled my equilibrium.

It would take time, the doctors said, to recover.

The night of Notre Dame's fire, I was in the midst of the most recent concussion, from a car accident weeks before. The glow was extra-rosy and the cries of onlookers too loud as the crowd edged ever closer to my claustrophobic brain.

The next day, President Emmanuel Macron addressed the people of Paris: "Notre Dame is our history, it's our literature, it's our imagery. It's the place we live our greatest moments, from wars to pandemics to liberations."

Notre Dame is France's kilomètre zéro—the precise center of the starting point of all roads in the city and country. Her many lives have been tumultuous. Her first stone was laid in 1163, with the faithful gathering to light candles. She took roughly two hundred years to build, and upon completion, received her bell towers and her best feature—the north and south rose windows—glittering eyes from which her spirit shone forth.

When Notre Dame was just three centuries old, Catholics slaughtered Protestant Huguenots en masse over a three-day killing spree, then celebrated their victory at her altar. Soon afterward, Huguenots attacked her façade, hacking the heads off of her statues—a fad that would continue for centuries.

When she was four hundred years old, Louis XIV, realizing Gothic was out and Baroque was in, had Our Lady's eyes ripped out and replaced with white glass. (Later, Hugo would rant: *Who has installed cold white glass in the place of those stained glass windows that caused the astonished eyes of our ancestors to pause between the rose window of the main entrance and the pointed arches of the apse?*)

Fanatics came after her again when she was five centuries old: Revolutionaries hacked off more statues' heads, attacked the arrow atop her spire, melted down her bells to make cannons, and renamed her The Temple of Reason.

Through all of this, people continued to light candles under bright or colorless glass, in turmoil and in peacetime, in sorrow or in joy.

The week following the fire, I was a guest writer at a literary event and had chosen to read from an essay I wrote on Notre Dame. I'd always felt a strong affinity for the cathedral, and in this piece, I analyzed her extensively, going deep and using my intellect, for my brain was my center, my own kilomètre zéro. I had written the best essay it could conjure.

But that night, my thinking was dulled. My chest burned, and chills wracked my body. By the time I took the stage in an underground cavern packed with poets, artists, and musicians, my throat raged and my voice faltered.

"Her scars and sweetnesses were mine," I read, wondering if my connection to this cathedral was a blessing or a curse.

Within weeks of the fire, the cause was narrowed to either a cigarette tossed by a construction worker or a short in the electrical system of the bells. Iron scaffolding on the exterior of the spire welded together that night, increasing the chance of collapse. Hundreds of tons of lead in the spire and roof were released into the night sky, putting surrounding neighborhoods at risk.

The bell towers had been fifteen minutes from crumbling due to the heat, but the firefighters had arced water over the blaze to dampen them. The water saved her towers but seeped into the mortar between her stones. Moving just one—even to rescue her from ruin—might cause her to cave in.

Nothing could be moved, because all had not yet settled.

I was in a similar state.

Even so much as a sip of wine caused vertigo, social events siphoned my energy at an alarming rate, and I required extreme focus to maneuver around the once familiar streets of Paris, as if I'd lost my compass arrow. I was in France to work on a novel, but now writing took twice as long; I couldn't fit my scenes into the book.

I began to doubt the wisdom of being in Paris. Notre Dame was a ruin, I had bronchitis, and the *gilet jaunes* (Yellow Vests) angrily prowled the streets on Saturdays en masse, the cost of renovating the cathedral making it a new target for protest.

In 1830, when Victor Hugo took up his pen to write *The Hunchback of Notre Dame*, he created a character so intertwined with the cathedral that....

He was its soul. To such a point was he, that those who knew that Quasimodo once existed, now find that the cathedral seems deserted, inanimate, dead. You feel that there is something missing. This immense body is empty; it is a skeleton. The spirit has departed; you see the place it left, and that is all. It is like a skull: the sockets of the eyes are still there, but the gaze has disappeared.

At the time, Notre Dame was a spectral wreck, matching Hugo's image. The people rallied and the city renovated, but Quasimodo had to wait twenty-five years for his new home to be completed.

Nearly one hundred years after Hugo published his novel, bombs, bullets, and shrapnel punctured Notre Dame's stone as World War I shook Europe. The cathedral was built to last, but by this time, she may have felt disaster-prone.

During World War II, Our Lady's eyes were removed again, and she endured four long years of blind silence, her bells mute. By the liberation of Paris in August 1944, her demise was imminent. But when Hitler ordered his general in Paris to detonate her, Dietrich von Choltitz refused.

On the day of the celebration, Charles de Gaulle approached Notre Dame. Parisians had fought the Germans from barricades—piles of tables and chairs and stools, with any weapon they could find—and chaos still reigned. German snipers remained high in the Gothic arches.

BBC correspondent Bob Reid's radio broadcast described the scene:

And now, here comes General de Gaulle.

The general's now turned to face the square and this huge crowd of Parisians [machine gun fire]. He's being presented to people [machine gun fire]. He's being received [shouts of crowd, shots]…even while the general is marching [sudden sharp outburst of continued fire]…into the cathedral.

De Gaulle walked straight ahead—shoulders high, his tall frame never flinching as bullets zinged from all sides and people scampered for shelter—into Notre Dame's interior to a blizzard of fire from the rafters. He remained for a fifteen-minute celebration.

Our Lady of Paris had been waiting a long time for this, and her bells rang out.

It's been said that Louis XIV, that long-haired hippie of a monarch, so hated to suffer waiting that after one courtier appeared late, he drawled, *"J'ai failli attendre"*—I almost had to wait! He considered it his divine right never to suffer a delay. But Parisians have learned—through revolutions, wars, reigns, and riots, in queues and métro stations, in bistros and museums—that most of us have to wait a little.

In the days following the fire, I dragged myself out to observe the people of Paris and scrutinize the incinerated cathedral from all sides. Access to Notre Dame was blocked, so crowds flocked to Île Saint Louis to ponder her cinders and ash, the gaping hole in the center of her flying buttresses, her singed but intact rose windows, like eyes with smudged mascara. I heard other languages, but the French voices were silent. The people of Paris—an elegant Parisienne in white, a swarthy father holding the hands of twin boys, two elderly men dressed with old-fashioned tidiness—quietly contemplated Notre Dame.

I had seen this kind of homage a few years before, when the bells of Notre Dame were replaced. That winter, the new bells were displayed in the cathedral's nave. Bleachers were set out, and people sat on freezing metal seats to meditate on the bell towers. Tourists fidgeted, but Parisians stayed still as statues. Three dignified ladies in black wool coats and colorful scarves and hats, their lipstick fresh, sat just so; a young couple snuggled side by side with intertwined legs. All listened to the chiming of the old bells—and imagined the sound of the new. Would they be sharper or gentler, hollow or full?

Attendre is French for "to wait." It also means "to expect."

Perhaps the French take the long view; the past is pro-
logue. To honor the old and envision the new are one and the
same. To wait is to anticipate.

All summer, the cathedral's sanctuary was open to the
elements. Her interior remained a jumble of accumulated
debris. Charred wood like Pick-up sticks and stone chunks
lay on the floor in pinpoint rays of sunlight, on shredded cane
chairs, among piles of ashes. Everything could cave in at any
moment. Even months after the fire, Notre Dame was still
considered a triage site.

Meanwhile, my own condition worsened. Neurological
testing revealed a chasm in memory, in word retrieval, in
vision. The latest concussion had sparked the cumulative
effects of all four concussions and the stroke, and my brain
remained in chaotic clutter along with the issues I'd traveled
to Paris to escape.

Even with my divorce finalized, I did not see a way forward. I raged at the ravages of age on my appearance—the
last time I'd dated, I was in my twenties, but I had no desire
to be a nun. The few times I ventured out, I chocked up dull,
time-wasting endeavors with Louis XIV types that fizzled out.

Friends endured my scatterbrained spaciness, my last-minute cancelations, my need for solitude. Writing was an act
of faith: I couldn't type well, so I wrote random scenes in
longhand. I often woke up alone with an iron band of fear
sinking into my chest: My brain was not strong enough to be
my center, and this left a terrifying void.

But in those instants, I tried to take a longer view. I came
to see that Hugo's belief in Quasimodo swinging from those
flammable rafters, and Charles de Gaulle's heroic stride, and
the resilience that Our Lady herself displayed in all her bro-
kenness were not qualities of the brain. They were qualities
of the heart.

———

Recently, my family scattered my dad's ashes into Puget Sound, Washington. He'd been gone three years; we agreed that we were glad we waited. As his ashes floated and swirled, then sank into the murkiness, chips and clumps mingling with the water, we spoke of his humor, the music he played on the piano and drums, and his fiercely loyal love—all that abides now that the ashes are gone.

Winter has come, and I am free of many concussion symptoms. My vision is clear, I can drive, and the scenes I wrote in longhand are fitting neatly into my novel.

I look around my home at the relics of my previous life: the Greek vase and Swedish plate on my mantle, crystal candle holders, photos of the four of us as a family, my dad's bongo drums. Like Quasimodo, I've had to wait, but my home has become the place where I live my greatest moments, my wars, my pandemics, my liberations.

Our Lady persists, on pause. Her roof was carefully covered last fall, but she stays bound inside within her melted iron scaffolding. Christmas came and went with no mass, no movement, no restoration of her sanctuary. But inside the cathedral, among the detritus and dust, stands the altar with its gold cross, and next to that, the marble *pietà* where Notre Dame's namesake holds her departed with love.

The center of the center remains, and the rest is reimagined.

Each night, I light three candles in a row and contemplate them in the way I learned from the people of Paris, who find layers of meaning in the combination of past, present, and future. Sometimes the past fizzles out (gratefully), or it's time for a new present (a fresh start), or the future grows dim (but still illuminated).

A few nights ago, the past and the future went out at exactly the same moment. So tonight, fresh candles burn on either side of the present, creating a silhouette of Notre Dame as she now stands—her tall spire gone, and her low center flanked by her bell towers. I remember that cauldron of violent flames licking the sky.

Parisien magazine wrote, "*La catastrophe nous renvoie à nous humilité et notre impuissance.*" The catastrophe refers to our humility and our helplessness.

It is during these times, when I'm aware of both, that what endures becomes clear.

What will Notre Dame's next life be like? An international contest is on to design a new spire, with hundreds of ideas flooding in: a glass solar roof with an urban farm; a greenhouse sanctuary for birds; a new home for her 180,000 bees; a blue-tiled roof made from recycled ocean plastic; a swimming pool. But Paris's chief architect has threatened to resign rather than allow a modern spire.

Until Our Ravaged Lady rises from the ashes, we will just have to do as she does: feel our universal humanity and stand with dignity in our humility and helplessness. Light a few candles…and wait a little.

❧ ❧ ❧

Erin Byrne is author of Wings: Gifts of Art, Life, and Travel in France, *editor of* Vignettes & Postcards from Paris *and* Vignettes & Postcards from Morocco, *and writer of* The Storykeeper *film. Her work has won many awards, she has taught writing all across the globe, and she hosts LitWings literary salon, which features writers, photographers, and filmmakers, in the Bay Area and Paris. Erin is Collaborating Curator of Travel Writing and Photography for The Creative Process Exhibition, which travels to the world's leading universities. She is working on a novel set in occupied Paris,* Illuminations. *Erin has unwittingly hosted parties in Paris on the nights of the 2015 terrorist attacks, the Notre Dame fire, and the covid-19 pandemic. www.e-byrne.com.*

✍ ✍ ✍

Key Change

What happens when the places we love start to disappear?

*H*ot, humid air, like a weighted blanket, draped itself around me as I exited Miami International Airport. As a native Miamian who now lives on the opposite side of the country, I live for this sensation. It's something I crave when I've been away too long, though my northern friends can't fathom why. One of the reasons South Florida feels like home to those born here is that nowhere else in the country quite *feels* like South Florida. It's the only stretch of the contiguous United States that sits in the tropical climate zone.

When I was a kid growing up here in the early '90s, I spent my weeks in Miami with my nose buried in one book or another. But weekends were spent far from the city center with my father, paddling through the Everglades or, more frequently, road-tripping through the Florida Keys—the 44 islands connected by 42 bridges, stretching 113 miles from Key Largo to Key West.

I've revisited the Keys frequently over the years, first as a teenager with an eye for adventure and later as an adult desperate for a soft place to unplug from the world. Yet two years had passed since I'd been back, and I wanted to come to terms with what Hurricane Irma had wrought when it pummeled the fragile island chain in 2017. I also wanted to camp in the more distant Dry Tortugas, a national park in the Gulf of Mexico made up of seven small islands seventy miles off the coast of Key West. The islands are among the most vulnerable to climate change, and I had never seen them. To put it bluntly: If I ever wanted to visit, now was the time.

For Miamians, a trip to the Keys starts where the Ronald Reagan Turnpike dead-ends into the South Dixie Highway, which itself ceases to exist once it hits the Miami-Dade County line near Manatee Creek. From there on out, you are on the southernmost stretch of U.S. Highway 1, known as the Overseas Highway. With Miami in the rearview, the twin seas of blue sky and ocean ahead throw the islands of the Keys, a mix of limestone and luck, into sharp relief.

Just south of Florida City, my father and I would often opt for the Card Sound Road instead of U.S. 1 as our path for leaving the mainland, driving needless extra miles sandwiched between aisles of mangroves bowed in brackish water, the air thick with the scent of decaying vegetation. All this in order to have a soda and a chat with locals at the divey shack-on-the-water Alabama Jack's before cruising over one of South Florida's least traveled bridges, Card Sound Bridge. As we'd cross, I'd lean my head out the window until the sea air stung my eyes, my senses alive with the dizzying brilliance of home. Later, we'd snorkel with angelfish and snapper at John Pennekamp Coral Reef State Park before heading to Mrs. Mac's Kitchen, three miles down the road, where we licked the salt from our lips before filling up on fish (dad) and key lime pie (me). Now, as I eased onto Card Sound Road, I felt welcomed home.

You could drive nonstop from Miami to Key West in three to four hours, but it's better to take your time. Weird things happen on Florida's fringes, and the Overseas Highway travels through some of the weirdest.

In Key Largo, the first key you encounter on the journey south, you can snorkel past a massive statue of Jesus called *Christ of the Abyss*. Or stay at an underwater hotel named after Jules Verne. Or ride the African Queen—yes, the cinematic steamboat that carried Hepburn and Bogart. A few keys south, in the village of Islamorada, you can take a snack break while sunburned tourists crouch on their hands and knees on a dock to feed the fish at Robbie's. Eager, gigantic tarpon leap out of the water toward a blanket of quivering bait dangling from visitors' hands.

There's the random sculpture of a large shark sticking out of the side of a building. The enormous red-and-white fishing bobber towering dozens of feet above a sign that reads WEDDING RESERVATIONS. And Betsy, a beloved forty-foot-wide spiny lobster sculpture, as Instagram-ready as anything in Florida ever will be, despite predating the app by decades.

The Keys are where the garish and irreverent come to create something unique, unshackled from propriety. They exist in stark contrast to Florida's panhandle—home to the buttoned-up state capital of Tallahassee—which could not be physically or figuratively further. The considerable aversion the two ends of the long state have for each other today belies their common history defined by absurd levels of capital amassed in the nineteenth century. In the Keys, it was attained by "wrecking," or salvaging cargo from crashed ships. Up north, it was attained by subjugation: In the early 1800s, nearly three-quarters of the population of Leon County was enslaved. Currently, the power to determine the fate of Florida lies in the hands of individuals who sit in the state capital, many of whom refuse to confront the realities of climate change. The fact that South Florida threatened to secede in 2014, due to the state government's inaction on climate change, only underscores how dire the situation has become.

As the miles ticked by on my drive through paradise, I passed monuments to Keysian resilience and stubbornness. New homes on stilts designed to perch above rising seas and withstand high winds. Updated and reopened resorts. It felt simultaneously inspiring and masochistic. Would efforts to rebuild work, and were they worth it in the long run?

After hours of driving past banyan trees and a stop to sift through the brightly colored offerings of Shell World, the Seven Mile Bridge appeared, the span to Bahia Honda Key. It's a transformational view with nothing but miles of water on either side. Every time I cross it, I feel as though the sea is consuming me, that I'm a car-size dart zooming across the ocean. The land fades until there's nothing but gliding pelicans and endless turquoise waters from there to eternity.

Late in the afternoon, I pulled into Bahia Honda State Park. The lush island had been my favorite place growing up, one where my family and I had spent long afternoons swimming and birding. I parked in the far lot near the park's western end, took a deep breath, and stepped outside to survey the damage.

Hurricane Irma had taken everything.

The old bathhouse where I'd aged out of countless bathing suits was destroyed. The canopies and many of the shade trees were swept away. Sandspur Beach, where I'd napped on beach chairs in shallow waters, was blocked by a chain-link fence. Some of the oceanside beaches—the crown jewels of Bahia Honda Key—were no more. The butterfly garden, too, gone completely, exiled now to memory.

Efforts are under way to rebuild, whatever that means. And I am happy for them, whatever that does. Apparently, a colony of least tern birds has taken up residence on Sandspur for the first time in thirty years. A seawall could help maintain the remaining beaches. But the backdrop to the time capsule of my childhood—flown kites and walks at low tide while tiny crabs scurried around my feet—is gone.

That night, after driving to Key West, I buried my grief in packing. In anticipation of my date with an unrelenting sun (the Dry Tortugas have neither potable water nor much shade), I'd brought along the following: a cooler with wheels to transport five gallons of water, electrolyte powder, a forty-eight-ounce Nalgene, three days' worth of food, a knife, a spork, a plate, a tent, a sleeping bag, a sleeping pad, cash for the campground fee of fifteen dollars a night, pajamas, a jacket, quick-drying shorts, underwear, a long-sleeved sun shirt, flip-flops, sneakers, mosquito repellant, two books, a headlamp, ChapStick, sunblock, sunglasses, a hat, two towels, body wipes, a bathing suit, prescription swim goggles, a nose clip, a snorkel, a rainbow kite named Fred, and a giant ocean float in the shape of a red macaw.

The next morning, when I arrived at the ferry terminal with my gear, I was greeted by a large group of children. Fifty-three excited fifth graders from Horace O'Bryant, a public school in Key West, were joining me on what would be a first trip to the Dry Tortugas for all of us. The diverse group of Conch kids (i.e., young native Key Westers) seemed as surprised to see me as I was to see them—the other passengers were older, mostly white, and could just as easily have been guests at a yacht show.

The Yankee Freedom III, the high-speed catamaran that ferries visitors to the Dry Tortugas, has a capacity of two hundred fifty as well as flush toilets, ice water, air-conditioning, coffee, breakfast, lunch, snacks, beer, and whatever else a customer who can afford the nearly two-hundred-dollar ticket might require. The ferry makes only one round-trip journey a day, depositing its passengers on Garden Key, home to historic Fort Jefferson, a massive brick hexagon built in the 1800s. In their allotted four or so hours, visitors are encouraged to snorkel, stroll, and take a tour of the fort before boarding the ferry for the two-hour trip back. Few elect to camp, so I, with my stuffed backpack and tent, stood out considerably. The most common question I received from strangers was "How?" To which I'd respond, honestly: practice, a knowledge of my comfort levels, and a lifelong willingness to sweat.

After we docked in Garden Key, the day-trippers were allowed to disembark, while we campers were held back to be briefed on how to leave no trace of our stay and what to do in case of an emergency. I then dragged my pack and cooler a few hundred feet from the ferry to a somewhat shaded area, flanked by sea grapes, where I began setting up my tent. The mosquitoes descended at once. And truly, I should have known better. It had rained a few days prior, but I'd let my eagerness to finish camp chores get the better of me. One of the rangers who saw me suggested I move my camp to an area in the open sun beside Fort Jefferson, a spot where the prevailing winds would sweep away not only the mosquitoes but also the stifling heat of the night. I heeded his advice, and by the time I had hammered my last tent stake into the ground, a crowd had gathered near the fort for a tour.

In 1513, Juan Ponce de León became the first European to encounter Las Tortugas. The "dry" was added later by British cartographers to signal the lack of water on the islets, which numbered eleven before storms and tides engulfed four of them. The Dry Tortugas ring a natural deep-water harbor, which meant ships in the Gulf could seek shelter there when bad weather loomed or when vessels needed repair. As the name indicates, the other items of interest were turtles. Many delicious turtles.

"If you were to write Las Tortugas on a map in 1513 it would be like writing McDonald's on an island today," said a ferry crewman named Hollywood, who led the tour.

Turtles still ply the waters, but all five species that call the Dry Tortugas home are listed as either threatened or endangered. Fort Jefferson, on Garden Key, remains. The Dry Tortugas' position in the Florida Reef—the third-largest coral reef system on the planet—meant that any large ship or invading army wishing to enter the Gulf of Mexico from the east had to sail south of the islands, which essentially made the Dry Tortugas the keys to the Gulf of Mexico. At Fort Jefferson's peak, it featured some of the most powerful weapons of its day, including twenty-five-ton cannons that could fire at any ship within three miles of the island.

Never in the fort's history was a single cannon fired in battle.

The never-fully-realized fort was also used as a prison during and after the Civil War. By the early 1900s it was mostly abandoned, paving the way for its transition to a bird reserve, then a national monument, and finally a national park in 1992.

After the crowds left on the three P.M. ferry back to the mainland, the quiet of the place was staggering. There were about a dozen other campers with me that night, among them Stacie and Mike, a pair of Key Westers with whom I'd become fast friends. We felt the strange and selfish pleasure of silence in a space usually flooded by crowds. A tropical island Magic Kingdom all our own.

Once the golden hour struck, Stacie, Mike, and I climbed up to the top of Fort Jefferson. The air was thick and humid that evening. The clouds blocked the sunset. But as night descended, the island came alive, slow-moving hermit crabs by the hundreds blanketing the campground, their sound dampened by the grass. A new moon rendered the sky the darkest I'd ever seen, as I stood within earshot of the crash of waves.

The next morning, I walked with Stacie along the shoreline trail from our campground to another of the Dry Tortugas, Bush Key. The half-mile path, closed most of the year to protect nesting birds, had only recently reopened. While we strolled, we saw conch and starfish. Jerry, one of the other campers, had beaten us out to the trail and drawn a smiling sun in the sand. At a certain point, the white coral fragments beneath our feet made it look like we were walking on bones. We kept an eye out for masked boobies while magnificent frigate birds soared above us, the throats of the males hot-rod red, and we talked about Audubon, who spent a lifetime killing avian life so he could paint it for posterity.

Back at the campground, Stacie and I watched the next batch of tourists disembark from the ferry and gather in front of the fort. Save for the birds and sea life, it felt like few things had come to exist naturally in the Dry Tortugas; Fort Jefferson seemed made of impossibility itself. The worn granite staircase slabs that spiraled through each bastion had been shipped from the north. Drinking water had been produced by steam condensers, also shipped in, powered by fuel brought from the mainland.

And now, Fort Jefferson is up against rising seas and a national park system with a $12 billion maintenance backlog. A plaque at the fort's visitor center reads, "Time, weather, and water continue to take their toll, necessitating ongoing stabilization and restoration projects." But to what end? How long can a state as susceptible to climate change as Florida continue to bet against itself by electing politicians who refuse to grapple with its vulnerability? We may very well be living in the dismantling, you and I, whether we choose to watch or not. And how does one build among constant erosion? Where do we go?

I spent my last day in the Dry Tortugas walking the brick perimeter of the fort, pausing to stare at the deeper patches of dark blue scattered amid the shallow turquoise, the water undulating up and down, up and down, like the drowsy breaths of an aquatic Dalmatian.

From my campsite, I could see the lighthouse on Loggerhead Key, where, for decades, Cuban refugees had landed at night, far from the Coast Guard's reach. Until recently, the "wet foot, dry foot" policy allowed any Cuban who reached land to eventually become a permanent resident—and Dry Tortugas park rangers were often the first to officially welcome them. Now, Cubans wishing to enter the United States face the same process as any other immigrant group.

"For generations of Cubans," Hollywood had shared with me after the tour, "Loggerhead Key served as their Statue of Liberty and Garden Key as their Ellis Island." An old chug, one of the small boats used by Cubans seeking refuge, is on display at Fort Jefferson. As I watched the waters swirling around the lighthouse, I wondered what the quest for refuge would look like for South Floridians as the seas continue to rise.

Still, I kept returning to the unexpected relief I had felt upon seeing the rebuilding efforts at Bahia Honda, even though I suspected it was a losing battle. How painfully easy it is to blur the lines between irrationality and hope, especially when it comes to our home. Maybe nothing will make Floridians give up on Florida—not yet anyway. Our love runs too deep for our own good.

ॐ ॐ ॐ

Rahawa Haile is an Eritrean-American writer from Miami, Florida. Her work has appeared in The New York Times Magazine, The New Yorker, Outside, Pitchfork, Rolling Stone, AFAR, Audubon, *and* Pacific Standard. *In* Open Country, *her memoir about thru-hiking the Appalachian Trail, explores what it means to move through America and the world as a Black woman and is forthcoming from Harper.*

FAITH ADIELE

❧ ❧ ❧

A Family Project

A Nordic-Nigerian's homecoming.

he six men encircling me all have a good foot-and-a-half on me; each towers between 6'3" and 7 feet, or as they measure it in Finland, 1.9 to 2.13 meters. I swing my head around the circle, blinded by their gleaming-white teeth, flushed-pink skin, and white-blond hair. They nudge one another's lean, broad shoulders and whisper in Finnish, a soft stream of sing-songy inhalations, eight liquid vowels, feathery sibilants. It's like being surrounded by a wall of white noise. Their mouths open and close like fish, widening and rounding, vocal cords vibrating: *sss, oww, nah*. Their eyes—as blue-blue as the lakes and rivers and fjords and seas around us—take me in.

The whispering men raise their eyebrows and nod, coming to urgent, sibilant agreement: *Sa vu!* They breathe. *Sa vu soww nah!*

The spokesman turns to me. "We want to know you," he says, giving his shirt a tug with long, pale fingers. Another nods eagerly and pulls at the drawstring on his trousers.

Alarmed at the prospect that he might undo them, I step back. Glancing down, I notice my golden-brown fists press against my legs. I breathe deeply to slow the fluttering in my chest. *You're a traveler. You've been around the world. You know how to get out of this.*

The six strangers, my affable Finnish cousins, crowd closer and smile. They smell green, the scent of birch and eucalyptus, the aroma of the branches used to whip one another in the sauna.

"*Savusauna* isn't easy," says one with bright cheeks like Mom, "but we think you'll learn to like it."

The challenge has been issued.

A week ago, after my mother and I had exhausted Stockholm's historic sights, we departed Sweden, her father's homeland, for Finland, her mother's. On the Värtahamnen docks, waiting in an orderly line for the 7:30 P.M. ferry to Turku, I leafed through the guidebook our cousins had sent in preparation for this generation's first reunion.

"Wow, Mom, Sweden ruled Finland for 589 years!"

She tore her eyes away from Kungliga slottet, Sweden's waterfront answer to Versailles, and turned slowly, shaking her head like the disappointed ex-schoolteacher she was. Lips pursed, she regarded me with hooded eyes. "Um, *what* kind of Nordic-Nigerian are you?"

"Um, the kind who surprised you with a trip to the homeland for your sixtieth birthday." I smirked. "You're welcome, by the way!"

"Okay. But seriously, think about your *morfar*." My Swedish grandfather had famously dominated my Finnish grandmother. He was bold and extroverted, one of twelve kids born to a sheriff and hot-tempered housewife. My *mummi* was soft-spoken and introverted, one of three children born

to a quiet carpenter who went insane. "Six centuries of dom-
ineering sounds about right!"

A whistle alerted us to begin boarding the Baltic Princess
cruise from Sweden's capital to Finland's oldest city. After
dropping our bags in our room, which was filled with the
blond wood and built-ins of my Washington State childhood,
we headed up on deck for a typical Nordic dinner of pickled
fishy things. The dining room was strangely empty, so we
had the view—the lights of Stockholm fading into dark blue
sea and sky—to ourselves.

"Who are we meeting tomorrow?" I asked, between bites
of gravlax and vinegary red cabbage.

Mom's eyes lit up, the orange stain in the right one a small
sunrise on a blue horizon. Ever the teacher, she launched into
the names, ages, and interests of our Turku cousins. "It's in
your packet," she reminded me. "Along with our itinerary,
there are letters from each set of cousins along the way, and
I marked their connection to us on the master family tree."

"Okay, so you get an A."

She laughed. "And yet I managed to raise a daughter who
insists on cramming for tests the night before!"

I leaned back in my chair and smiled. "Do they know I'm
Black?"

"Yes. We've exchanged family photos, and they know your
poppie was Nigerian. I think they've even read some of your
essays about meeting him and your siblings in Nigeria."

An hour later, when we'd had our fill of salmon and her-
ring and mackerel, we turned our backs on a soft blue horizon,
dark with night, a mere shimmering line separating sky from
sea. We headed downstairs to our cabin.

Below deck, a completely different world spilled into the
promenade. Red-faced Finns of all shapes and sizes stumbled, sprinted, and crawled along the nautical-themed carpet,
clutching entire liters of *koskenkorva*, Finland's answer to
vodka, and *akkavitti*, caraway-infused aquavit.

We shot each other dismayed looks. We knew Finns were hard-drinking, but out of control? And loud? All our family stereotypes were upending, it seemed. Stockholm's hushed orderliness had been almost oppressive. If they believed in bragging, Swedes would brag about *lagöm*, their philosophy of balance, of "just enough." In crowded parks, we'd laughed at the clusters of picnickers self-regulating their music and conversations to such extent that nary a molecule of sound escaped the invisible circle around them. We'd expected Swedes to be bold and Finns to be quiet. As another lanky Finn staggered down the hall, my limbic system switched to high alert.

I pressed against our cabin door, shrinking-shrinking, willing my blackness into invisibility, as Mom fumbled with the keys. With my nose ring, my curls in constant rotation between bleached-blond and crimson, my designer eyeglass collection, my comfort onstage with the mic, I am not the shrinking type. Normally. But the night before, our last in Sweden, had also been a shock. Skinheads from the countryside and their girlfriends, glittering eyes blackened with eyeliner, had flooded Stockholm's pristine, sedate downtown to celebrate the beginning of the weekend. From our hotel balcony, I watched them cruise below, strangely quiet, their Swastika-bedecked convertibles making slow turns at the edge of the Baltic.

And so this night began, us trapped in our cabin while a Bacchanal raged outside.

"Holy shit, I'm beginning to see why Swedes always gave us those looks when we mentioned going to Finland," Mom said, after our cabin door received its third frenzied pounding.

"Yeah, I thought Finns were supposed to be quiet and depressed."

Mom laughed. "Finns may not have been Vikings, but it's like some pagan blood lust out there."

When she leaned the desk chair against the door, I widened my eyes.

She shrugged, flashing her palms. "Hey, better safe than sorry."

All night, drunken Finns careened, fought, and carried on up and down the corridors. Through the door we heard muffled off-key singing, the clink of bottles, and shouted toasts of "*Kippis!*"

"Damn," I muttered. "Welcome home."

Come morning, Mom poked her head outside and laughed. "C'mon, they're all passed out." She waved me toward the door.

We tiptoed out, stepping gingerly over the sleeping Finns strewn, heads askew, along the garish gold and blue wall-to-wall carpet, and headed up on deck.

Morning on the Baltic resembled those educational films we watched in geography class—impossibly pristine and picturesque, unbroken horizon of blue sky and sea, placid with a hint of ice. The occasional island glittering with birch forests and gingerbread summer cottages. At the announcement in Finnish, Swedish, and English of our pending arrival to Port of Turku, everyone crowded onto the deck.

Below, among the warren of sailboats nestled into berths and cranes next to bright containers and cement docks, stood families in standard Nordic uniform: trim capri pants, long-sleeved boatneck tees with dark horizontal stripes, sculptural leather shoes, and rain anoraks.

"Look!" Mom cried with a trill of laughter, "how sweet!" A smiling family of blonds and gingers—father, mother, two daughters, and a son—held a cardboard sign: WELCOME HOLLY & FAITH.

Behind them, dark-haired Romany women in long, black velvet skirts and petticoats milled about, looking straight out of something from Romanian history. Above them, graffitied onto a tall warehouse tower, was a shaky swastika and the English phrase, "WHITES ONLY."

Mom paused her frantic waving. "Oh shit."

"Hmm." I quipped, "for a return to the homeland, I'm getting mixed signals."

She chuckled. "Yeah, that's quite a juxtaposition."

I kept my eyes trained on the smiling family below, our family.

Maybe this juxtaposition was why people always made such a big deal about me being Nigerian and Nordic. "How in the world did *that* happen?" they've been asking my whole life, as if Nordic was so northern hemisphere-white and Nigerian so southern hemisphere-Black that the cultures could never possibly intersect. As if humankind hasn't been traveling and intermixing for millennia. As if people don't hop on planes (or in my father's case, a steamship) and relocate for jobs, education, love.

Sure, I'd briefly wondered if our Finnish relatives would embrace me, but I didn't expect the country to have a say. Of course there were white supremacists in Finland, though it did seem like overkill.

"Seriously," I said, "isn't over ninety percent of the population white?"

Mom snorted. "Yeah, I'm not exactly sure what they're worried about. Some of the cousins mentioned the rise of national groups, but they said, 'These people are so stupid, who would follow them?'"

We joined the hungover crowds on the skybridge linking the ship to the terminal and made our way toward our relatives. As we met for the first time, I imagined how we must look: us—two brunettes, one half-African—and them—two redheads and three blonds—nodding and beaming. The mother and father stuck out their hands. *Hello, hello.*

It was hard not to feel like a commercial for air travel or DNA testing.

Later, back at their farmhouse, sitting around a picture-perfect table with colorful Marimekko linens and Iittala glassware, the commercial became real. In anticipation of the second family visit in 110 years, our relatives had clearly been practicing their conversational skills. Either that or as with the boat Finns, we'd been radically misinformed about the notorious Finnish reticence. Over lunch the ruddy, fit family of five chatted easily about Mom's favorite topics: U.S. versus European politics, the American versus Finnish educational systems, and travel, specifically, the excursions they had planned for us in their medieval city of Turku.

During dessert, Mom threw caution to the wind and confessed what we were both thinking. "Whew! This is certainly a relief." She giggled, smoothing her fingers over the flowers and shapes of the tablecloth. "Based on the men in my family—and what I've heard about Finns for, well, sixty years—we were afraid that we'd scare you silly with our talkativeness!" The modulation in her voice ramped up, returning to retired-schoolteacher volume. "In fact, I've been holding back."

Cousin Marja, irrepressible and dimpled, laughed. "We've been practicing!" she announced proudly, placing a flat buttery cake studded with bright summer berries in the center of the table. The family nodded.

"Yes," her jolly, handy-around-the-house husband piped up. "We heard that Americans don't like silence like we Finns do, that they especially like to talk at the dinner table. So we've been preparing, eh, Little Conversation."

"It was a family project," a tween contributed. "After we heard your interests, we went to all the tourist sites in town, collected the pamphlets, studied them, and then prepared The Small Talk!"

"Wait." I leaned across the bold geometric tablecloth. "You already toured everything?"

"Just to make sure it was worthwhile," Marja explained. She perked up. "It turns out that our city is quite interesting!" Her tone was half sincere, half droll.

The younger daughter, a redhead, added, "And it gave us topics for Our Chitchat!"

Okko, a sturdy eight-year-old, shoveled boiled potatoes into his mouth, chuckling to himself.

We spent a week touring Turun Linna, the Medieval castle that was the seat of Swedish rule, and the Sibelius Museum dedicated to Mom's favorite composer, browsing the stalls in Market Hall, and island hopping by boat in service of Marja's Midsommar food cravings. Everywhere we spread the gospel of Smalltalk; nowhere was there any indication that Turku, while certainly white, was for "whites only."

On day seven, the family took us to the train station and waited patiently while the other passengers openly eyed our bizarre family with the Chitchat and the brown skin. We were on to the next leg of our trip—traveling inland for another round of meet-and-greets, more family reunions where the long-lost American cousins were the main event.

"Don't worry about the train," Marja winked. "It's very orderly—not like the boat."

I turned to Mom, alarmed that her tendency to overshare might have offended our new relatives. She grinned. "Marja says the tax on alcohol is so high that Finns ride the boats to Sweden just to drink on tax-free liquor! Isn't that a hoot?"

"Yes, the ones with the alcohol problem," Marja added. "Most of them don't even get off in Sweden. They just drink on the way, turn around, and drink on the way back!"

First we went east to Helsinki, the capital, where we poked around more museums and a church carved into a giant boulder and accompanied a cousin to Tango Night, middle-aged Finns shuffling around a social hall in absolute silence. Then we went up north to our ancestral Savo, an eastern region near the Russian border known throughout Finland for producing strangely talkative folk. Each week, each town drew entire families—silent, smiley men, chatty women with bobbed hair, well-behaved children, vibrant elders who grabbed my mother's rosy cheeks and burst into tears. They rushed in with gifts of hand-knit woolen socks and embroidered table linens and bottles of perfume. They dragged out embossed family albums with actual photographs of us inside, and set down bowls of wild berries, and threw open their city apartments and summer cottages to welcome in family members they hadn't seen in a hundred years. It was almost enough to make a Nigerian-Nordic girl cry.

But it's in our final stop, our actual maternal village of Kiuruvesi, that I find myself standing on the lawn dotted with yellow and white and lavender wildflowers outside a white clapboard farmhouse, encircled by six sets of blue eyes, gleaming teeth, pink skin, and blond hair. Being invited to a type of sauna I've never heard of.

Upon entering each new family household, Mom has learned to declare immediately and unequivocally her no-sauna policy, tapping her chest, as if her heart couldn't take it. She's lucky she's a guest and that she knows so much about Finnish and family history; otherwise, we'd have an international incident on our hands, seeing as sauna is Finland's primary pastime. Instead, she offers me up: "Faith loves sauna!"

Up until now, that's been true. I've learned not to flinch when dinner ends with a virtual stranger nodding approval and then stripping in close quarters. And these distant cousins have been gentle, dividing themselves into shifts by gender, allowing me to go with the women and girls while the men and boys keep Mom company before taking their turn. As we lounge in our towels, clinking beers, I marvel. It's an amazing thing—the Black body accepted into the family with no fantasies, either dangerous or erotic.

"Smoke sauna is traditional to Savo," my cousin explains, pronouncing sauna the same way I learned growing up (and was later ridiculed for at college), the right way: SOW-na. "Anyone can do hot rocks and steam, but smoke is for the serious, the—how you say?—connoisseur."

"We plug the chimney," another cousin chimes in enthusiastically.

The *savusauna* is a return to the original, pre-chimney sauna. Wood is burned in a large stove, and the smoke fills the room. Once the sauna is hot enough, the fire is allowed to go out, and the smoke is ventilated.

"Because you want to die?"

I'm only half kidding. Just a few decades ago, sauna was the transitional space between life and death, the gateway between this life and the next. Sauna was where women gave birth. Sauna was where the dead received their final wash.

My cousins laugh, a sound like a mountain stream tumbling over rocks. "We like it; it's good for purifying."

I wonder if this is literal—an alcoholic detox—or figurative. In either case, it can't be wise to steep in six men's smoky karmas. Even if we are related.

"As you know," says the gregarious, rosy cousin who first issued the invitation, "SOW-na is how we welcome guests. It's the best way to get to know someone." The six nod eagerly, their flopping blond hair reminiscent of overgrown golden retrievers. "Will you join us?"

For a split second, I am a someone free to say yes. I imagine watching a cousin lean forward, tiny beads of sweat rolling down his blotchy-red back, to dip the long-handled ladle into the wooden bucket with a *bloop*. As he dribbles water over the hot coals, they sizzle and hiss. The *löyly*, thick white steam, billows around us, settles over us as heat presses against my sternum.

My mouth pops open, knee-jerk reaction to the danger of suffocation. My nostrils flare like billows, dragging at the thick wet air. I lean back, spine melting against the rough warm wood of the sauna wall. I breathe consciously, deep meditation breaths that will my heart to slow, to have faith that beneath the blanket of wet heat, there is enough air.

The man coughs and flicks a branch against my legs. Immediately the tiny room blooms with the crisp bite of eucalyptus and pine. I glance down to see pinpricks tingling red up my calves, green fronds against brown skin. One by one, my muscles loosen and puddle, as if they're being massaged. I feel supported and weightless, the way I imagine the womb must have felt. I glance up at the tall, blue-eyed, blond male stranger sweating and grinning inches away from me, a Black woman. I glance around at the five other naked men surrounding me, their tobacco breath thick and grassy on my neck and shoulders.

Will you join us?

I shake my head, ending my daydream. How do I tell them, these Finnish cousins? Much as I love sauna (a friend in Minnesota once sent his red-faced teenaged son out to knock on the door to see if I was alive, as no one had ever spent so much time in his sauna), I'm wearing a lifetime of being a Black woman in America. How can I strip naked and enter a dark, smoky box with six naked white men?

Will you join us?

The one stipulation I gave Mom when announcing her sixtieth birthday gift, a Midsommar trip to Finland and Sweden, was that we had to track down our Finnish relatives. She agreed. I knew she would; it involved research, after all, and her teacherly instincts prevailed. Mom began rifling through her mother's and aunt's diaries and letters, and in no time at all she had regular pen pals, the most devoted being a cousin in northern Finland named Pirjo who planned out our entire visit, complete with a family "reunion" and host in each town. According to Pirjo, my grandmother in the U.S. and her sister in Finland had been writing and exchanging family photos for years before they died; all the Finnish cousins knew about us and had been waiting.

"I did what you wanted," Mom reported during one of our logistical phone calls, after the usual gush of *Pirjo-this* and *Pirjo-that.* "But I don't think we should stay with strangers."

I took a deep breath. "Well, frankly, Nordic countries are so expensive, I don't think we can afford *not* to stay with them. And besides, you've wanted to visit Finland and Sweden your whole life!"

"Mmm," she conceded, skeptical.

I pressed on. "*Mummi* got cancer before she could return home. Our connection to the place *is* family. Why not go all in?"

She made a show of grousing a bit more, and I chuckled. She was the one who had supported my desire to go to Nigeria twelve years ago and find my father and siblings. She is the one who encourages me to write about our scattered-over-three-continents family. And she will be the one who falls hard, sending letters and packages for years to come to these Finnish strangers who are also, now, our family.

And I am the one who brought us this far and who stands sweating on the edge of one world, poised to step into a smoky unknown one.

"Not this time," I say, smiling at my six cousins. "Not yet."

❧ ❧ ❧

Faith Adiele is founder of VONA Travel, the nation's first workshop for travel writers of color, and author of the travel memoir, Meeting Faith, *an account of becoming Thailand's first Black Buddhist nun, which won the PEN Open Book Award. The PBS documentary* My Journey Home *documents her journey to Nigeria to find her father and siblings. She is also co-editor of* Coming of Age Around the World: A Multicultural Anthology; *author/narrator of the audio/e-book,* The Nigerian-Nordic Girl's Guide to Lady Problems; *and senior editor at* Panorama: The Journal of Intelligent Travel. *She penned the introduction to* The Best Women's Travel Writing 2009, *and her stories appear in the 2014, 2006, and 2005 editions, as well as in the Travelers' Tales' anthology* A Woman's Asia. *Faith lives in the San Francisco Bay Area and at adiele.com and @meetingfaith.*

Ann Leary

❦ ❦ ❦

The Godfather Town

They weren't afraid. Really.

My husband, Denis, and I aren't big travelers. When we do take a trip, we usually go to Italy, but we like to float other options first.

"Why not Istanbul?" I'll suggest.

"We never did that African safari," Denis says, and we carry on with this charade for a few days, tossing out increasingly implausible ideas as if we're the kind of tourists who get their kicks trekking through Colombian cocaine plantations or paddleboarding in shark-infested waters. We're not adventurous—we're afraid of pretty much everything—but mostly we're afraid to visit places we might not love. We already know we love Italy, so we go there. We're not Italian, but we understand the language, and because of ravioli and the works of Scorsese and Coppola, we feel a sort of complicity with the Italian people. We're *practically* Italian, as far as we're concerned, so, especially in recent years, our European holidays have been to Italy—Venice, Rome, Florence, Tuscany, the Amalfi Coast, and most recently, Sicily.

When I said that we understand the Italian language, I didn't mean to imply that we understand *all* the words. No, what I mean is we understand that we are hearing the Italian language when it's spoken. Not all of the time, but most of the time, especially when we're in Italy. I do know a few words and am constantly trilling *buongiorno, grazie,* and *permesso* at hapless waiters and passersby, gesticulating wildly, all my accents on the wrong syllables and my spittle bouncing off the wrong consonants.

Denis just says, "Howsit goin?" To everybody. Everywhere.

For our Sicily trip, we rented a car in order to drive around and see the sights, even though an Italian friend had advised against this.

"Most Americans find the Autostrade a little intimidating," she had warned.

We are *not* most Americans, so we insisted on the rental car, and on our second day we drove off to find a scenic town a man named Enzo had told us about. We'd met Enzo on a beach that morning and he'd informed us that we were just a short drive from the most scenic of all Sicilian towns. "It is the town in *The Godfather*—the film, *The Godfather*," Enzo had proclaimed. And then we had to go see this real Sicilian town, this amazing *Godfather* town, so we jumped in the car and set off.

The road was winding and a little scary at first. I could see how some Americans would be frightened.

"This isn't so bad," I said to Denis as he drove along. "I think it's sad that people are so limited by their fears, because you can't really experience a place until you drive its roads, just like we are. Really, it's only by poking along the byways and in and out of the sleepy villages off the beaten track that one may really get to know a place."

Denis told me I was blocking his view. He was trying to pull out of the long, steep driveway we'd just ascended. I had thought we were on a road, but it was the driveway from our hotel.

"Nothing coming this way...no, STOP!" I said as three motorcycles whizzed past. The road we were entering was narrow, and it was hard to see approaching cars because of all the curves. "O.K., go now, NO, WAIT!" I screamed. Then after a truck flew past, I shouted, "GO...GO...GO...GO... GO...STOP!"

"Sit back so I can see," Denis said, through clenched teeth. Then he steered us onto the road, and we were off.

The thing to do, when you're traveling in unknown places, is to get lost right off the bat. That way you get it over with, and you don't have to worry about it anymore. We tried to enter the Autostrade heading north, but instead found ourselves ascending steep, sometimes seemingly vertical switchbacks that brought us to the lovely but very congested town of Taormina. We could see how others might think driving in Sicily is scary. But we weren't afraid. We said this quite a few times as we sped around tight turns, the road dropping off thousands of feet beside us, a honking bus on our tail and motorcycles flying at us from the opposite direction. Once we got on the Autostrade, it would be better, we reassured each other.

And then we entered the Autostrade.

Apparently, when they built the Autostrade, on this part of the Sicilian coast, the tunneling through mountains and cliffs became too tiresome, so they engineered a sort of Jetsons-style space highway. You just speed along at ninety mph on a twisting, turning superhighway suspended thousands of feet—oh, I beg your pardon, *meters*—above the land or sea below. I really don't mind driving across bridges, because bridges have fences or walls to keep cars from falling off. The Autostrade has a little guardrail. Do you know how easy it is to flip a car over a guardrail? Denis does, I know, because I asked him. My head was buried between my knees, but I was able to shout, "DO YOU KNOW HOW EASY IT IS

TO FLIP A CAR OVER A GUARDRAIL? Do you know you JUST HAVE TO TOUCH THE RAIL WITH YOUR TIRE and you'll be...."

"Yup, thanks, got it," he said.

We eventually climbed a long, narrow road that led us to the hilltop village of Savoca. In addition to being one of the locations for *The Godfather*, Savoca is a beautiful medieval village with ancient stone walkways and views of the surrounding countryside and, in the distance, the Ionian Sea.

Though the village was relatively empty when we arrived, we'd since eaten lunch in a café, and in that time, a tour bus had pulled up in front of The Church of San Nicolò—the church where Michael Corleone and Apollonia were married! We decided to have a quick look inside before the others crowded in.

While I was trying to force Denis to take my photograph in front of the church, an older man approached me with a shawl and a smile. He had other, similar shawls draped across his arm. I admired them politely, but told him I really wasn't in the market for a shawl. He ignored me and continued to thrust his wares at me, and I admit, I got a little huffy. I wasn't going to be hoodwinked into buying a shawl. I was there to see *The Godfather* church, if he didn't mind!

He did mind, very much. He pointed angrily at a placard that said, in both Italian and English, that the Church of San Nicolò is, and has long been, a house of God, not just *The Godfather* church, and that those entering are asked to show respect by covering bare shoulders and legs. He wasn't selling the shawls, he was loaning them. I apologized profusely, pulled a sweatshirt out of my bag, and put it over my sleeveless top. Then we followed the tour-bus crowd inside.

The next day, we hired a young guide named Luca to take us to visit Mt. Etna, mostly because he would do all the driving. We'd heard it was a lovely hike to the summit. On the way, Luca told us about Mt. Etna's previous eruptions, some of which had happened during the past half-century.

The most devastating recent eruption was in 1992, when lava flowed down the mountain, threatening various towns and destroying numerous buildings. You can see Mt. Etna for miles. It smokes—it's a heavy smoker—but somehow we hadn't understood, until Luca informed us, that the volcano was still active and could erupt again at any moment.

"I think we might be going to the wrong volcano," I suggested helpfully.

Not far from the base of Mt. Etna is the village of Zafferana. Luca wanted us to see this village where a miracle had happened not once, but twice. We wondered if the miracles somehow involved *The Godfather*. Perhaps the actress who played Apollonia was discovered there, or Al Pacino bought everyone a round of sambuca in some crowded *ristorante*. In fact, holy miracles happened in Zafferana. According to legend, one of the more serious Mt. Etna eruptions occurred in the seventeenth century. The villagers of Zafferana, upon seeing the lava flowing toward their homes, prayed to the Virgin Mary and carried a statue of her to a point in the lava's path just above town. It was at that very spot that the lava stopped. So, when the 1992 eruption occurred, the townspeople again carried a statue of the Blessed Mother to the place where they hoped the lava would cease—and again, the lava stopped flowing there.

Luca parked next to a cottage at the bottom of a steep hill, and we climbed out to see where the miracle transpired. He pointed to a wide ridge of hard volcanic rock—a former molten lava tsunami—that snaked down a long slope and ended right behind the cottage.

Denis and I were marveling at how close to the house the lava had come, and Luca seemed to mistake our horror for fascination.

"Today you'll only climb Etna, but another day, you must book a cave tour," he said. "You wear a harness and are lowered into tiny cracks in the side of the volcano, very popular." He mentioned something about another tour that involved jeep rides along live lava trails, but he'd lost me at the part about lowering tourists into an active, smoldering volcano.

Had these people never heard of Pompeii? I imagined a tour guide centuries from now—perhaps a descendent of our own Luca—guiding tourists through the archeological site where we now stood. I imagined him showing the group a recently unearthed finding—the remains of a couple, so perfectly preserved you could read their American passports. I imagined the looks of disgust as he explained that nearby were the remains of two young children, crushed by the American tourists who'd trampled them in their attempt to flee the flowing lava.

Nevertheless, after leaving Zafferana, Denis and I decided to hike a little way up the volcano. It wasn't that we were afraid to climb all the way to the top, to the part that smokes, where lava could erupt at any moment with zero warning. It was merely that it was midday, and hot.

The landscape on Mt. Etna in September is eerie and lunar, mostly barren, but with surprising waves of color from wildflowers that grow here and there in the black volcanic soil along the steep path. When we reached the summit of one of the lower craters, a couple of hippies were there, sitting against their backpacks, smoking a joint. I've climbed a few small mountains and hills, and in my experience, there are always hippies smoking a joint at the summit.

Denis wanted to get a photo of me. "Back up," he kept saying. I backed up. "Just a little more. A little more."

The hippies laughed and laughed. Finally, I got the joke. He had backed me up to within inches of the edge of the plateau surrounding the crater. Behind me was nothing but the faint outlines of distant craters. Another step back and I would have plummeted thousands of meters to my death, but of course Denis stopped me.

We put the camera away and just gazed down at the world below. The sky around us was a thin blue color—almost white. We weren't sure if we were in a low-hanging cloud or volcanic smoke. Probably both. Many meters below, we knew Luca waited next to his car. Somewhere in the distance was Zafferana, preserved and protected by its benefactress, the Blessed Mother, and far away was Savoca, *The Godfather* town. But here, where we stood, perched on a crater of an active volcano, it was quiet and the air smelled faintly of sulphur, marijuana, and something else, some fragrant desert plant like eucalyptus or mimosa. It was quite something; it was like being in heaven, and we wondered why on earth we'd been so afraid.

જી જી જી

Ann Leary is the author of the novels The Children, The Good House, *and* Outtakes from a Marriage, *and the memoir,* An Innocent, A Broad. *Her bestselling novel,* The Good House, *has recently been adapted as a motion picture starring Sigourney Weaver and Kevin Kline. Ann's* New York Times *essay, "Rallying to Keep the Game Alive," was adapted for the Amazon "Modern Love" TV Series and stars Tina Fey and John Slattery. She is currently working on a new novel and a collection of essays for Simon and Schuster. Her work has been translated into eighteen languages, and she has written for numerous publications, including* Ploughshares, NPR, Real Simple, *and* the New York Times. *Ann and her husband, Denis Leary, live in New York.*

SUSAN ORLEAN

🙟 🙟 🙟

Zooming in on Petra

Dust, donkeys, drones, and the exquisite
pleasure of delayed gratification.

*O*nce you've been to Petra, it stays with you. Long after
you've left you will find grit from Petra's red sandstone
in the tread of your shoes; your fingernails will have a faint
rosy tinge; a fine pinkish dust will cling to your clothing. For
some time you will close your eyes and still be able to relive the
startling moment you first saw this ancient stone city rising out
of the desert floor; you will savor the memory of this place, its
grandeur and strangeness, even after you manage to wash away
the traces of its red rocks.

Driving southwest across the dull plateau from Amman
for a few hours, you suddenly tip into the dry basin of Jordan's Arabah Valley and tumble down through mountain
passes. The landscape is cracked and sandy, seared and
unpromising. It is hardly the setting in which you expect to
find a city of any sort, let alone one this rich and extravagant

and refined. There seems to be no water, no possibility of agriculture, no means of livelihood or sustenance. The fact that the Nabatean people, the nomadic Arabs who criss-crossed the region until they grew wealthy from trade, made Petra the capital of their empire by the fourth century B.C. is baffling. Yet here, at the valley's center, are the remains of this once-lavish city, watered by hidden aqueducts that run for miles from an underground spring. It looks like no other place I've ever seen. The "buildings" are punched into the rock cliffs—in other words, they are elaborate caves, recessed in the sandstone and fronted with miraculously carved ornate facades. It is probably one of the world's only cities that was made by subtraction rather than addition, a city you literally enter into, penetrate, rather than approach.

Petra will draw you in, but at the same time, it is always threatening to disappear. The sandstone is fragile. The wind through the mountains, the pounding of feet, the universe's bent toward disintegration—all conspire to grind it away. My trip here was to see the place and take a measure of its evanescent beauty, and to watch Virtual Wonders, a company devoted to sharing and documenting the world's natural and cultural wonders, use all manner of modern technology to create a virtual model of the site so precise that it will, in effect, freeze Petra in time.

I arrived in Petra just as the summer sun cranked up from roast to broil; the sky was a bowl of blue and the midday air was piping hot. The paths inside the Petra Archaeological Park were clogged. Horse-drawn buggies clattered by at a bone-joggling speed. Packs of visitors inched along, brandish-ing maps and sunscreen. In a spot of shade, guides dressed as Nabateans kneeled to conduct their midday prayers.

At its peak, two thousand years ago, Petra was home to as many as thirty thousand people, full of temples, theaters, gardens, tombs, villas, Roman baths, and the camel caravans and marketplace bustle befitting the center of an ancient crossroads between east and west. After the Roman Empire annexed the city in the early second century A.D., it continued to thrive until an earthquake rattled it hard in A.D. 363. Then trade routes shifted, and by the middle of the seventh century what remained of Petra was largely deserted. No one lived in it anymore except for a small tribe of Bedouins, who took up residence in some of the caves and, in more recent centuries, whiled away their spare time shooting bullets into the buildings in hopes of cracking open the vaults of gold rumored to be inside.

In its period of abandonment, the city could easily have been lost forever to all but the tribes who lived nearby. But in 1812, a Swiss explorer named Johann Ludwig Burckhardt, intrigued by stories he'd heard about a lost city, dressed as an Arab sheikh to beguile his Bedouin guide into leading him to it. His reports of Petra's remarkable sites and its fanciful caves began drawing oglers and adventurers, and they have continued coming ever since.

Two hundred years later, I mounted a donkey named Shakira and rode the dusty paths of the city to ogle some of those sites myself. This happened to be the middle of the week in the middle of Ramadan. My guide, Ahmed, explained to me that he had gotten permission to take his blood pressure medication despite the Ramadan fast, and he gobbled a handful of pills as our donkeys scrambled up rock-hewn steps.

Ahmed is a broad man with green eyes, a grizzled beard, a smoker's cough, and an air of bemused weariness. He told me that he was Bedouin, and his family had been in Petra "since time began." He was born in one of Petra's caves, where his family had been living for generations. They would still be living there, he said, except that in 1985, Petra was listed as a UNESCO World Heritage Site, a designation that discourages ongoing habitation. Nearly all the Bedouin families living in Petra were resettled—sometimes against their wishes—in housing built outside the boundaries of the new Petra Archaeological Park. I asked Ahmed if he preferred his family's cave or his house in the new village. His house has electricity and running water and Wi-Fi. "I liked the cave," he said. He fumbled for his phone, which was chirping. We rode on, the donkeys' hard hooves tapping a rhythmic beat on the stone trail.

Petra sprawls and snakes through the mountains, with most of its significant features collected in a flat valley. Royal tombs line one side of the valley; religious sites line the other. A wide, paved, colonnaded street was once Petra's main thoroughfare; nearby are the ruins of a grand public fountain or "nymphaeum," and those of several temples, the largest of which was probably dedicated to the Nabatean sun god Dushara. Another, the once free-standing Great Temple—which probably served as a financial and civic center in addition to a religious one—includes a six-hundred-seat auditorium and a complex system of subterranean aqueducts. On a small rise overlooking the Great Temple sits a Byzantine church with beautiful intact mosaic floors decorated with prancing, pastel animals including birds, lions, fish, and bears.

The grander buildings—that is, the grander caves—are as high and spacious as ballrooms, and the hills are pocked with smaller caves as well, their ceilings blackened by the soot left from decades of Bedouin campfires. Some of the caves are truly imposing, like the Urn Tomb, with its classical facade carved into the cliff on top of a base of stone-built arches, and an eroding statue of a man (perhaps the king) wearing a toga. Others are easy to miss, such as the cave known as the Triclinium, which has no facade at all but possesses the only intricately carved *interior* at Petra, with stone benches and walls lined with fluted half-columns. Standing inside the valley it is easy to see why Petra thrived. The mountains contain it, looming like sentries in every direction, but the valley itself is wide and bright.

So much of Petra feels like a sly surprise that I became convinced the Nabateans must have had a sense of humor to have built the city the way they did. They were gifted people in many ways. They had a knack for business and cornered the market in frankincense and myrrh. They had real estate savvy, establishing their city at the meeting point of several routes on which caravans shipped spices, ivory, precious metals, silk, and other goods from China, India, and the Persian Gulf to the ports of the Mediterranean. They had a talent for melding the dust and dirt around them into a hard, russet clay from which they made perfume bottles and tiles and bowls. They were expert artisans. And while it isn't recorded in historical texts, they clearly appreciated the hallmarks of architectural showmanship—a good sense of timing, a flair for theatrical siting.

The most convincing evidence of this begins with the Siq, the main entrance to the city, a natural ravine that splits the towering rocks for almost a mile. It's a compressed, confined space; its rock walls lean this way and that. Once you inch your way through it, you are spilled out onto a sandy apron and confronted with the most dramatic structure in Petra— Al Khazneh, or the Treasury, a cave more than a hundred feet high, its facade a fantastical mashup of a Greco-Roman doorway, an Egyptian "broken" pediment, and two levels of columns and statues etched into the sheer face of the mountain.

The Treasury wasn't actually a treasury at all—it gets its name from the riches said to have been stored in the great urn atop the circular building at the facade's center. The statues adorning the colonnaded niches suggest it may have been a temple, but most scholars think it was a tomb housing the remains of an important early king. (A favorite candidate is the first century B.C. Aretas III, who used the word Philhellenos on his coins—"friend of the Greeks"—which might explain the building's Hellenistic flair.) Inside the cave there are just three bare chambers, today empty of whatever remains once rested there.

Perhaps the Nabateans placed this grand building here because the Siq served as a buffer to marauders, much like a wall or a moat. But I have to believe they knew that forcing visitors to approach the Treasury via a long, slow walk through the Siq would make a perfect lead-up to a great reveal, designed to delight and astonish. The gradual approach also leaves the world with a timeless pun, because coming upon the Treasury this way makes you feel as if you've found a treasure at the end of a secret grotto.

As Ahmed and I rode along, I could just make out in the distance the team from Virtual Wonders, who had spent the day flying a drone over the Great Temple, shooting high-resolution images of it from above. The company was formed in 2018 by three friends with complementary talents. Mark Bauman, a longtime journalist and former executive at Smithsonian Enterprises and National Geographic, knew the people in charge of historical locations like Petra and how to work with local authorities. Corey Jaskolski, a one-time high school dropout/computer whisperer (he eventually earned a graduate degree from MIT in electrical engineering), who has patented systems for impossible-seeming robotic cameras and 3-D scanning for use underwater, on land and from the air, would manage the technological challenges of image capture and digital modeling. Kenny Broad, an environmental anthropologist at the University of Miami, is a world-class cave diver and explorer for whom scrambling around a place like Petra was a piece of cake; he would serve as chief exploration officer. The three of them shared a passion for nature and archaeology and a concern with how to preserve important sites.

While outfits such as the Getty Research Institute and the nonprofit CyArk have been capturing 3-D images of historical sites for some time, Virtual Wonders proposed a new approach. They would create infinitesimally detailed 3-D models. For Petra, for instance, they would capture the equivalent of two hundred fifty thousand ultra-high-resolution images, which will be computer-rendered into a virtual model of the city and its breathtaking structures that can be viewed—even walked through and interacted with—using a virtual-reality headset, gaming console or other high-tech "projected environments." Virtual Wonders will share these renderings with authorities and other scholarly and educational partners (in this case, the Petra National Trust). Detailed modeling of this kind is at the leading edge of archaeological best practices, and according to Jordan's Princess Dana Firas, the head of the Petra National Trust, the data will help identify and measure the site's deterioration and assist in developing plans for preservation and managing visitors. "It's a long-term investment," Firas told me.

By the time I arrived in Petra, the Virtual Wonders team had scanned and imaged more than half of Petra and its significant buildings using an assortment of high-tech methods. A DJI Inspire drone—for which a military escort is required, because drones are illegal in Jordan—uses a high-resolution camera to collect aerial views, shot in overlapping "stripes" so every inch is recorded. Exact measurements are done by photogrammetry, with powerful lenses on 35-millimeter cameras, and Lidar, which stands for Light Detection and Ranging, a revolving laser mechanism that records minute calculations at the rate of a million measurements per second. When combined and rendered by computers those measurements form a detailed "texture map" of an object's surface. All of this data will be poured into computers, which will need about eight months to render a virtual model.

None of this is cheap. In Petra, the Virtual Wonders team hiked around with about a half-million dollars' worth of gear. According to Bauman, the company's hope is that the cost of the projects will be recouped, and exceeded, by licensing the data to film companies, game developers and the like, with a portion of the revenue going back to whoever oversees the site, in this case the Petra National Trust. This isn't an idle hope. Petra is so spectacular that it has been used as a location in films, most famously *Indiana Jones and the Last*

Crusade; countless music videos; and as a setting in at least ten video games including Spy Hunter, OutRun 2, and LEGO Indiana Jones. If its approach succeeded, Virtual Wonders hoped to move on to similar projects around the world, and since I left Jordan the company has begun work at Chichen Itza, the Mayan city in the Yucatán. It has also scored a clear success with an immersive virtual reality exhibit titled "Tomb of Christ: the Church of the Holy Sepulchre Experience," at the National Geographic Museum in Washington, D.C.

I left my donkey and crossed through the ruins of the flat valley to join the team on a ridge overlooking the Great Temple. "We're shooting stripes," Jaskolski called out as the buglike drone rose and jetted across the open sky toward the temple. Jaskolski's wife, Ann, was monitoring the drone on an iPad. She reached out and adjusted the drone's landing pad, a gray rubber mat, which was weighed down with a rock to keep the gusty breeze from toying with it. The drone made a burbling sizzle as it darted over the temple. Somewhere in the distance a donkey brayed. A generator coughed and then commenced its low grumbling. "We're *killing* it!" Jaskolski called to Bauman, sounding a little like a teenager playing Fortnite. "I'm really crushing the overlap!"

Bauman and I hiked along the ridge to another building known as the Blue Chapel. A few crooked fingers of rebar stuck out of some of the rock—evidence that some clumsy restoration had been attempted. But otherwise, the structure was untouched, another remnant of the city that Petra once had been, a bustling capital, where lives were lived and lost; an empire etched in time, where the city's carapace is all that remains.

On the far side of the valley from the Treasury, across the plain, Petra's architects kept another great trick up their sleeve: Ad Deir, or the Monastery. This ancient temple is thought to have been dedicated to a deified Nabatean king named Obodas I, and possesses Petra's largest carved facade.

But the path there gives you no glimpse of it at all. For forty minutes Ahmed and I clung on as our donkeys climbed up the steep path. I kept my eyes glued to the back of Ahmed's head so I wouldn't have to see the sheer drop-off along the edge of the trail.

As we made yet another turn with no building in sight, I began to wonder if I had misunderstood our destination. Even when Ahmed stopped and announced that we had arrived, there was nothing to see. The heat was getting to me and I was impatient. I grumbled that I didn't see anything. "Over there," Ahmed said, gesturing around a ragged rock wall. When I turned the corner, I was met with the full-frontal view of an enormous facade with an array of columns and doorway-shaped niches, almost 160 feet wide and nearly as tall, carved into a rocky outcropping. It was so startling and beautiful that I gasped out loud.

Like so many of the monuments here, the Monastery's interior is deceptively simple: a single rectangular room with a niche carved into the back wall, which probably once held a stone Nabatean icon. The walls of the niche itself are carved with crosses, suggesting the temple became a church during the Byzantine era—hence the name. The Monastery is said to be the best example of traditional Nabatean architecture— simplified geometric forms, the urn atop a rounded building at the center. It is believed that the Monastery's architect took inspiration from the Treasury but pointedly stripped away most of its Greco-Roman flourishes. There are no statues in the spaces cut between the columns, and overall it's rougher, simpler. But out here, all alone, in front of a wide stone court- yard where Nabateans and travelers from across the ancient world came to worship or feast, the sight of the Monastery is profound.

I stared at Ad Deir for what felt like an eternity, marvel- ing not only at the building but the way it had provided the exquisite pleasure of delayed gratification. When I returned to Ahmed, he was on the phone with his two-year-old daughter, who was begging to get a new teddy bear on their upcoming trip to town. Ahmed has five other children. His oldest son, Khaleel, also works as a guide in the park. Khaleel had taken me earlier in the day to a ledge above the Treasury, a view even more vertiginous than the trail to Ad Deir. I needed several minutes before I could inch to the edge and appreciate the view. When I steadied my nerves and was able to peek out through squeezed eyes, I could grasp the monumentality of the Treasury—how it loomed, emerging out of the mountainside like an apparition, a building that wasn't a building, a place that was there but not there.

What will it mean to create a perfect model of a place like Petra—one that you might be able to visit sitting in your living room? Will it seem less urgent to see Petra in person if you can stick on a pair of virtual reality goggles and make your way through the Siq, gawk at the Treasury, hike up to the Monastery, and inspect ruins that are thousands of years old? Or will having access to an almost-real version of Petra make it easier for more people to learn about it, and that, in turn, will make more people care about it, even if they never walk over its red rocks or slide their way through the Siq? The preservation aspect of projects like Virtual Wonders' is undeniably valuable; it saves, for posterity, precise images of the world's great sites, and will allow people who won't ever have the opportunity to travel this far to see the place and experience it almost as it is.

But visiting a place—breathing in its ancient dust, confronting it in real time, meeting its residents, elbowing its tourists, sweating as you clamber up its hills, even seeing how time has punished it—will always be different, more magical, more challenging. Technology makes it easier to see the world almost as it is, but sometimes the harder parts are what make travel memorable. The long climb to Ad Deir, with its scary path and surprising reveal, is what I will remember, long after the specific details of the building's appearance have faded from my memory. The way Petra is laid out

means you work for every gorgeous vision, which is exactly
what I imagine the Nabateans had in mind.

As soon as I left Petra, I found myself staring at the pictures I
had taken and finding it hard to believe I had been there; the
images, out of context, were so fantastical that they seemed
surreal, a dream of a red stone city dug into the mountainside, so perfectly camouflaged that as soon as you drive the
steep road out of the park, it seems to disappear, as if it were
never there.

In Amman, where signs advertised this fall's Dead Sea
Fashion Week ("Bloggers and Influencers Welcome!"), my
driver pulled up to the front door of my hotel and I stepped
out, passing a sign directing Fashion Week attendees to the
ballroom. The hotel had just opened for business—it was a
glossy, glassy building that advertised itself as being in the
heart of the new, modern Amman. But ancient Jordan was
here as well. The entry was puzzlingly dark and small, with
a narrow opening that led to a long hallway with walls that
were akimbo, leaning in at some points and flaring out in
others, with sharp angles jutting out. I inched along, dragging
my suitcase and banging a corner here and there. Finally, the
dark hall opened wide onto a big, bright lobby, so unexpected
that I stopped cold, blinking until my eyes adjusted to the
light. The young man at the reception desk nodded at me and
asked if I liked the entrance. "It's something special," he said.
"We call it the Siq."

Susan Orlean is the author of eight books, including The
Bullfighter Checks Her Makeup, My Kind of Place, Saturday
Night, *and* Lazy Little Loafers. *In 1999, she published* The
Orchid Thief*, which was made into the Academy Award-
winning film* "Adaptation," *starring Nicolas Cage and Meryl*

Streep. Her book, Rin Tin Tin: The Life and the Legend, a New York Times Notable book, won the Ohioana Book Award and the Richard Wall Memorial Award. In 2018, she published The Library Book, about the arson fire at the Los Angeles Public Library. It won the California Book Award and the Marfield Prize, was nominated for the Andrew Carnegie Medal, and was a New York Times Notable Book of 2018. Orlean has been a staff writer for the New Yorker since 1992, and has also contributed to Vogue, Rolling Stone, Outside, and Esquire. She has written about taxidermy, fashion, umbrellas, origami, dogs, chickens, and a wide range of other subjects. She is currently adapting The Library Book for television. She lives with her husband and son in Los Angeles.

AUDREY FERBER

፨ ፨ ፨

A Daughter's Guide to Florence

What to see, what to miss.

HISTORY

The summer I was thirteen, my mother, Florence, visited Florence, Italy. I was so busy French kissing and throwing pots at an arty camp for teenagers in the Berkshires, I didn't think much about my parents' trip. But when they arrived for visiting day, my mother's blouse was open one button lower than usual. She wore startling chartreuse pointy-toed flats, and every time she moved, a buttery new handbag warmed in the crook of her arm released a rich emollient scent. My mother always looked great, everyone commented on her sense of style, but she seemed different that day, more vivid than before the trip.

"Florence was magnificent!" she squeezed my forearm. "The art, the food...."

199

"*Firenze,*" my father trilled, in one of his funny voices. He gave everyone nicknames and had been calling her that since they'd arrived. "Tell her about the museums."

"Fantastic. And the shopping!" My mother drew me to her. "You'll love it," she whispered huskily in my ear. "Promise me you'll go."

"All right. I'll go." I pulled away from the scent at her collarbones. *Antilope,* the perfume she always wore.

I had more important things on my mind than their stupid vacation. Did she even know that my story about the cruelty of circuses had been chosen for the camp literary magazine? Or that I'd decided to get my own apartment in Greenwich Village when we returned to Brooklyn, since everyone said I was "very mature" for a thirteen-year old? Or that I'd had three boyfriends in three weeks?

She used to call me "Messy Bessy" because I didn't hang up my clothes. She criticized the "moat of books" on the floor around my bed, told me I drank "like a truck driver" when I held my mug in both hands, and that I sounded like a "fishwife" when I stood on our front porch and yelled to my friend who lived at the end of the block. I looked at her pearly fingernails and pristine outfits and wondered if she was my mother at all.

GETTING THERE

She died too early at the age of seventy. A decade later, my father died, my husband celebrated his seventieth birthday, and I turned fifty-four. By even the most generous calculations, I had lived half my life. I'd traveled to Ecuador, to Israel, to Mexico and Morocco, but never to Florence. I had not kept my promise to visit the city she'd loved. So, without my usual procrastination, I booked the trip from San Francisco to Italy. I bought the tickets quickly because time no longer seemed limitless. I bought the tickets because she told me I'd love it, and grudgingly, I'd begun to admit that her instincts about me were usually right.

ACCOMMODATIONS

From the outside, our Santa Croce B&B looked ancient. Dark, rough stone hung with spidery ironwork. But inside, renovation had lightened and brightened the rooms. The parlor retained a few old-world touches, a carved, dove-grey marble fireplace and a ceiling painted with clouds and an array of Biblical figures, but the open kitchen, fitted with a massive professional stove and a long stone counter lined with stools, was state of the art.

Happily, I had signed on for a cooking lesson with Mariangela, the owner. On our second day in Florence, while my husband went off to revisit the Medici Chapel he'd loved on his first trip to Italy many years before, we prepared *crostini di fegatini,* the traditional start of a Tuscan meal. After we cleaned the chicken livers, Mariangela added them to a saucepan of sautéed garlic, carrots, and parsley. Next, we poured in broth and wine.

"My mother fried her chicken livers with onions in chicken fat. My grandmother's recipe," I told her. "Then she chopped them in a wooden bowl with hard boiled eggs."

"Jewish chopped liver. I know it," Mariangela said. "Very good."

Not very good. When I was a kid, my grandmother's liver, glistening with ladles of chicken fat, had given me the reflux of an old man. I still hated the slimy, internal look of raw liver. Cooked, I couldn't separate it from its function, and tasted only filtration sponge. But as much as I disliked the chopped liver of my youth, and even with my adult gourmet pretensions, Mariangela's version, with two heaping tablespoons of capers and four anchovies, just seemed wrong.

She handed me a round of toasted bread spread with the liver paste. I nibbled to be polite. First, the velvet texture, then the salt of the fish, the sour briny capers, the musky liver, the undertone of wine; an umami tsunami exploded in my mouth. I ate another round, then another. I couldn't get enough.

I hoped that my mother had eaten crostini while she was here. Perhaps the lusty tastes still lingered when she visited me at camp. She'd continued to make her mother's traditional chopped liver but lightened the recipe, less chicken fat, more onions, a little parsley. She'd challenged her mother's wisdom, made the recipe her own.

ART

At the Uffizi Gallery the next day, my husband and I wove through the din of guides competing in French, German, Italian, and Spanish to the large crowd surrounding Botticelli's *The Birth of Venus*. My mother had kept her postcard of Venus from the Uffizi pinned over her desk for more than thirty years. The image always left me cold. Venus's pastel beauty, the regularity of her features, her demure stance and classic femininity represented everything I detested as a teenager. I experienced life in slashes of bright color, ironic juxtapositions. If I were a painting, I'd have been a Magritte with a tart green apple face or one of R. Crumb's *zoftig* Amazon women, strutting my power in shit-kicker boots. Venus was the light, traditionally pretty daughter I suspected my mother would have preferred. Where was Venus's anger? Where was her rage?

Magically, the crowds thinned. My husband and I stood in front of the canvas. Venus served up on a clamshell, hands placed strategically to cover her breasts and mound. One knee bent, she tilted sexual but shy, beautiful yet unsure, a behavior primer for women and girls. Practice modesty, don't be aggressive, keep your assets under wraps. The only male in Botticelli's painting, a handsome angel with puffed cheeks, sent a stream of air in her direction and reinforced my mother's worldview: women needed men, not just for marriage and children, but to bring them to life!

"You should have been a better role model!" I'd screamed at her after two meetings of my college women's group. "You should have shown me how to get a career, not a man."

When I was still single in my thirties, no matter how gentle her tone, her questions about my dating life made me defensive and sad. She romanticized her courtship with my father, his brilliance, his good looks. My relationships seemed both more exciting and less productive than theirs. I craved variety, experience, couldn't imagine limiting my libido to partners with whom I might eventually share a checking account and children.

As I got older, my mother admitted regrets and doubts. That didn't please me either. With friends, I was a wise listener, the giver of good advice. But I didn't want to see my mother's pain, her problems. Although my father's faults were legion, any words against him eviscerated me. I recoiled from a truth less pleasant than the early romances, less regular than Venus's classic lines. What was the right distance between a mother and daughter? When she stuck to the early stories, I dismissed her as irrelevant. When she confided more fully, I turned away. She couldn't do anything right.

FOOD

Long ago, when I preferred my spaghetti sauced with ketchup and my ice cream pink, my mother's food choices repelled me. But on our third day in Florence, in a terraced restaurant overlooking the Arno, I unintentionally ordered the lunch she would have chosen: assorted *salumi*, strong cheeses, oil-cured olives, and crusty bread.

That night, we followed Mariangela's directions to her favorite *gelateria*. We stood in a crowd of Italian families, young couples, old people, in front of a counter that opened onto the street. Two little boys crouching on the ground ran toy cars over our feet. Finally, close enough to see the tubs, I recognized *stracciatella,* a velvety white gelato with slivers of dark chocolate; *spumoni*, the strawberry, pistachio, and chocolate concoction layered with candied fruits and nuts that was so popular in my childhood Brooklyn; and a dense *cioccolato*, almost black. I chose *nocciola*, hazelnut, my mother's favorite.

The subtle flavor expanded in my mouth, tasted of nut-oil, moist earth, and adult life.

Maybe all humans traveled the same taste road, from pablum to salt and spice, then back to gumming soft, sweet food again. Or were my mother and I uniquely alike, our receptors, our saliva, our tongues, her preferences passed to me in utero?

One of the last times I saw her, I made rice pudding, her favorite nursery dish, while she recovered in the guest room from another asthma attack. I boiled the rice, then mixed it with cinnamon, vanilla, eggs, and raisins. The kitchen sweated a soft, starchy warmth. Instead of milk, I used vanilla yogurt and hoped she liked the tang, the taste of California I'd added. She had little appetite, but I wanted to cook soup, bake muffins. I was desperate to care for her in the way she'd cared for me. All the thermoses of sweet milky tea she left at my bedside when I had a sore throat, the endless pans of spare ribs she'd roasted for me, the stacks of potato pancakes I'd taken for granted.

SIGHTSEEING

One sunny afternoon at the Boboli Gardens, I asked a stranger to photograph my husband and me in a maze to mimic a photo of my parents. Then I raced up the rock stairs to search for the exact vista she had photographed. If I stood where she stood, saw what she saw, if my foot miraculously touched one speck of earth that hers had tread, maybe she'd come back to me again. But my knees hurt on the stairs. I couldn't see the map without reading glasses. I had waited too long to come to Florence, too long to appreciate my mother. No matter how I posed or where I stepped, she was gone.

"You're Florence," my mother's best friend in Florida had said the last time I visited. "Your style, the way you hold yourself, your sense of humor. It's like she's in the room."

"My mother, funny?" The words were out before I could make them polite.

"Hilarious. Her little insights, the way she noticed everything. She could be very wicked, too."

When I was in my thirties and starting to get published, my mother showed me a story she'd written about a date with my father when she was seventeen. She'd captured the noise and grit of their Brooklyn neighborhood, the Socialists on soapboxes, the grinding metal streetcars, vinegary mustard on a crisp deli frankfurter, my father's voice, the way he used to call her "kid."

I'd long ago inherited her passion for style and clothes but now her best friend insisted she was funny. And she wrote, too! How had I missed it all those years? My mother and I were twins!

Perhaps I wasn't the original "interesting" woman. My mother read books, wrote stories. She had deep, long-lasting friendships and a keen observer's eye. She'd probably felt unique, passionate, and disappointed in her own mother, too. I'd shaded the colors completely black and white: She was uptight, repressed, a study in cleanliness and rectitude; I was a bright exploding star. All children need to individuate. Maybe defining myself in complete opposition to her gave me the push I needed to get out the door.

After university, I moved to California and created a life there. I found work, friends, and a marriage that sustained me. But as my parents aged, I questioned my decision to remain across the country, so far away.

"You followed your dreams. I'm happy for you," my mother insisted. But she cried each time we kissed goodbye at the airport.

SHOPPING

One evening near the end of our time in Florence, my husband set off for the Medici chapel again, and I went to buy gloves. My mother had returned from her trip with more than a dozen pairs. I was the only customer in the small drawer-lined shop perfumed with the crisp, almost alcoholic scent of leather. The salesman fanned a selection on the counter. When I tried to stuff my hand into a silk-lined orange kid glove, he looked down the length of his Roman nose and shook his finger at me. He took it from me, inserted a metal tube, and blew into each finger. His cheeks expanded, like Botticelli's angel, as he opened the leather with his breath. Patiently, he worked the tight glove onto my hand, one finger at a time, starting at the tip of each digit, prodding, coaxing the leather down. The shop was silent except for the chuffing of his breath.

"I think they're too small." My words broke the intimacy.

He shook his finger at me again. "You want a tight. You wear and it shape to you hand."

About the fourth pair, I leaned back in the chair and relaxed. I pictured my mother in a glove shop like this one, dreamy, sad, passionate, exacting, living a full complicated life that had nothing to do with me.

When I was about nine, we'd gone to one of the many pizza places in our Jewish/Italian neighborhood for a slice. The discs of rising dough gave off a live yeasty scent. The counterman's black hair hung in a low wave on his forehead. His sleeveless undershirt showed smooth muscled arms and a neck full of good luck charms on gold chains. He looked at my mother, a long appreciative stare. She didn't look away.

"I changed my mind. Orange instead of Coke." I tried to get his attention.

But he filled a second cup without taking his eyes off my mother. "The pretty lady's daughter getsa both."

We took our slices and my two sodas to a table in the back. I didn't have the language to ask her what had happened. But the event, seeing her through someone else's eyes, was unusual enough for me to stow away. His gaze split a hairline crack in my ownership of her, forced me, for a second, to see her outside myself.

FLORENCE AFTER DARK

When I left the glove shop, it was dark outside. I crossed the plaza to the fountain where I'd arranged to meet my husband. It was Friday night, and we had a reservation at a restaurant famous for wood-roasted chicken. The guidebook promised "moist velvet breast meat" and the "crisp perfection of herbed skin."

"Chicken again?" I'd whined during my childhood when my mother served the same meal every Friday night.

"There's nothing better than a good roasted chicken. And we're Jewish. That's what we do."

We weren't observant. We didn't mark the Sabbath but she stuck to the ritual meal that would have been a cele-bration to our ancestors in the *shtetl*. She described her first taste of Chinese food as the "discovery of a new world," rebelled against her mother's heavy Old World cooking, but honored our history as well. Looking back, she seemed a graceful vessel, able to hold both old and new.

Of course, she'd been right about me adoring Florence. I felt as if she'd led me to the trove of velvet slippers in a stall at the edge of the Ponte Vecchio, that she'd stood beside me as I bought sweet almond soap in a sixteenth-century muse-um-like perfume shop started by Dominican friars, rested with me on a bench in an intimate courtyard, the stone pat-inated the color of caramel. I toasted her with biscotti and figgy Vin Santo every night.

We were compatible, cozy together. I'd lived inside her body and she'd seen inside me.

"You're a 'red' girl. Not 'pink,'" she'd told me when I was seven or eight and trying to convince her to buy me a cheap pink frilly dress.

"You'd be good at that," she said softly, lovingly, not long before she died, as we watched a brilliant woman journalist reporting on PBS.

But in all the ways she'd seen me, and in all the ways we were similar, we were not twins. I was louder, ruder, more outgoing and confident. The generation I'd been born into gave me more opportunities. My personality allowed me to take more risks.

"You say what I'm thinking but would never say out loud," she told me once.

A gust of March wind whipped around me. I thought of ripping into my parcel of new gloves, each pair taped inside a sheath of gilded Florentine paper, but reached inside my handbag for an old pair of my mother's instead. Black unlined doeskin, her favorites. Traces of her *Antilope* lingered in the soft skins. My fingers rested in the indentations hers had left. The gloves didn't fit exactly. Her fingers had been longer and slenderer than mine. Still, wearing them comforted me, as if we were holding hands.

Audrey Ferber's essays and stories have appeared in the New York Times, LILITH *Magazine, the* Cimarron Review, Fiction International, A Woman's World Again*, and elsewhere. She teaches writing and Women's Literature at the City College of San Francisco. She received an MFA from Mills College and is a proud member of the Writers Grotto. As soon as the Covid 19 crisis ends, she wants to go to New York City, Barcelona, San Miguel de Allende, anywhere and everywhere outside her house.*

ﬥ ﬥ ﬥ

Frangipani

A young girl teaches a scholar
about the politics of desire.

E very evening, the limbs of the frangipani tree that shaded
our second-story apartment shivered and rustled, strew-
ing star-shaped blossoms onto our balcony's tiled floor. Balmy
lake breezes mixed the petals' thick perfume with the aromas
of brewing coffee and fried snacks wafting from our neighbor's
kitchen windows. In the distance, auto rickshaws and motorcycles revved their engines, announcing the start of Bangalore's
evening commute.

The minute I heard the creaking branches, I'd stop whatever I was doing to come outside. Leaning over the balcony's
wrought iron railing, I'd smile and wave at the black-haired
girl who was, inevitably, perched somewhere on the tree's
trunk, her bare feet tight against the rough bark, her long
fingers plucking flowers.

"*Namaskara*, Varuna," I'd call out. "*Hege ideera?* How are you?"

"*Namaskara*, Akka! I am fine," Varuna would reply, waving back.

"Good," I'd say, reaching for clusters of newly opened flowers nestled between the leaves. I handed them to Varuna in fistfuls, careful not to crush the petals, delicate as wishes.

Varuna's body was like a stretched rubber band, long and thin and taut with momentum. Ropey muscles lined her arms, and her hair, which looked like it had never been cut, hung past her hips in a straight, tightly wound braid. She wore sun-faded cotton salwar kameez and always had a plastic shopping bag looped around her wrist. She never wore shoes.

Varuna's mother tongue was Kannada, a language she chirped like a parakeet, and one I was just beginning to learn. I'd greet her, ask how she was doing (always fine, big sister, always fine), and what she had for lunch (biryani or roti or halwa). Once I asked her what class she was in at school (third standard) and how old she was (eleven) and why she wasn't wearing a school uniform (I don't go to school, big sister). When my husband was home, he'd translate, falling easily into the Kannada he spoke while growing up in Bangalore in the 1990s.

"Can you ask her what the flowers are for?" I asked him once.

After a few rapid exchanges, my husband translated, "She says that they're for puja. They're auspicious. Her mother is praying for something, and she needs them."

I didn't ask what Varuna's mother was praying for. I didn't have to. If she needed the flowers badly enough to send her daughter climbing strangers' trees, it must be something important.

Once, my landlady—who lived downstairs—caught Varuna climbing the tree, and flew into a rage.

"Get down from there," my landlady yelled, shaking her fist. Her hennaed hair quivered, and her cheeks flushed an angry pink. "Those aren't yours."

"They're just flowers," I said. "Why can't she have them?"

"They're *my* flowers," my landlady said. "She can't just *take* things. It's not right."

For the next week, my landlady sat vigil in her front room, ready to spring outside the second she saw Varuna within a few yards of the tree. Through our floor—which was her ceiling—I could hear her muttering about how poor people in Bangalore are out of control.

During those weeks of hypervigilance, Varuna and I developed a system. She would turn onto our street and look up at me. If my landlady was home, I'd signal that Varuna should leave. If she wasn't home, I'd beckon frantically. Varuna would flash up the tree, a brown streak of manic limbs, and the two of us would pluck furiously, filling her bag before we were discovered.

I was in Bangalore because I had received a Fulbright fellowship to study India's publicly funded early childhood education centers. Most of these centers were in slums. During my fieldwork, I found myself spending less time observing lessons, and more time gossiping and giggling with the mothers who stopped by for rations, forms, or moments of rest.

The women were curious about me, and the incongruous combination of my dark, Indian skin and twangy, Western accent. They asked me about my parents, my husband, my job. Inevitably, they'd ask me when my husband and I were going to have kids.

"Soon," I'd say.

"When you want children, here's what you do. Buy a packet of milk and take it to the *koil* just here," one mother told me, gesturing in the direction of about four different Hindu temples.

"Or else you can go to another *koil* down the road there and ask for a special puja," another said. "The priest will give you ghee. If you eat that ghee, you'll get pregnant immediately."

"Don't forget to bring flowers," they all reminded me. "Puja is always better with flowers."

I wondered what kind of pujas were prescribed for women who wished for something besides marriage or children. What if a woman wanted a college degree, or a book deal, or a visa to another country? What if she wanted to leave her husband, or move into her own home, or start a career?

I never asked, not because I didn't want to know, but because it didn't seem right. In the slums, women live in worlds that prohibited too much wanting or wishing, too much hoping: women who test the limits of hope shouldn't expect help, human or divine. Men want, women provide. That's the way the world works.

No one told me this, specifically. But somehow, they made sure I knew.

One day, after another morning in the slums, I came home and stopped in front of the frangipani tree. Lost in thought, I plucked a plush bunch of blossoms and buried my nose in them, inhaling a fragrance like starlight. My landlady stepped outside, clutching an expensive purse and a set of house keys.

"Oh!" I said, holding up the flowers. "I'm so sorry."

"Don't be silly. Take, take!" she said, breaking off a few more and handing them to me.

"Thank you," I said. After a minute, I asked, "So it's O.K. to take these?"

"Of course! Why do you ask?"

"When Varuna came, you didn't want her to have any," I said. When my landlady looked at me blankly, I said, "The little girl with the long braid?"

"That girl? Chee! That's different," she said, wrinkling her nose in recognition. "You, you please take as many as you like."

One of the last times Varuna visited me, she attracted the attention of the gang of nine- and ten-year-old boys who ruled our street. They gathered at the foot of the tree, peering up into the branches, their faces wrinkled with suspicion.

"What is she doing?" the leader called up to me.

"Ask her," I told him.

"O.K.," he said, nodding. He turned to Varuna and, switching into Kannada, asked, "What are you doing?"

She spoke to him so rapidly that I only understood every third or fourth word. Still, I knew it had something to do with pujas and flowers and her mother.

"Did she tell you?" I asked.

"Yes," he said. "She's doing it for puja."

"Can you help her?"

After a minute, he said, nodding approvingly, "O.K. Puja is good. We can help."

He sent the youngest boy to get a plastic bag, then delegated the other two to go to the other frangipani trees on our block. The boys weren't very good at climbing trees—they were too young—but they managed to fill their bags. Varuna dropped onto the pavement and accepted them graciously, her smile tight and proud.

Then my landlady's red Toyota pulled into the driveway.

"How dare you!" she yelled as she let herself out of the car, not even waiting for her driver to open the door, as she usually did. "Those are mine!"

The boys watched curiously, but didn't say anything. Neither did I.

Varuna turned on her heels and walked away, her steps rhythmic and measured, her back as straight and poised as a queen's.

A few days before, when I had been caught with frangi-pani in my hand, I had stuttered out an apology.

But Varuna knew that those precious flowers, and the power they held, belonged to her just as much as they belonged to me or my landlady or the boys on my street. Knew that the poor deserve as much desire as the rich, that women and girls ought to be allowed the same number of wishes as boys and men. Knew that, despite what anyone told her, she and her mother were entitled to their dreams.

Varuna's gods hadn't showered her with luck. But they weren't interested in withholding it. Only humans were interested in that.

I watched her retreating back and, for the first time in years, I had the urge to pray.

Mathangi Subramanian is an award-winning writer and educator based in San Jose. Her novel A People's History of Heaven *was long listed for the PEN/Faulkner Award and the Center for Fiction First Novel Prize and was a finalist for the Lambda Literary Award. Her middle grades book* Dear Mrs. Naidu *won the South Asia Book Award. Her work has appeared in* The Washington Post, Ms. Magazine, Al Jazeera America, *and* Zora Magazine, *among others. A former Fulbright-Nehru Scholar, she received her doctorate in education from Columbia University Teachers College. She is the proud daughter, wife, and mother of Indian immigrants.*

ॐ ॐ ॐ

Journey Proud

Danger will always win out over safety.

The engines start up, rumble to life, and the ferry to Croatia gives a monstrous shudder, a vibration that travels up the body, from stern to stem. Everything inside shakes loose and reconfigures—organs, opinions, neural pathways. There's a feeling of internal teeter. How easy now to lose your footing and stumble into the new.

From the top deck, I look back at the sad lot left on the Ancona docks, waving goodbye with their hankies. Passengers onboard lean over the railing and blow final kisses. Translation: *Miss me, miss me, miss me, but for Christ's sake, let me go.*

Every departure brings back a memory from childhood: standing on the dock in Everett, Washington, watching my fisherman father leave for Alaska, for somewhere, anywhere, away from bills and worry. The sea gave him the perfect excuse. Where else is a farewell as unquestioned as when the captain leaves to support the family, who must stay and carry that worry? They trudge home shouldering the new burden, will be weighted with it until he returns unharmed. All I ever wanted was to go with him and ride those seas, to head for that somewhere, anywhere world.

For all the sorrowful looks, there's nothing you can say to dissuade the voyagers now. Danger will always win out over safety, thrill over the known. If real perils await, they're no match for the stronger desire to cross over to a place that may help you figure out who you are. Perhaps it's the last lost piece in the ten-thousand-piece puzzle, a picture of the ocean, all wave, all blue.

To find that piece is the reason for this trip. I'm traveling to a homeland where I've never set foot but where people have my father's eyes, my mother's hair, my sister's gait. Maybe there I'll learn why there is a hole in my puzzle the size of a Dalmatian island; the size of Korcula, where the name Mirosevich is as common as Croatian dirt.

Unless you're forced to leave the country you love, torn away from family and friends, each journey holds promise. I am as prepared for that promise as I will ever be. My wife, Shots, is prepared for something else. She takes out a pill case and we toast each other with a paper cup full of water, then swallow the small yellow Dramamine pills, though the harbor waters are as flat as a blue-green pane of glass.

As the ferry pulls into open sea, I take one last look back. From a bluff on the south end of the city, a neon sign shines green and welcoming: BAR. A starboard beacon. A hopeful light. Are the customers inside toasting our departure or does something else bring them to that perch? Everyone seeks a view. Everyone wants to look out, see a horizon line and try to imagine a point past that line, where the water spills over the edge.

In a pivotal scene in Andrei Tarkovsky's 1983 film, *Nostalghia,* the pool at the center of Bagno Vignoni is empty, completely drained. At the bottom of the pool all that once lay submerged is now visible: A rusted tin cup. A few wooden boards. An old twisted bicycle. A high-heeled shoe, flung off a foot during someone's moment of wild abandon.

The protagonist in the film, a Russian writer named Andrei Gorchakov, has come to Tuscany to research the life of an eighteenth-century composer, but soon his quest turns into a search for himself. Like all searches, he must face something he fears. A fear of life? Of death? Maybe it's unimportant, for soon a challenge materializes. He must walk across the width of the town's drained *piscina*, from one side to the other side, with a lit candle.

He lights a candle, touches one side of the pool, and begins the walk toward the other side. Before he goes very far, a wind comes up and blows the candle out. He must go back to the beginning, relight the candle, and start again. This time he walks more slowly. Once again, the candle is whiffed out. He employs protective measures, shelters the candle with his coat, throws his shoulder to the wind, and still, and still. Each attempt to make it across fails. It's a very, very long sequence in the film. Tarkovsky either had great patience or poor editing skills.

Finally, after numerous attempts, Gorchakov succeeds, and that's the end of the scene. It's also the end of Gorchakov, who dies with that final accomplishment.

Nostalghia. The title applies. You go back and back—to a memory, to a familiar place you never knew—and the candle blows out. You keep lighting it again and again. Each time you start anew you feel you're getting closer to the other side. Your fingertips can almost reach. You can almost touch the other shore.

It's the perfect timing for a departure. The sunset takes the sky through the color spectrum: from pale yellow to golden to orange to red, then deep blood red. The sky's a transformer rose. Did the *Jadrolinija* ferry line plan it this way, to optimize the romance of sunset, to soften our introduction to the Adriatic?

Out toward the bow, we find those who can't or won't look back, who are pointed toward the next frame in the story, toward the sea. Passengers hang on the rim—laughing, smoking. I hear someone say, "We're not in Kansas anymore, Mildred," in a thick Midwestern accent. We soon learn there's a large contingent of American tourists on board making a pilgrimage to Medjugorje, the site where, in 1981, the Blessed Virgin Mary appeared before six Croatian youth and conveyed the first fundamental—and somewhat redundant—message: "Peace, peace, peace, and only peace!" Mary knew the power of repetition.

The pilgrims have a cheer that's hard to manufacture, a belief that buoys better than any life preserver. They sit on the deck in tightly formed circles. A guitar materializes and they sing, a peppy "Up With People" kind of tune. One woman wears a large button with a picture of the Virgin's face in laminated plastic, like an advertisement for a missing pet.

I suspect if Shots and I dare hold hands and flaunt "the love that has no name," we'll be toast. Yet I can identify with these faithful on one level: there's nothing as potent and non-denominational as belief. It's everyone's little ticket to ride. I'm as ready as they are to court the miraculous. I want to be changed, where I've always dreamed of being changed. Out there, on the sea.

Past the bar, a light rain starts up. That's odd. The sky was cloudless a second ago. The ferry deck rocks forward, then side-to-side. The waves below us are caught in some indecision. We're riding a confused sea. A sea that can't make up its mind.

The pilgrims rise together as a single organism and head inside en masse. The loving couples leave. The romantic embrace at the bow will have to wait. Then only the hardy remain. Dark clouds race in from the west, throw a gray ceiling on the sky and on thought. The rocking gets a little rougher. The sea spray, refreshing a moment ago, pierces my skin like acupuncture needles.

I try to convince myself I'm not like those fearful ones, the go-insides. Nor the ones who never made the journey. The stay-at-homes. The never-beens. I will remain on the helm until the sky darkens into night. Departure is where every thrilling memory resides.

Shots convinces me otherwise. "Don't worry," she says. "We'll come back out when it calms down."

Our ferry is tall, with steep sides like a deep-dish pie. Royal blue piping runs from stem to stern. The vessel inspires confidence in all things naval, in captains and chains of command, from the navigator on the bridge on down to the swabbies who scrub the deck. It's not hard to give myself over to this command, to the neat white and blue of it. And a giving over is what's required. Control is already out of our hands.

For the first time, we take a good look at our cabin—a dark, dank cubby. One small porthole provides a tiny circle of light. Two narrow bunks attached to the wall will prevent any attempt at intimacy. Nothing is very clean. In my idea of ocean travel, I pictured a cabin similar to the one Bette Davis occupied in *Now Voyager*, full of light and blond wood, with a complete vanity and a well-stocked wet bar.

I couldn't have romanticized all this, could I?

The ferry gives a weird jolt, as if we've hit the wall.

"Don't bother knockin' if this cabin's rockin'," I say to Shots, the bumper sticker message plastered to the back doors of Winnebagos or trailers, the joke told around a camp-ground campfire by an old snowbird with a gleam in his eye. The line nets me a weak smile.

I find our provisions and open the bottle of wine, a bit early into the trip, but it's unnerving, this rocking, and we might as well roll with it.

We begin to roll. We roll into worry. With sea travel the worry is about sinking, with a plane it's crashing, with a train, derailing. Disaster fear is specific to the vehicle doing the transporting, and lucky that or we'd have nothing to contain the fear that accompanies any voyage to a new world—and the fear would grow wild, gangly, unspecified. Soon there'd be no going to the corner store for a carton of milk.

I try and rustle up some courage. I remember what a friend told me: that right before she's about to leave on a trip she gets *journey proud*. "It's what happens the night before you travel," she said. "You're full of the desire to be gone, and because any journey into the unknown takes a kind of bravado—genuine or quickly fabricated—you're full of yourself. Puffed up. No one can stop you; nothing can get in the way. There's a funny pride that replaces common sense or caution, and all is go, go, go."

Until something beyond your control orders you to stop.

Everything is motion. How far are we from shore? How many hours equal how many miles? The ferry bucks into a gale, makes no forward progress, like a bird you see on a stormy day, stationary in the sky, held in one buffeted position.

I notice how quiet Shots has become. Earlier we heard a group of German men in the next cabin, their booming drunken voices penetrating the thin wall. I feared they'd keep us up all night with one continuous beer barrel polka. Now there's not a peep coming from the other side. We hit a wave that rocks us backwards, and I hear one of the men attempt to laugh, but the laugh falters, halts midway, like that bird. Then their cabin falls silent again.

The storm ratchets up another notch. Another. We descend into a tense present tense. The future is removed from the mind. Here we are, on the Adriatic, the beautiful Adriatic, the blue Adriatic that has turned black and white. Whitecaps, torn white curtains, race past the porthole. This is a very tall vessel. If I can see the tops of waves in the sky....

Shots decides to risk a look. She gets up from the bunk just as another wave hits, and is knocked over flat, onto the floor. She rises to her knees, can't stay upright so crawls on all fours to the porthole. Holding a chair, she pulls herself up, looks out, and quickly turns away.

"Is this it?" she asks.

There it is. The question each of us carries within ourselves. For years the question waits on some internal shelf, available yet never used, for while we may *think* of asking it on the turbulent transcontinental flight or when the technician reviewing the mammogram asks for a second look or when footsteps behind us quicken on a dark street at night, we hold off each time. We save it, because you can only *say* the question once out loud. It can be used only in the direst of circumstances, not before.

"Is this it?" she asks again. I know what she's really thinking: *And now a word from Mr. Death.*

I lie. "No, we'll make it through. It'll be fine by morning."

She nods like she believes me, for to not nod would be bad luck and now we are believing in luck and fate and we are so very much afraid.

I pray, or what passes for prayer. The quibbling and odds-making that accompany deals. If this then that. If that then this. I only know that in the morning, if we make it to Split, we're booking the first flight home.

I need to replace the image now popping up on replay: the ferry going down, the Titanic plunge. That's when I see him. There, on deck. My father smiling, his cap pushed back on his forehead. Yes, it's him, that gleeful look in his eye. *A life on the sea?* he shouts over the sound of the wind. *Here it is, sweetie. Here's the chance to prove your mettle.*

Thank God he never saw me like this before he died. What a disappointment I would be. The girliest of girls.

Shots and I lie together on one bunk, hold on tight. With each new wave the mattress under us lifts, suspends in air as the ferry rises up, shoots the face of the curl. We fly until the laws of gravity apply, then straight down she falls. When we hit the floor of the swell, there's the sound of a loud crack, a slat that breaks, a plank that gives. Splinters fly, we hear them fly, we're falling. Up we go and down again, the boat is now a tiny boat, a plastic toy in a large black tub, around us all is dark and howl. Look Ma, look how small we are, make it stop, please make it stop.

And now we face our deepest fears, were we ever truly loved, and will I see my home again, and someone scale the ladder quick and test the crow's nest rock and sway. Someone have the guts to climb and tell us if there's land. There is no land mass, there never was, get ready, girl, to let it go, there's nothing left to buoy us.

Shots yells above the sea's roar that sooner or later we will come under the protective arm of some landmass, that the worst part is being in the middle of the sea between shores. She's right. In the middle *is* the most treacherous place to be.

All through the night: a door that just keeps slamming.

There is light out. The sky goes from black to black and blue to gunshot gray to dirty white. Our bodies feel bruised from the battering night. Out in the common area, we find other passengers in varying states of shock. One woman says that at the first sign of the storm, the crew disappeared.

While Shots tries to find coffee, I take a bench seat next to a window and look out at the gray sky, the sea choppy with whitecaps. A woman from Indiana leans over from the seat opposite and offers me some *Tic Tacs*, a reward for getting through the rough passage. The little white mints cheer me beyond belief.

The ferry trudges through the heavy chop. Outside, the air is electric after the storm. Few passengers are willing to brave the wind, but I need to go out on the deck to find out what has survived. Who survived? The sea has taken a beating, been sucker punched. I can see the physical evidence of that beating in the waves, the imprint of a fist. Thin slashes crisscross the water, marks left from an uppercut. The waves roll by like swollen black eyes.

I look down at the deck's wooden railing. Names and dates are etched into the wood: *Anton '76, Mirka, '82*. Whether scratched in with a bobby pin, a pocketknife, or the edge of a coin, the angular, blocky lettering is easy to decipher, serves as evidence of other crossings, records of passage. Maybe there's always a need to record where you are when you first spot land.

Two men stand farther down the railing, silently smoking, flicking their ashes into the Adriatic wake. The taller of the two takes a puff, there's a small flare of red flame at the tip, a second of warmth, a heartbeat. He taps the cigarette on the railing. The ash falls into the waves and is gone. The men don't look Slav, and I can't quite figure out where they're from. I recall the little German and French I remember from high school, toss in my one all-purpose word in Italian, and cobble together a question.

"*Scusi. Es'cuse moi. Wo ist Korcula, bitte?*"

Neither makes an audible reply. Then, with some sense of agitation, the taller of the two points toward a large, dark blue mound on the horizon, darker blue than the surrounding sea.

A shore coming into view. The place where all the stories began, the place my ancestors left, boarded a ship, forded this very sea, and never returned. Once they stepped onboard, they would never see home again. That journey was their test of faith. They were willing to bet that the new world offered something more than the old world they were leaving behind. Just as I am willing to bet the old world will offer something new.

When the ferry docks, the pilgrims rush to the exits, the first to depart. They're anxious to get going, to be rewarded for their belief. I gather up our suitcases, take Shots's hand,

and follow them down the departure ramp. On shore, a *Jadrolinija* staff person, a young woman in a vaguely nautical suit jacket, greets us with a forced smile. "How did you like your trip?"

I ignore the question and ask her where the nearest church is located. She looks miffed, then gives in and says there's one nearby, two blocks away, close to the center of town.

We head down the street. I tell Shots we've survived the worst, that we can now face whatever headwind comes our way. Once we get to church, I plan to light a candle. I plan to light two. If they blow out, I'll light them again.

❧ ❧ ❧

Toni Mirosevich is the author of six collections of poetry and prose, including a book of nonfiction stories, Pink Harvest, *which received the First Series in Creative Nonfiction Award and was a Lambda Literary Award Finalist. Her multi-genre writings are anthologized in* Best of the Bellevue Literary Review, The Best American Travel Writing, The Gastronomica Reader, *and* The Discovery of Poetry. *Essays have appeared in* Fourth Genre, North American Review, The San Francisco Chronicle, Michigan Quarterly, *and elsewhere. She received the Astraea Emerging Lesbian Writer in Fiction Award, Frank O'Hara Award, residencies with the MacDowell Colony, Hedgebrook, and others, and multiple Pushcart nominations. She is a professor of creative writing at San Francisco State University.*

PEGGY ORENSTEIN

๛ ๛ ๛

Why I Took My Daughter to Auschwitz

Knowing our past, what is our responsibility to the future?

There's a poem that went viral a few years back that contained the verse, "The world is at least 50 percent terrible, and that's a conservative estimate, though I keep this from my children."

I thought about that line on a foggy November morning, as my husband, daughter, and I drove to the Auschwitz-Birkenau Memorial and Museum in Poland, the site of the largest death factory of the Nazi regime. Visiting had not exactly been on my travel bucket list, but my husband, a documentary filmmaker who is Japanese-American, was asked to judge a film festival in another part of the country, and since we were here anyway—and since our daughter,

Daisy, and I are Jewish—it seemed an opportunity and, even more, an obligation.

Still, I'd been dreading this moment the entire trip. Truthfully, I'd been dreading it since we'd made the plane reservations. And not only for myself, but for Daisy. At fourteen, she was the youngest age suggested by the museum for visitors. I knew the tour would traumatize her, but traumatize her how? By giving her nightmares for which there was no solace? By inspiring her to delve deeper into her heritage, identify more strongly as a Jew? By making her want to turn away from that identity forever?

I was raised in Minneapolis in the 1970s, part of a small, insular Jewish community, some of whom were survivors of the genocide. They told us their stories every year on Holocaust Remembrance Day in old-world accents, some revealing a tattoo on a forearm. As a girl, the mother of one of my friends had been among ninety women forced into a field during a death march; when the Germans opened fire, she saw her own mother fall dead in the snow, yet had to keep running to escape. The ten who lived were liberated by Russians the next morning. We learned about gas chambers and forced sterilization of women. We learned about the lampshades. In fifth grade, we were shown *Night and Fog* in Hebrew school. It was, perhaps, a little too much too soon.

Daisy's Jewish life has had less context, less grounding. We don't belong to a synagogue. She didn't go to Hebrew school (though for two years she did, along with a friend, study religion with a rabbi). Her Judaism is more about family and holidays, something you participate in out of choice, not because if you don't, you will be accused of colluding with Hitler. I've struggled with how to tell this child I love, whom I want to protect from pain and harm, about the existence of pure evil. There's no real right moment to mention the millions systematically murdered, or that, had we been there, we would have been among them. It feels like willfully robbing her of innocence.

Nor is my husband much help. His parents, grandparents, aunts, uncles, and cousins were forced into the Japanese-American prison camps, stripped of citizenship, property, savings, and livelihoods. When Daisy was eight, we attended the opening of the Heart Mountain Interpretive Center, a former internment camp in Wyoming transformed into a museum where one of my husband's films plays on a perpetual loop. On the plane from Salt Lake City to Cody, Wyoming, I asked him what he had told Daisy about the internment. He paled. "Nothing," he said. "I guess I should before we get there?"

I had prepared us for our visit to Auschwitz—as much as one can prepare—by visiting other Jewish sites in Poland first, to understand not only the tragedy of the genocide but the vibrancy of the community that once existed there. In Warsaw, we spent a day at the POLIN Museum, which traces a thousand years of Jewish life in Poland. In Kraków, we went to Oskar Schindler's enamel factory, which had, after the film *Schindler's List*, been turned into an interactive museum about life for both Jews and Poles under the German occupation.

At that time, Jews comprised nearly 10 percent of the Polish population—3.1 million people. They formed their own political parties, youth groups, and schools. There were around one hundred fifty Yiddish publications, and Yiddish theater flourished. Although anti-Semitism was endemic (as it seems to be again) and most Jews, as a result, were poor, they still made up more than half the country's doctors and a third of its lawyers. I realized my own grasp of my people's history had been pretty shallow: As far as I knew, Moses parted the Red Sea, Tevye was exiled from Anatevka, six million Jews were murdered in Europe, Philip Roth won a Pulitzer, and then came Notorious R.B.G.

It's about an hour's drive from Kraków to Auschwitz, and on the way Daisy piped up that she'd never studied the Holocaust in her former K–8 school. "I think you should write the principal a letter, Mom," she said.

I nodded. "That's a good idea, honey." I was proud of her for thinking of it.

By the time we arrived, the movie-set-like mist had lifted; the sun was warm, and I could smell the loaminess of the earth. Our guide, a former journalist who now works for the memorial's press office, led us through the historic gate with its ironwork sign that reads, WORK SETS YOU FREE. Tourists snapped photos beneath, but we declined; among other things, I couldn't imagine what the appropriate facial expression would be.

Of course, I was destroyed. What other reaction could there be? We walked through the barracks where prisoners had slept crowded on the floor, on straw-stuffed mattresses; the one-square-meter "standing cells" of Block 11, into which four inmates at a time would be crammed upright, in total darkness, unable to move. We saw the sites of medical experiments; the courtyard that ran slick with blood from executions; a gas chamber and the crematoriums. A modern-day exhibit held a vertical book, thousands of pages long, inscribed with the names of all of the dead. I looked up my own last name: There were eleven pages, in tiny type, rows upon rows upon rows of Orensteins, Ornsteins, Ohrensteins, Orenshteins. I wondered if any were my cousins. I wondered how old they were, what their lives were like, whether they'd had children, whether those children were dead too. I thought about the generations lost, the descendants unborn, and felt my knees buckle.

In another building we filed by stacks of shoes, hairbrushes, hair itself shaved from prisoners' heads and saved by the Nazis. We paused before a pile of suitcases that towered above our heads. Names had been neatly painted on each one. Our guide pointed out a suitcase belonging to a small child, an orphan named Gertrude Neubeuer. "Look," he said, "her birthday was two days ago." So, as it happened, was mine. Daisy wrapped her arms around me, leaned her head against my shoulder.

Auschwitz was a work camp. Many died there, but it was nearby Birkenau that was built for mass extermination. Seven-hundred or more people lived in each of its hastily erected horse-barn barracks, sleeping five or six to a shelf. There was no heat, no water, little food. Typhus was rampant. Close to 1 million Jews—as well as 122,000 Poles, Roma, Soviet prisoners of war, and others—died here, most murdered in the gas chambers.

The Nazis had bombed those crematoria as they retreated from the Red Army, but the ruins remained, and that is where we finished our day. I watched as Daisy took pictures of a memorial plaque, and wondered: What more can I say? The rationality with which the Nazis carried out their atrocities is inexplicable, and, of course, they are not the only ones. All people have the capacity, in one way or another, to turn hatred into ideology. We are all capable of evil, big and small. We all have within us the monstrous, the conniving, the cruel. Yet we are also capable of selflessness, bravery, and resilience.

There is good luck and bad. Faith and its loss. Sacrifice and survivalism. Faced with a test of character, what would we do? Who would we be? Knowing our past, what is our responsibility to the future?

The sun was setting through the leafless trees, turning the sky lavender, salmon, and neon pink. Lights blinked on along the path to the exit, and we pulled our jackets tighter against the fall chill. We were warm enough, and we could leave this place. But before we did, our guide shook our hands. "Now you, too, are a witness," he said.

On the drive back, we were quiet, absorbing what we'd seen. I glanced at Daisy, whose eyes were closed. I thought she'd fallen asleep. But suddenly she lifted her head. "Mom, I don't want you to write that letter to the principal," she said.

"You don't?" I replied, surprised.

"No," she said. "Because I think I should do it myself."

The world is at least 50 percent terrible, and that's a conservative estimate, though I keep this from my children.

But now my daughter knows. And truthfully? I think she is stronger for it.

ॐ ॐ ॐ

Peggy Orenstein is the author of the New York Times best sellers Boys & Sex, Girls & Sex, Cinderella Ate My Daughter, *and* Waiting for Daisy, *as well as* Don't Call Me Princess, Flux, *and the classic* SchoolGirls. *A contributing writer for* The New York Times Magazine *and* AFAR, *Peggy has also written for such publications as* The Los Angeles Times, The Washington Post, New York, The Atlantic, *and* The New Yorker, *and has contributed commentaries to NPR's* All Things Considered. *She has been featured on, among other programs,* Good Morning America, CBS This Morning, The Today Show, Morning Joe, NPR's Fresh Air *and* The PBS News Hour. *Her TED Talk, "What Young Women Believe About Their Own Sexual Pleasure," has been viewed more than 4.8 million times.*

✍ ✍ ✍

Convivencia

A Tale of Two Pilgrimages.

*L*ast spring I followed my friend Anna to the town of Ávila, Spain, where she'd felt called to research the fifteenth-century mystic Saint Teresa. Anna had read Saint Teresa's seminal work, *The Interior Castle*, in her twenties and was captured by the nun's blueprint of the soul as a many-roomed castle, the center of which could be entered through the gateways of prayer and meditation. By going straight to the source—to the very convent where the Carmelite nun lived, to the cobbled lanes she'd walked, to the cathedrals where she'd prayed, Anna hoped to find inspiration for a collection of poetry she aimed to write. "I also hope to get an epiphany myself," she admitted.

I held no personal ambitions for the trip, but loved the concept of traveling to a place for artistic inspiration—even as a tagalong. So although this "town of stones and saints" wasn't my personal pilgrimage, when we arrived to the picturesque city on a sunny spring afternoon, I was happy to be there. We'd just finished up leading a group of twelve travelers through the rowdy medinas of Morocco, so quiet, unstructured time in a tranquil city seemed like the perfect way to unwind. Tapas bars lined the old streets, wide squares were clustered with silver chairs and conversation, and there was that warm honey light that felt so quintessentially Spain.

We trundled our suitcases from the train station until the pavement of the new city yielded to cobblestone inside the old, walled part of town. Our apartment was in Santa Teresa Square, and we were relieved on arrival to find a spacious living room with a wide window. Best of all, there were two separate bedrooms.

To cut costs, Anna and I mostly share rooms when we travel, an arrangement that works surprising well given we are opposites in many—if not most—ways. For example, Anna cleans while she cooks, while I prefer to do the dishes after. She hangs her clothes in the closet straight away, while I work straight from my suitcase. In sum: I'm messy, and Anna is neat. But these surface differences are easily resolved, and I rein in my mess the best I can.

The real secret to our harmony is in our quiet style of traveling. We spend whole days apart, solitary *flâneurs* who keep good company with journals until dinnertime. Then, over glasses of *Rioja* and wedges of *manchego*, we unpack the day's ideas and adventures. Perhaps most important, though, is that we share the same killjoy early-to-bed and early-to-rise circadian rhythm. Our idea of a great night is to nest in with a book.

Still, four weeks traveling together is a very long time, and since every traveler must pin her drifting existential discontent on something, a travel companion—even a perfect one—is an easy target. In fact, it was Anna's very perfection that I began to home in on, imagining it was being imposed on me in the form of seemingly innocuous statements, which I took as cloaked suggestions. "I am going to go to the bathroom now—you never know, there might not be one on the bus!" she'd declare. Or she'd pour a can of nuts into a Ziploc, saying, "It's always good to bring a snack on the train!"

I even found myself sighing at her perfect eating habits—the whole-kernel oatmeal she'd soak each night before going to bed. *Why not a carefree cinnamon bun, or a naughty sugar-laced churro?* I wondered.

After taking stock of the apartment and enjoying the bright view of the square, we picked rooms and began to freshen up. In my own space now, and free to be me, I stationed my overstuffed suitcase on the floor and let its contents eviscerate across the tiles—rumpled t-shirts, ticket stubs, uncoupled socks. After my shower, I tossed a wet towel across my bed in gleeful rebellion.

Come afternoon, we wandered together out into the square, each with our respective books. Anna had Teresa's *Interior Castle,* of course, and I carried *The Dream at the End of the World*, a book by Michelle Green about Paul Bowles and the Lost Generation in Tangier, Morocco.

Since college, I'd been captured with Bowles and his rowdy and defiant literary comrades—Kerouac and Burroughs. Their rebellion echoed my own discontent with society, and the lawless zone that was Tangier in the fifties seemed an enchanting place to question mainstream norms. Now nearing the end of the book, I was eager to finish it.

We found a table in the square and ordered. Anna opened her heavily marked copy of *The Interior Castle*, and I resumed the section describing Woolworth heiress Barbara Hutton's elaborate *fêtes*. At her mansion above Tangier, Hutton dazzled guests like Truman Capote with belly dancers, camel drivers, nomadic tribesman, monkeys, and snake charmers. As usual, drugs, sex, and guns were in ample supply.

I looked up from my pages and chuckled at the opposite nature of our books. While in Anna's book, the fifteenth-century Saint Teresa furnished her metaphoric interior castle with virtue and penance, the characters in my pages cavorted and indulged in actual brick-and-mortar castles. While Saint Teresa sought to make the monasteries stricter and more austere, in The City of Vice nothing was forbidden, except murder and rape.

After completing a chapter, I stirred my hot chocolate and wondered when I had last eaten fruit. "I think the last piece of fruit I had was in that dessert back in Tangier," I confessed, admiring Anna's porcelain complexion.

The next day we split. I carried *The Dream at the End of the World* to a sidewalk café, and Anna set off to research Saint Teresa. I ordered an espresso and opened my book. Now Phyllis della Faille, a Tangier socialite, was chartering a cargo ship to ferry her menagerie of cats, rodents, horses, and other pets to Portugal where she had just purchased an old castle. Like many of the Tangier expats living there in the '50s, Phyllis's life seemed so easy as to be borderline boring, and so she had to manufacture her own predicaments.

After a couple of chapters, I paid my bill and decided to take the audio tour of the impressive walls that earned Ávila UNESCO World Heritage status. I rented my headset at the tourist stand and ascended the stairs to begin my procession around the 2,516-meter-long fortification. Along the way, I pushed numbered buttons and listened to historical commentaries through the earpiece.

Constructed between the eleventh and fifteenth centuries to ward off Moorish invasions, the walls were a scenic remnant of the religious conflicts between Morocco and Spain. The Moors took over the Iberian Peninsula in 711, and then the Christians took it back in the *Reconquista*. But in the eighth century, a new era took hold: *La Convivencia*. During this time, Muslims, Jews, and Christians purportedly shared *Al-Andalus* in peace. This *Convivencia* broke down with the Inquisition, however, when even Saint Teresa herself was subject to interrogation. Her Jewish merchant grandfather made her suspect, as did her visions and spiritual ecstasies—which were seen as potentially false.

Church bells chimed, and I paused for a rest. I stared out at the Castilian plateau through the wall's crenellations, seeing vineyards, stone habitations, and the Sierra Gredos Mountains in the distance. My thoughts returned to Paul Bowles and how much in my twenties I had admired his atheistic worldview. In his novel *The Sheltering Sky*, his characters Kit and Port ventured into the vast Sahara to shed the fortifications of mainstream religion and ideologies and face down the Infinite straight-on. Bowles and his wife, Jane, did the very same thing in real life—smoking *kif*, taking *majoun*, and courting the void among the dunes. It seemed so cool to me at the time—so honest and brave—and echoed my own youthful desire to shed my conservative religious Midwestern upbringing. Stepping outside of norms like marrying early and having a conventional job felt like a way to live more vividly and fully. Now in my forties, I questioned that theory.

A lot had happened to me in the intervening decades, and this was the first time I'd paused to take stock of my hero. Since then, I'd suffered broken-heartedness, periods of aimlessness, despair, and confusion about my purpose. A near-death paragliding accident left me with an increased sense of mortality, and with maturity, my political consciousness had evolved. I looked at the world with all of its violence and inequality and now wondered: *Why did evil exist, and why was it allotted so unjustly?*

All at once, standing there on Ávila's walls, Bowles's vision of a world without meaning struck me as too harsh. In his world, there were no bounds, and pleasures were pursued without limits. Morocco seemed merely a decorative playground where he and his friends could indulge cheaply and lawlessly. They bought mansions, collected expensive rare fish, and carried out their gin-fizz lifestyles. Meanwhile, riots

waged in the background as impoverished Moroccans struggled to wrest their independence from the French colonists.

Perhaps this deep lifestyle of denial is why, in *The Sheltering Sky,* Bowles's character Kit goes insane in the desert
at the end of the book or why, in real life, Barbara Hutton
attempted suicide twice. Maybe it's why Burroughs stayed
high on opium all the time, or why so many of the expats who
inspired Bowles's books were so disaffected. An undeniable
undercurrent of despair ran through the Tangier scene. I had
tasted some of that despair in the quiet lonely moments of my
own solo travels, writing questions in my journal: *What do I
believe in? Who am I connected to?*

That night, Anna and I convened for dinner. We ordered
a round of tapas, and she recapped her day—describing the
cathedrals and the convent where she viewed Saint Teresa's
wooden pillow. She then announced that online check-in was
available for our flight, and perhaps we should return to the
apartment and log on to the internet to avoid hassles at the
airport the next day.

But before we turned in, we took one last stroll to admire
Ávila's walls, now lit from the bottom in evening light. She
loved Ávila and felt inspired to write her book of poetry
about Saint Teresa. I, too, felt inspired and confessed my
unexpected revelation.

"I think I have outgrown nihilism," I declared.

On the train to Madrid the next day, Anna pulled a tissue out
and began wiping down the greasy window, reminding me
again of how opposite we were. It never would have occurred
to me to wipe down the window. But as the train lurched
forward and we entered orchards hung with bright oranges,
I was happy for the clearer view.

As we coursed through the arid hills of Andalusia, I
realized we now had more in common. Though I wasn't
going to adopt Saint Teresa as my new hero anytime soon,

I could suddenly empathize with my friend's more ordered and meaningful view of the world. What the meaning was I didn't know, but I suspected at the very least it involved kindness, the indispensable ingredient that seemed to elude the expats in Tangier. I pulled out a round of the *Casera* cheese I'd purchased in the square, and Anna produced some crackers from her bag. And then we ate, drank, and in the spirit of *convivencia*, resumed our reading.

Christina Ammon has penned stories for BBC, Orion Magazine, Hemispheres, The San Francisco Chronicle, Conde Nast, *and numerous travel anthologies. She is the recipient of an Oregon Literary Arts Fellowship for nonfiction, and her stories have earned several awards from Travelers' Tales publishers. In the winters, she organizes writing and storytelling workshops in Morocco, Mexico, Nepal, and Spain through her company, Deep Travel Workshops (www.deeptravelworkshops.com). When not traveling, she lives in rural Oregon near her fellow pilgrim, Anna Elkins—who went on to publish a poetry collection about Saint Teresa with Press 53.*

Abbie Kozolchyk

꿩 꿩 꿩

Making the Rounds

Exploring the Andean town where
a bread is never just a bread.

*W*inding my way out of Cusco at two A.M. on a
Sunday—past the club-hopping crews in the Plaza
de Armas and the undulating silhouettes along a nearby lovers'
lane—I had no idea that the scene I was headed for was expo-
nentially crazier. My destination? Oropesa, a small town about
fifteen miles to the southeast, where the bakers who turn out
the region's most iconic bread were about to clock in for the day.

Here in the "National Bread Capital," so designated for its
absurdly fertile alluvial soil, you've got to get up pretty early
in the morning if you're going to compete in the *pan chuta*
space: Breakfast is one of the most popular times to tear into
these spongy, subtly sweet mega-rounds, even the daintiest of
which are a foot in diameter (the jumbos, generally reserved
for religious holidays and altar offerings, span twenty inches).
Though the oven-to-mouth version is best—because you're
still practically taking hits of the oven's eucalyptus smoke off

the soft, brown crust at that point—locals also eat *pan chuta* throughout the day, whether with butter, marmalade, cream, or nothing at all.

The Oropesa bread ladies dominate an entire aisle of Cusco's Mercado San Pedro in their lavishly pleated jewel-toned skirts and impossibly tall white hats. But even in plain clothes, an Oropesina at market is easy to spot: She's the one doing a brisk business behind a pile of outsized, disc-like loaves. And, after more than a decade of writing about Peru, I'm the one who's often in line for them.

Still, for someone who'd eaten her weight many times over in *pan chuta*, I knew shockingly little about the staple—a deficiency I hoped to change during my last trip to Peru, when I heard that some of Oropesa's old-school, family-run ovens were increasingly open to visitors. A few emails and phone calls later, I had a date with Modesta Castelo Farfán, owner and grande dame of T'anta Wasi (House of Bread in Quechua), and an award-winning baker known for consistently stellar *pan chuta*. (She's even nabbed the cover of *Amasando Exito*, a magazine published by the region's chief shortening supplier.)

After a half-hour drive down a two-lane highway that wound past tiny farming enclaves—none visible in the inky darkness of my middle-of-the-night drive, but some detectable in the rainy season's pregnant air—I rolled up to her compound just before two A.M. I was hardly the first to arrive. The "maestro"—a twenty-something bakery foreman named Delfin—was already on hand to tend to the first batch of dough and fire up the domed adobe oven, a scene that was unfolding in *panaderia* after *panaderia* for blocks in either direction.

T'anta Wasi sits right in the middle of the main commercial drag, where wall-to-wall bakeries form a seductive carb corridor along the narrow highway that links Cusco to Lake Titicaca and Bolivia. A lot of hungry travelers pass through here, as do bands of itinerant sheep, even at this cockamamie hour. As I watched in general disbelief, drivers of tuk-tuks, big rigs, and every motor vehicle in between would pull over, cueing the sales team from the nearest open bakery to dart out—often across the highway—bags of *pan chuta* in hand.

While I waited for the lady of the house, whose return from a weekend in Lima was rain-delayed, I happily accepted Delfin's invitation to the bakery's inner sanctum—all vats, troughs, and long wooden surfaces—where my demo (really, just a normal morning's worth of bread-making) would begin. As a remarkably speedy and coordinated team of five worked around me, I learned a number of lessons. For example, that pan chuta is believed to take its name from an old Quechua word for stretching or flattening. And that while all local bakers add their individual flourishes to their loaves, every *pan chuta* uses the same basic recipe: flour, salt, sugar, yeast, shortening, eggs, anise, cinnamon, vanilla, and—the pièce de résistance—glacial water from the nearby *apu* Pachatusan. (An *apu* is any sacred Andean peak that, despite centuries of imported Catholicism, remains a divinity to indigenous locals. Pachatusan is one such divinity, whose name means sustainer of the world.)

Though people have tried to replicate *pan chuta* throughout Peru—and have gone so far as to pre-clean their ovens with branches of wet eucalyptus leaves, as Oropesinos do for extra flavor—the taste is supposedly never the same without Pachatusan's water and implied blessing. Delfin seeks the additional blessing of Pachamama (the Andean version of mother earth) daily as he's firing up the oven, where he spills the first sip of whatever he's drinking in deference to her.

There's a whole metaphysical component to this bread that outsiders would need a doctorate in syncretic belief systems to understand. Possessed of no such degree, I questioned everyone I could, starting with Doña Modesta, who—having finally gotten back to Oropesa—emerged in all her azure-skirted glory at around seven A.M.

As she gave me the owner's tour of the joint, and paused with particular pride beneath the frescoed images of two locally venerated Virgenes, I took the opportunity to seek some clarification:

"So both Virgins are patron saints of Oropesa?"

"The Virgen Asunta is venerated on one side of town, the Virgen Reyna Estrella on the other, and the church of San Salvador sits in the middle."

"And all of their blessings—plus the *apu* Pachatusan's—are believed to filter into the local bread?"

"Yes," she answered, adding—as if nothing could be simpler—that there was also the regionally venerated Virgen del Carmen to consider, plus Saint Francis of Assisi, to whom every baking family in Oropesa dedicates an altar, because at least here, he's the patron saint of bakers.

In fact, I learned during a later conversation with Mario Samanez—onetime mayor of Oropesa—that when the statue of Saint Francis in the local church started to seem a bit puny for a patron saint, none other than the aforementioned shortening supplier bestowed a new and improved version upon the community. Samanez noted another venerated church statue: El Niño Panadero—a baby Jesus clutching some *pan chuta* in a nod to the local legend that he used to pose as a young bakery assistant and distribute bread to poor children, until one day he vanished, only to reappear in the Virgin Mary's arms during a holiday procession.

Lest I start to feel I understood the extent of *chuta* symbology, another subsequent conversation disabused me of that notion. This time, I was speaking with the noted Cusqueño professor Alfredo Hinojosa, whom I'd sought out for his reported expertise in the history of the region—and who opened with no less than this: "To eat bread in Oropesa is to visit the soul of a Cusqueño."

He went on to explain, among other things, that *pan chuta* is the Andean representation of the Host. And that if you look at things through a colonial-era indigenous lens, the *chuta*-as-Eucharist also represents—however indirectly—the desire for freedom from Spanish rule.

So when is a bread just a bread? Not yet.

Pan chuta is also a major token of affection here. "When we're young and in love," according to the former mayor, "we don't have the habit of taking flowers to our girlfriends—we make special bread with a little more shortening or butter, and we take that as a gift to our beloved." Another custom that continues to this day: "If you want to name someone a godparent, you offer three *chutas*," Samanez explained.

How far back these traditions go, no one knows for sure. But what historians do know is that the arrival of Cusco's first bull—imported by a Spanish viceroy who wanted to start cultivating wheat here—was such big news, local kids ditched school to catch a glimpse. Among the truants that day was none other than Garcilasco de la Vega, the famed chronicler of early colonial Peruvian life, who noted in his writings that he got spanked for the infraction, according to professor Hinojosa. And thus do we have a record of the sixteenth-century arrival of wheat cultivation to the area. As for that viceroy, he hailed from Oropesa, Spain—and named his newly acquired turf for his old stomping grounds in 1571.

Over the next few centuries, Oropesa, Peru, would grow to a town of one hundred or so family-run ovens, dozens of bakeries, and all manner of bread-themed events. "La Reina del Pan," for one, is the local answer to the Miss American pageant, except that every contestant has the same talent. And that skill has such a far-reaching reputation in the bread-making world that Doña Modesta's daughter, Liz—along with then-mayor Samanez—jointly represented Peru at Italy's Gran Festa del Pane in 2009.

The proud mamá used her gallery-mounted photos of the occasion as the grand finale of our tour—and a life lesson: Keeping family tradition alive is everything, as generations' worth of bakers in her family (and her husband's) affirm.

As we exited the little photo gallery, we could see that the fab five—Delfin, Guillermo, Elvita, Olga, and Veronica— were just wrapping up their last batch of *chutas* for the day. "Want to go decorate your own?" Doña Modesta offered. She didn't have to ask me twice.

But when I got to the work space and picked up the decorating tool of choice—a Gillette Super Delgada razor blade with which the other women had been creating all manner of lovely motifs atop the day's *chutas*—only one adornment came to mind. I slowly etched the word *Gracias*.

The great-grandchild of someone who used to get around Havana with homemade rolls in place of bus fare, Abbie Kozolchyk has deeply held associations between bread and travel. She also bakes at home in California, where she's happily upstaged by an amazing fourteen-year-old tart maker. Outside the kitchen, Kozolchyk has authored National Geographic's The World's Most Romantic Destinations *and contributed to* The New York Times, The Wall Street Journal, *and* Condé Nast Traveler, *among many other publications.*

COLETTE HANNAHAN

≈ ≈ ≈

Call of the Sirens

She should have seen it coming.

*I*t sounded like a manatee-sized pumice stone exfoliating the bottom of the van. Then came a bucking-bronco jolt. Thrown forward, we braced ourselves on whatever we could: amps, boxes, a cooler, my backpack, one another.

The driver said something in German. Everyone laughed but me.

The girl translated. "We are stuck. Stuck on a rock."

At this point I knew four things: I had climbed into the back of a windowless van with seven strangers, mostly men; we'd been driving for over an hour on the highway; we'd turned onto a dirt road, and now we were in the middle of the woods somewhere in France.

My head got hot and prickly. My chest felt heavy, like a small animal had curled up on it.

The night before I left for my trip, in the kitchen at my parents' house, my dad had given me a short father-daughter

244

talk. "Remember, Coletta," he'd said, making eye contact over the counter, "all men are scum."

My brother, eating a chicken wing at the sink, looked up. "Yep."

My other brother, sitting next to me, nodded with raised eyebrows.

I was fresh off a lucrative summer business venture as a cutlery saleswoman in Minnesota. It was one neighborhood, Sunfish Lake, that had put me on the map. I'd made my way around the lake in my brother's Camaro selling hundreds of knives: Bird's Beak paring knives, fishing knives with built-in rulers, hunting knives, boning knives, turkey-carving knives, knives designed with warm bread in mind, flexible pop-your-brownies-out-of-a-pan-intact knives (a favorite among my ten-and-under market), and most popular, the Super Shears, which I'd cut a penny with to conclude my slicing-and-dicing demo. It was all effortless, and I was astonished.

At the end of the summer, I found myself onstage at a convention somewhere in South Dakota. Hundreds of people were standing and applauding as I accepted a two-foot trophy adorned with flaming knives.

"Hannahan, I have big plans for you," said my manager later that night.

But I had plans of my own. I'd saved enough money from my cutlery enterprise to take a semester off from college and travel abroad for the first time. I planned to see Ireland, France, Italy, Spain, England, and Scotland for five months.

A sepia-toned slideshow of me, a Midwestern girl coming of age in Europe, flashed through my mind. I imagined myself strolling the streets of Paris at sunrise wearing a white scarf tied with a sophisticated knot and red lipstick, as the scent of chocolate croissants wafted from a bakery. Befriending an Irish band at a Galway pub and learning to play the fiddle. Standing up to help row a gondola in Venice.

My Eurail pass would not only be my ticket to meeting adventurous, open-minded friends from all over the world, it would also be my ticket to inspiration. I saw myself at the Musée d'Orsay, inches from great paintings I'd seen only on slides in art history classes, my eyes tearing up. I'd learn a little Italian here, pick up some French there. I'd discover how to say, "I'm a self-made woman," in Spanish. Maybe even find my calling.

But a month in, the only things sepia-toned were my teeth, from chain-drinking cups of Barry's Irish tea. I was hovering in Ireland, afraid to move on, and sinking into a routine. I'd spend my days wandering the streets of Dublin, Belfast, and Galway, getting damp and cold, and then return to my hostel dorm room to read left-behind novels in my bunk and listen to Van Morrison on my Walkman. At night I'd venture to a café, eat a bowl of leek soup, and journal about all the ways I would live differently when I returned to the U.S.

Meanwhile, the scenes I had scripted for myself in my European tourism commercial were rare and fleeting. I'd stand on a bridge with a pretty view, peel an orange, and while eating it, feel at peace—and like I was onto something. Then, when it was gone, I'd think, *O.K., now what?*

One morning, I woke up early in the top bunk of a Galway hostel, sad to the bone.

I slipped out of the thick-aired dorm room and made my way to the dining hall. As I waited for my brown bread to toast, I scouted a place to sit. All the tables were filled with early-rising backpackers, but I noticed one open spot across from a slight man twice my age. I hoped I wouldn't have to make conversation.

"Good morning," said the man, looking up with kind eyes. "How are you?"

I immediately broke into tears. "I didn't think it was going to be like this. I'm really lonely."

He took a sip of tea. "Well, that's good."

"What do you mean?" I wondered if he'd heard me correctly.

"Don't fight it," he said, smiling. "When you feel a feeling really deeply, and you don't fight it, that's when life opens up and you see it in a new color."

He took another sip. I was silent.

"And with every new color, the world is more beautiful. The loneliness won't last, but the color will. It's yours to keep."

Walking around in the rain later that day, thinking about sleeping another night with my hat on, I decided it was time to head out of Ireland and get my trip back on track. It was mid-March; France would surely be warmer, bursting with flowers and fresh starts. Paris, the Riviera, Provence—I couldn't go wrong.

But when I arrived in Avignon, I was still lonely.

I should have seen this coming. I had grown up an observer—always fascinated by my siblings' and friends' ability to fully enjoy themselves. On beach days and trips to amusement parks, at birthday parties—all the classic I-was-so-excited-I-barely-slept-last-night activities—I couldn't match their level of enthusiasm. I began to suspect I was miswired.

Thankfully, my mom was studying to be a psychologist, so I had access to her massive bookshelves full of self-help material; in high school I listened to character-development cassette tapes and read *What Color is Your Parachute?, How to Be a No-Limit Person,* and several volumes of *Chicken Soup for the Soul.* At night, I lay in bed replaying my day, taking note of all my interactions until I fell asleep. I often wondered how it would feel to stop overthinking and live like everyone else.

My older cousin—the one who'd assured me (against my academic advisor's strong advice) that it was a smart move to switch my major from advertising to English—had lived in Eritrea for a year. He'd sent my family long letters detailing his life on the coast of the Red Sea in East Africa: what he was learning, whom he was meeting, all the sounds and smells and tastes of his village across the world. Rereading those letters over and over, I noticed an aliveness bubbling up in me. I was sure travel could change me.

But in Europe, as the days passed, I felt like I'd failed in all the things I had set out to do. I was only going further inward—wrapping myself in layers and layers of gauze.

On my last day in Avignon, I wandered the cobblestone paths looking for a shady spot to read while waiting for my train to Paris that night. People always found what they needed in Paris, it seemed.

Decked out in my baggy cords, t-shirt, and running shoes, I lugged my backpack, which had grown to the size of a well-fed seal.

Then I saw them.

Willowy bodies fanned across the lawn by the Palais des Papes. They looked like a shoot for an edgy perfume ad. A mating call. So much bare skin. So much snug fabric. There were six guys and one girl, who was wearing a rose-colored velour bustier. One guy played guitar. Another a drum. Some sang along. Others were just splayed out on the grass, soaking in their collective coolness. Modern-day Sirens. I couldn't stop staring.

The girl motioned for me to sit down. "Come," she said, smiling.

Any other time, I would have made up an excuse, but I was so desperate to escape my own thoughts, I sat down. She asked if I was from the US, and I asked if it was obvious. We laughed. I asked if she was from Ireland. She was German, but her English teacher was Irish. She pulled a German/English dictionary from her purse. Her friends didn't speak English well, she said, but she wanted to learn because she was a poet.

"Why English?" I asked.

"It's simple. The word 'strawberry.' It's so beautiful. In German, it's *'die erdbeere.'*" Her face pinched up as she said it.

"Straw-ber-ry," she repeated, smiling, like she was tasting one for the first time.

Then the guy in pleather pants stood up and said something in German.

"Come," said the girl, gathering her things. "It's time to dance."

"Thanks, but I have a train to catch."

"What time does it depart?"

I considered lying, but couldn't. "Ahh, eight o'clock. The last train to Paris."

"Not a problem." She turned to her friends with a hand in the air. "She will join us."

The guy with the sleeveless half-shirt slung my bag over his shoulder and stepped into the pack of guys walking away.

What was that my dad had said about men?

I smiled at the girl, trying to hide my apprehension, and followed.

We stopped in the parking lot by a dirty white van with no windows and, as I soon saw, no back seats—the exact vehicle I'd been warned about in elementary school Stranger Danger classes. I hesitated, then ducked into the back.

"Colette, we are stuck," the girl repeated. "We have to get out."

Damn it, I thought. *Drug cartel? Organ poachers? Is the cooler for icing my kidneys?*

I cleared my head. *No, the girl is nice. I can trust them. They just love to dance in the middle of the day…in the middle of the week…in isolated places far away from where they could have danced.*

The guy in the passenger seat hopped out and slid open the side door. I pushed myself up from the ratty blanket covering the floor of the van and crawled over all kinds of cords snaked into tight piles. The tops of spiny trees appeared as the wake of dust settled behind us.

Then the girl turned to me. "We are close. We will walk."

She laced her arm through mine, and I faked a smile.

The cratered road ended at a clearing. We were on a peninsula on a lake, with no sign of another human in any direction. A few minutes later, the guys pulled up and unloaded a generator, a card table, two huge amps, and a turntable.

One of them cracked open the cooler and passed around cold, stubby bottles of Bière Spéciale, as the music started and the punctuated beat climbed. The weight on my chest began to dissolve. The same three notes repeated. Then faster.

Woven into the mix, a deep voice boomed, *"Tanz, tanz, tanz, tanz."* Then on a loop, a woman with a sexy voice inhaled, exhaled, inhaled, exhaled. The music ramped up until we were like stones being polished in a rock tumbler. There were only eight of us, but we stayed close as penguins. Bumping into each other, trying on one another's moves. We danced like this for hours. Wild. Drumming up clouds of russet dust.

I looked at the girl. Her eyes were closed, and her head rode the beat like a boat in the waves. She was the queen, and this her land. She swirled her arms through the air and moved her hips in her first language.

The sun toasted our heads and noses and cheeks. At one point, the guy with bleached hair passed around an economy-sized cardboard tray of croissants, and we kept dancing. The guys pranced with spaghetti legs around the girl and me. I couldn't stop smiling. If we had spontaneously combusted, I wouldn't have been surprised.

And then, when my limbs felt phantom, the beat cranked up again until it exploded. Our hands shot up into the sky like it was the end of a twenty-year drought. And we danced even harder.

The lake breeze crawled over the peninsula and threaded though the tall grass, clearing the dust. The pretty, controlled movements I learned in dance class as a girl unfastened until I was a crane building up momentum to fly off the lake. I thrashed my arms, fanned out my chest, lifted my face to the sun.

I wanted to run at life, jump up, wrap my arms and legs around it. Bury my face in it. Curl up with it till morning. I felt it sneak up the back of my shirt as I twirled. Years of self-consciousness and fear unspooled from around my body.

In a few hours, I would catch my train from Avignon to Paris, waving as the van pulled away. But for those moments, as I danced with strangers in the middle of the woods, thousands of miles from home, I saw the world set ablaze, filtered through the hues of spontaneity, trust, and abandon—colors that were now mine to keep.

Colette Hannahan is a San Francisco-based painter, illustrator, teacher, and writer who has had more jobs than birthdays. In addition to peddling knives in Minnesota, she has delivered mail at a retreat center in the woods of the Hudson Valley, applied makeup on brides-to-be at a salon in Brooklyn, steamed blouses for models in Manhattan, taught art and yoga to adults with autism in Chicago, mentored teens at a boarding school in New Mexico, sold computers from a kiosk in San Francisco (only one got stolen), and supervised a giant bounce house for NASCAR fans in Milwaukee. She also created the illustrations in this book. Her website is colettehannahan.com.

Jacqueline Luckett

ℬ ℬ ℬ

Single Woman
Traveling Alone

In Mexico, she finds unexpected
answers to life-changing questions.

ow can you even think of doing such a thing?
First you wake up in the middle of the night,
body aching for the sex it hasn't had in 461 days. Since you
left your now ex-husband sitting at the kitchen table, salmon
poised on his fork, disbelief in his almond eyes. Heat spreads
slowly. You want the delicious release.

Then you wonder, for the twenty-thousandth time, if
it will take twenty years of your future to feel at ease with
twenty years of your past. You have learned to let go of marriage, of family, a lovely house, laughter at corny jokes, the
promise of happily ever after. But, more often than not, what
is gone wrenches your insides and the sadness imprisons you

in bed. This hovering, dark cloud cannot last forever. If only your eighty-two-year-old mother understood.

"You're strong, like me," she tells you. She of the fifty-five-year marriage to your father, whom she'd loved since she was seventeen. The fifty-five-year love affair interrupted only by your father's death. No, not interrupted: she loves him still. Everlasting love is your inheritance, and you have squandered it.

But your mother is right. "I am strong. But sometimes I don't feel like it. Sometimes I don't want to be strong," you tell her. Tell your sister at two o'clock in the morning. Tell a good friend so many times she suggests you tell a therapist. Tell the therapist until you tell yourself you no longer want to hear it.

Three days later, you create a list of hopes and possibilities. A map for your future: the ideas, the actions you want to carry out. Not that you didn't have ideas or take action before—that was a list for family, for husband and wife. You need a list for you, all on your own again. The tools are aligned: glasses, determination, laptop. You create an Excel spreadsheet, excited by the order it will give your life. And then you realize: this is not the time for order. This is the time for chaos, for movement based on heart, not head. Hands grab paper and pad, heart commands your list: French classes in Provence, tango lessons in Argentina, discover San Miguel de Allende.

Mexico. A quick and easy getaway from California. Privilege has its privileges. Before you know it, you've booked a flight to a town whose website boasts pre-revolutionary history and charm. Blue skies, friendly people. *Gorditas*, red snapper tacos, and mezcal margaritas. Lots of North American expats.

What will happen if you drop dead in your hotel room?
Without engraved wedding band or spouse nearby, consider making your body easily identifiable. Shun the practical. Step

into your future. Get a bright tattoo. Something bold, serpentine, dragon-like. Ink another on your bicep, wrist, anyplace
easily noticed: next of kin or whom to call in case a bee fights
you for a taste of your Coke, flies into your can, and stings
you in the depths of your throat while you relax in the central
jardín and elderly Mexican men stare over their morning *café
con leche*, curious at your singleness. This is sort of what happened to someone you know who knows someone who went
to Puerto Vallarta last year and nearly died. Who can say? It
could happen to you.

What have you done?
The plane lands at 10:30 P.M. Pitch dark. The scent of mold
and sweat creeps into your nose as you enter the terminal.
You pray your feet will hold steady on the slick and shiny
linoleum. The moths fluttering around blaring lights remind
you of the summer night you and your sister were alone in
the house, and a huge moth flew through an open window,
drawn to the kitchen's lights. That fear punches you now.
The panic. Alone with yourself this night. The phone call
years ago that quickly brought your father home from his
weekly poker game to kill the moth. He didn't chastise you
for your cowardice, for separating him from his winning
hand. He smiled, and you could've sworn he tossed back his
hero's cape as he smashed the flapping wings, the inch-long
carcass, with the certainty he might have gathered had a
two-legged monster threatened your safety. Decades later,
you know fear shouldn't bother you. Should remind you to
be strong.

   Your heart is beating hard. Not all airports are the same,
especially when you're alone. You seek comfort in shadowing
passengers from your flight, the nods of the armed *federales*
pointing you toward customs, and a green light that allows
you to pass. To go wherever you please. No strings, no one
holding back. Not in this Mexican city, not at home. You
have made your list.

A week ago, you put your trust in Lisa, a comforting voice on the phone, the expat proprietor of the charming bed and breakfast so artfully photographed on the internet. "My flight arrives late at night," you said. "What should I do?" "Oh, don't worry, honey," Lisa had reassured. "I'll take care of everything."

Like some stupid movie scene, the hands of the clock in the airport entry hall make their way casually around its face. There is no driver waiting, bearing a sign with your name. "Where is he?" you whisper, yours among the only English spoken in this airport, a lighthouse in the 10:45 P.M. sky.

Seek refuge in the restroom. Hold back tears. Find a guard and ask, "*¿Hablas Ingles?* English?" He smiles, and you in your broken Spanish ask, and he in his broken English helps, pays for the phone call, talks to the operator. You reach Lisa. "Where is the driver you promised would be here?" Hear her sleepy voice, "Did they forget about you, dear?" Admit. "I don't know what to do." Her carefree voice. "Just take a cab, sweetie. It's not far."

How to find a taxi when you are without the words you need? You are remarkably American. Easily identifiable Black American. You believe your face screams, SUCKER! An old woman beckons you with a toothless whisper, "*¿A dónde vas, señorita?*" *Where are you going?* All four feet of her, wizened and bony, reminds you of a fairytale witch, the kind who steals children and bewildered tourists and cackles deep into the night. No child here. You are single woman traveling alone. You seek out your guard-friend, and the woman scuttles away. He points you in a safe direction and helps you use your limited vocabulary to barter for an official taxi. "*Cuanto. Qual. ¿Este?*"

¿A dónde vas?
The cab follows the dimly lit access road into the darkness. Nothing is familiar. Not the feel of the tires rolling smoothly over asphalt. Not the street signs: *pare, alto.* Nor the distance in kilometers. Behind you, the lights of the airport fade, along

with a distant, glimmering skyline. Though you don't know it now, it's Guanajuato. You've read about the city's pillared churches and rainbow virgins and streets paved with gold. But you cannot see them. Only the taxi headlights, cones of white. The driver speaks no English, and you suspect your Spanish resembles little he's heard before.

You forgot to ask the most important question: How long will it take to get to San Miguel de Allende? Just as you forgot to ask that now ex-husband how the two of you could fix what had gone wrong in your marriage. Now, the cab moves swiftly. You sit back in your seat. Think of your father driving the family cross-country to Detroit. "How much longer, Daddy? How many more days?" His confidence behind the wheel. "Just a few more," he said. "And then we'll be there." Never once were you afraid.

Your mouth is dry. Your breathing shallow. The driver's black hair is cut close. There is a wide space between his shirt collar and the nape of his neck. The radio is low, but the music sounds like a mariachi band. He whistles with the music in spurts as if he can't recall the entire song. You hate the sound of whistling, but not tonight.

Try to communicate with him, "*¿Cómo está usted?*" in the way you failed to with your ex in those last months of marriage, afraid of what he might say if you asked, "How are you?"

"*Bien, Señora,*" the driver says. "*¿Y usted?*" "*Bien!*" you reply, happy to be asked, happy to be heard. He prattles on but you don't understand. "*No comprendo, Señor. Lo siento.*"

"I don't understand." This was your husband's response when you said that you weren't happy. That you feared what unhappiness meant for your future. Fear kept you silent and still and small. But that's not why you are here. There is another fear to conquer: single woman traveling alone.

How will you stay safe?
Pray to the Holy Virgin to ride beside you, to protect you on this ride, not to mention the seven days ahead. Ask for

protection from the car suddenly tailgating yours, bright lights beaming so high you see the shadow of your breath. Ask for safety from things that go bump in the middle of nowhere, more than two thousand miles from home.

Beyond the window lies a pitch dark full of mesquite bushes. Animals scurry at the sight of this sole car on the road. Cows and dogs. *Vacas y perros.* Practice Spanish to stay awake. Even if the driver no more understands you than you him, you feel the connection. Safety in numbers. Or is loneliness the price of your emancipation?

Your road to independence is as winding as this mountainous highway. Surely you will get there soon. In the darkness, blacker than any black you have ever seen, you wish to say more to your driver. You wonder if this is how it will be in San Miguel de Allende, without the words to ask for a seat on the bus, a ride into town, a table for one. Your driver understands or perhaps he is more experienced at ferrying travelers on the road to autonomy. With a simple motion of his hand you think means thirst, he stops at a poorly lit grocery store in the middle of a block-long town.

Inside the open market, an old woman digs in the pockets of her windblown wrap and hands the driver his change, a Coke, and a chocolate bar. He strolls back to the cab. But not before a scruffy man walks into the headlights and bends down to peer in the cab. You are not concerned about his looks but what you imagine he might do.

This is an old delusion born of your mother's inexperience: "You never know what men will do if they know you're alone." And your aunts' precautions, leftovers from the racism of their Mississippi youth: "Don't talk to strange white men." And nuns who made you kneel to ensure the hem of your skirt touched the floor, who told you not to wear patent leather shoes because boys could see under your dress.

Even now, fear leaks down your throat. It tastes like vomit.

You slip the watch from your wrist, hide it between your sweaty palms, push your linen dress over your knees. Wonder why you traveled to Mexico with a Rolex, with diamonds in your ears. Wish for the crucifix you once wore around your neck in the days you believed in mass and Holy Communion, in saints, in love that lasted a lifetime.

Your driver shoos the man away. *"Esta bien, Señorita."* His voice is reassuring.

How much farther? Strain to see a road sign. San Miguel de Allende 90km. 50km. 15km. At last the driver points out flickering lights ahead, and you relax as the car approaches aged cobblestone streets, twinkling church spires, vendors selling dolls and bouquets of pink flowers, revelers whose white skin screams "tourist." Bougainvillea blood red in the dark of night.

For a second, you are furious with Lisa, for her failure to take care of you as she had promised. "Welcome," she says, stepping forward to hug you. Release this anger and much more. You're happy to be at her B&B, glad for the artificial torches lighting the garden path, for the fireplace in your cozy room that reminds you of home. You sip hibiscus tea and listen to the innkeeper's tales of the impotent, artistic, wealthy ex-husbands she's left behind, though it's well past three A.M. Is there a list like this in your future? A list of exes to enumerate and delight female strangers with indelicate, post-marital tales? You decide that is not your destiny. One ex is enough. Your list is different. You want the next time, if there is one, to be a better version of the love and commitment you thought you had. What your mother knew she had.

What will you do here, all by yourself?
Walk. Stroll aimlessly. Enjoy the peach and orange and turquoise facades of buildings in this town. Explore alleyways filled with local craftsmen, art galleries, and cafes. Wonder at delicate lanterns hanging on curlicued iron posts fixed to the sides of Colonial-style homes. Listen to the tales of ancient streets hewn by Chichimeca hands, of conquistadors who hid in rooms with twelve-inch-thick walls to keep their skin

white, to avoid the summer's heat and the sting of foreign mosquitoes.

Visit churches ten, twenty more. Stare at Jesus Christ's likeness in a glass coffin. Examine statuettes of long-forgotten saints carved into exterior corners of buildings meant, centuries ago, to lure indigenous people to pray to these smoothly whittled holy men—Christian substitutes for quarter-moon gods of harvest, birth, war, and death.

Photograph desiccated doors. When they open, point your lens at hibiscus- and jasmine-filled patios, swimming pools, silver and wooden crucifixes adorning the walls, hand-thrown ceramic pots overflowing with flowers whose sweet scent makes you swoon.

Savor the smell of *chalupas* and *gorditas*, too, *mole* and roasted poblano peppers ground in speckled *molcajetes*. Taste sweet *piñas* and green cantaloupe, the watermelon and pink papaya crammed into tall plastic containers from the Costco just thirteen miles north, on the outskirts of town. Ignore the loss of tradition for the betterment of the people and laugh because you left your membership card at home.

Get your palm read. Your eyes follow withered fingers tracing your lifeline, health line, lines marking what will be and what was. Mumbles in fragmented English of those you left behind who no longer care you are gone. How can she know, this palm reader? Of the ex pissed at your international frolicking? Of the angry stepdaughters, the confounded son, and the pain of losing them?

"Your future lies with you, *Señora*."

You gasp at her truths, her prediction.

Turn from your ex's shadow and delight in the gold trinkets, silver bracelets and earrings, the finely drawn patterns on blue and yellow pottery, the tin-framed mirrors hidden in corners of the Mercado de Artesanías. Barter gently as the ex taught you to do: Is this your best price? "*Sí, sí*. For you." Have fun haggling, saving two dollars. Assume the vendor thinks the joke is on you, just another stupid gringa, only brown like him.

How will you handle your new freedom?

Eat at Cantina Fresca. "*Sí, una persona, por favor.*" Hug the owner when he says, "Sometimes it is good to be alone." You nod yes, when you mean no. Flirt, just a little. Wander the streets, never taking the same path to and from the B&B. You feel obvious. Separated by the kink of your hair. Noticed by the color of your skin. Value your difference.

Move away when the white innkeeper tugs at your Afro, amazed at its thick softness. "Such a contrast to horse-haired Mexicans," she says, ignoring your astonished face. Does she think this is a compliment? She names for you the two Black people living in town, expects they'll be interested in you or you in them based solely on the color of your skin. She doesn't even know who you are.

Let go of the old delusion that trails in the wake of the men selling pink, red, and green straw baskets swinging from cal-loused hands. Don't assume these men know you're alone. Or will remember your face, your hips, the only Black woman in this brown and white town, or will speak of you at night to their wives who sat all day in the *mercadito* where tourists negotiated the price of trinkets the wives cannot afford and do not want.

In your youth, you did what your mother, aunts, and nuns expected. Now, you laugh out loud. Not your mother nor aunts nor any nun could do what you are doing right now.

Workmen whistle at you from the top of the holy *parro-quia*, watch your hips and full breasts from high above the streets—not the gray in your hair, the lines in your face, the no-longer smooth skin of your hands. You smile, take plea-sure in their whistles, swing your hips, swish your skirt to the music of their words, the joy their distant appreciation brings. Bless them for the blindness of height and continue in and out of more *mercados* and *gallerias,* calling out *buenos dias* when it is *buenas tardes*. But you don't care because you're glad to be able to speak, to smile, to know you're alive.

How will you meet people? You know how you are.

Oh, but how you miss your Black. In your grocery store and shopping mall. In your politicians and preachers. Not a day goes by that you do not think of the color of your skin, the reminder that you're alone in a sea of brown people, descendants of indigenous people conquered by men with swords and disease. You miss your Black, the sistuh talk, the hey girl, the right on, the I heard that, the unh huh, the say what, that rolls off the tongue, a language of its own.

For the first time, you listen to your girlfriends' counsel to keep an open mind and open face. Say hello to strangers lingering around umbrellaed tables in the smooth-stoned patio of your new B&B. Smile. Ask where they're from. Let them wonder why you've come to Mexico alone. Let the sun shine on your face, bring back the flame in your eyes. Tell them you're here to celebrate yourself as woman, not mother or wife or daughter. That you are learning to sleep in the middle of a king-sized bed, control the remote, watch sports on TV only if you want to.

Three women artists recognize you in the plaza. "You're staying at our bed and breakfast, aren't you?" You vaguely remember their faces. "Yes, I am. I love it." They do, too. "Join us for dinner." You don't hold back. You are thankful for these women who paint in the day and dine with you in the evening, praise your strength where no husband or bourgeois friends have. "So what brings you to San Miguel?"

A little question for which you have only a big answer prepared because you're embarrassed that the truth is a muck of blame and guilt and frustration and disappointment you don't want to explore. "My divorce was finalized in—" Before you can finish, they jump in. "I've been divorced for ten years." "I'm on my second marriage." "Have another drink, you deserve it." You laugh with them. Accept their blessings on your smoldering pain and let it slip through your fingers onto the floor, the cobbled stones outside, under the feet of the pineapple vendor and the woman who sells heart-shaped balloons on your first Valentine's Day alone in twenty years. Smile at these women and their wonder at your strength. At their inclusiveness. Their sisterhood-love the color of water.

And when you leave?
Hire a taxi and double-check your reservation for an English-speaking driver who takes the hairpin turns slowly so you can savor the view of the hills, the pink spike of the *parroquia* glistening in the sun. Ride to the airport in the comfort of daylight and air conditioning. Take one last look at the mines, recall the revolution.

And what will you do when you get back home?
Practice rolling r's. Rrrr. *Roja, recuerdo, restivo. Gracias, porque, libertad*.

Take a karate class. Write stories. Drink with new friends. Move into a new house.

Buy a tight black dress with a low neckline. Fall in love. Go to bed with a stranger.

Dance the tango on a tabletop in that small café on Jackson Street where no one knows who you are. Flirt with the guitar player, tickle his gray beard. Surrender to delicious urges.

Tell your mother a new kind of strength runs through your veins.

Sit on the edge of your bed pleased with yourself.

Get on with your list. Get on with your life.

ॐ ॐ ॐ

Jacqueline Luckett is the author of two novels, Passing Love *and* Searching for Tina Turner. *She has written essays for* The Huffington Post *and* The Best Women's Travel Writing 2011. *The Bay Area native lives in Oakland and continues traveling to nurture her passion for photography and cooking. She has yet to return to San Miguel de Allende to uncover answers the ancient city will reveal the second time around.*

Anne Sigmon

❦ ❦ ❦

Good Enough

How high must she climb to find herself?

*M*t. Kilimanjaro loomed in front of me, a black vertical mass just an arm's length away, too steep to peer up or down. *Just as well*, I thought. My heart pounded, my lungs screamed for air, and my hands burned with cold. I rapped them against my poles for warmth.

Ahead, the lights of other parties snaked up the mountain like prehistoric glowworms on Pleistocene terrain. The mountain soared upward, the result of some ancient volcanic thrust. Carefully, we sliced sideways across the rock face on the fragile scree.

I expected my legs would hurt, but it wasn't really pain—more like walking on two blocks of Jell-O. Reaching for my water bottle, I found solid ice. The wind snarled and the cold gnawed at my face. I shuddered on the ledge, suddenly realizing there was nothing below me but space.

"I'm frightened," I mumbled to no one.

It had all started six years earlier with two Moosehead beers, a new boyfriend, and a boast. It was 1991. A novice hiker in my late thirties, I was dating Jack, a die-hard outdoorsman.

"I'm not an athlete," I'd warned him when he invited me to Yosemite National Park. Did I tell him I was so uncoordinated I'd flunked jump-rope class in seventh grade? Probably not, but I stressed that my idea of hiking was a stroll in the park with my dogs.

"Just an easy walk," he'd assured me.

Easy? As I'd puffed my way up the eight-hundred-foot ascent to Sentinel Dome, my white leather tennis shoes had slipped on the steep granite trail. Every twenty minutes or so—too often to suit his jackrabbit pace—I'd paused to catch my breath and rest my shaky legs. But the rewards at the top had hooked me on hiking: the skeleton of a four-hundred-year-old Jeffery pine made famous by an iconic Ansel Adams photograph; a view of Yosemite falls tumbling two-thousand-five-hundred feet into a roiling pool. As we'd started back down, the ghost of a moon rose over Half Dome.

The way up Sentinel Dome that day had been hard. The descent was just plain scary. After I tripped over a loose rock—barely stopping myself from cartwheeling off the slope—I'd slowed to a turtle's pace, picking my way down the ridge. "Come on," Jack coaxed. "Almost there. I've got a couple of Mooseheads on ice in the car."

By the time we reached the parking lot, I was red-faced and thirsty, but not for beer. Jack opened Calistogas instead. "We'll save the Mooseheads for Kili," he announced. "One day, you and I are going to climb Mt. Kilimanjaro. We'll drink these two beers at the top."

Dream on, I thought.

Fifteen months and a dozen more backcountry treks after that Yosemite hike, I married Jack. Though I'd long since dismissed the preposterous idea of climbing Kilimanjaro, I noticed he saved those two Moosehead beers like talismans.

He kept them through our year-long engagement, our wedding, and two cross-country moves, from San Francisco to Chicago and back again. He finally stashed them on a back shelf in his woodshop. The beers were still there in 1996 when two friends invited us to join them on a trip to Africa.

"It'll be an old-style, tented-camp safari," I told Jack. "I've always wanted to go on safari. Haven't you?"

"Absolutely. We'll go early and climb Mt. Kilimanjaro. Meet the safari group afterward."

"You're not serious."

"Of course I am." His enthusiasm was tinged with an edgy determination. He studied my face, waiting.

The seconds ticked off while I took the measure of myself, breathing in, glancing out the window.

"Oh, why not?" I finally answered, certain I'd lost my mind.

Nobody had anything good to say about climbing Mt. Kilimanjaro. My research turned up vivid magazine articles that described in detail the grinding climb, bone-chilling cold, dirty huts, lousy food and—most graphic—the screaming headaches and retching nausea of altitude sickness.

"Sounds great," Jack said.

"Are you nuts?"

"Don't be a wuss. It'll be fantastic—a once-in-a-lifetime experience."

Jack's tender encouragement had faded with time and five years of marriage. As I got fitter, the hikes got tougher. Still, I was always just a bit too slow for him—never *quite* good enough. Our hikes, like our life together, were a hot-and-cold roller coaster of encouragement and disregard. Through it all, I just kept on trekking, enthralled by the backcountry grandeur.

After months of planning, twenty hours of flying, an overnight in Nairobi, and a jouncing four-hour minibus ride to the village at Kilimanjaro's base, I wasn't tired. I was pumped as a rookie boxer, feinting to mask anxiety. I wanted to face the mountain and size it up. But when I peered east from the lookout at our Arusha hotel where Mt. Kilimanjaro should have been, there was nothing but a clump of formless late-afternoon clouds.

The next morning, I saw it clearly—an Olympian mass hovering above the clouds, dismembered from the African plain below. A glacier spilled from the mountaintop like frozen white lava. I stood in speechless awe, thinking: *She who climbs it will surely touch the moon*. I willed myself not to wonder what effort, what reservoir of stamina, that might require.

We'd chosen the Marangu Route—supposedly the easiest ascent. On that choice I'd been adamant. We booked a six-day trip through the Dik-Dik Hotel in Arusha, just Jack and me, plus our two guides and a team of porters. We would climb for four days up the mountain, then speed down in two.

Our guides were rugged, wiry men of the Chagga tribe who lived scattered at Kilimanjaro's base. Alouise was a short, small-boned man of about forty who spoke in a raspy, cigarette-laced voice and laughed like Louis Armstrong. Damás smiled with easy confidence but never had much to say.

After a couple of hours' organizing at the foot of the mountain, we set out on a wide track through the rainforest. Speckles of lacy sunlight filtered through the forest canopy; loose, red dirt cushioned our steps. Tufts of olive-colored moss draped from cracked gray branches, and long vines slid down from century-old macaranga trees. Our steps were punctuated by the cackle of a far-off Colobus monkey. *A simple hike*, I thought. *What had I been so afraid of?*

Alouise set a relaxed pace as he demonstrated the secret of high-altitude hiking. In Swahili, the word is *"pole, pole"*—slowly, slowly. We hiked the gentle terrain for three miles to Mandara Hut, where we would spend the first of four nights on our ascent.

The *"pole"* pace suited me and allowed time to study the muted beauty of the mountain. With the altitude and cold, everything appeared in miniature except the rocks. From a distance, the landscape seemed a dull brown in low relief. But as we hiked, we discovered the colors of Kilimanjaro: pink impatiens; bold, cream-colored petals of the protea Kilimanjaro; phallus-shaped lobelia; and black-and-turquoise sunbirds darting around the flowers.

At twelve thousand feet, we reached Horombo, an enclave of spare A-frame huts where we camped for two nights to stave off altitude sickness. In our sleeping bags those evenings, Jack and I read aloud to each other by flashlight. "The Snows of Kilimanjaro" wasn't the story I remembered. Hemingway's writing was still exquisite, but the story was not, as a wounded adventurer dies an ugly death from gangrene provoked by a minor camping injury.

Where have my fantasies taken me? I wondered, as I shivered in my sleeping bag, listening to the wind moan, just before I fell asleep.

The next morning, we headed farther up the mountain. By fourteen thousand feet, the alpine meadow—with its easy hiking—was behind us. The temperature tumbled. I huffed as we made our way up the high desert saddle between the twin peaks of Kibo and Mawenzi. An untamed moonscape of barren red-gray rock, the saddle was wide and wild, as far from anywhere as I'd ever been.

It was steep, and I was breathing hard, reaching deep, fighting the cold. I was so focused on the physical demand required to put one foot in front of the other, I barely noticed the afternoon clouds rolling in until they let loose with hard pellets of hail that bounced off my jacket like a frenzy of buckshot. Wet snow mixed with sleet, just a dusting at first, then harder, blowing sideways in a pelting blizzard.

I adjusted the hood on my parka to cover my face, then switched off my mind, carefully, studiously, refusing to think about anything but the next step forward. It was a slow, breathless quarter-mile to the Kibo warming hut, the last stop before the push to the top.

———

At Kibo, our early, pre-summit dinner began ominously when the candle refused to light. *Was it a lack of oxygen? How much oxygen does a person need compared to a candle?* I wondered. Even lying down, breathing was an effort.

"We'll come for you at midnight," Alouise said. "There's better footing then, when the scree is frozen." For the five hours following dinner, I lay sleepless in a freezing lower bunk, staring out a dirty window at nothing. Even the storm had vanished.

Finally, midnight came. Shivering and struggling to catch my breath, I stood in the dirty hut, fifteen-thousand feet above the plain of Africa, bundled in down and Gore-Tex everything, and steeled myself for the night ahead.

Before we left the hut, Jack helped cinch up my hood; I slid my water bottle bandolier-style over my shoulder. It was hard to move in that extreme-weather gear. Alouise arrived carrying a gray metal box I hadn't seen before—oxygen and emergency first aid. Waiting outside was Damás, the "assistant guide" whose unspoken purpose was to serve as escort if one of us couldn't make it to the top.

We were lucky: the storm had passed. Outside, the moon's full, benevolent face illuminated the frozen scree. A thousand brilliant stars dangled just above my head, hot white on a black velvet sky. The footing was sure; the wind was calm. I dared to think I might make it.

But as we hiked up from the hut, the trail was steeper than anything I'd ever attempted—an incline that, to my unpracticed eye, looked almost perpendicular. Alouise moved in front to set the pace: *pole, pole*—slowly, slowly. I followed him. Jack stepped behind me with Damás in the rear.

A rhythm soon emerged with our hiking poles, hands, and feet. We swayed like camels loping across the desert, but uphill on loose, sandy scree. Upward we climbed, exertion warming us. The air was thin, and my chest heaved even at our *pole* pace. Before long, I had to stop for a breath and a drink of numbingly cold water—but to halt for even a moment meant losing the warmth generated by our movement. Each pause was quick, to lean on my hiking poles and reach deep, deep—grasping for a full breath, getting only half, but happy to have it.

Jack seemed hardly winded.

We climbed on, cutting narrow switchbacks across the endless, steep, black mountain. Upward progress was slow on the loose rock.

At the Hans Meyer cave, where we paused for a rest, I sat hard on the nearest boulder, gasping. Jack, on the alert for signs of mountain sickness, demanded my address.

Ludicrous, I thought, not wanting to waste precious air on conversation, needing every molecule to breathe. When I didn't answer, he persisted. "Anne, what's your address?"

"Johnson Road," I spat.

"Where? What number?"

"Eight-o-eight," I snapped. "I'm not...delusional...I...just...can't...breathe!"

He smiled. Satisfied that temper was a positive sign, he retreated.

We trudged on. I craned my neck, scanning the ridge above me where the yellow moon balanced precariously on the rim. *Could that really be the top?* Onward, onward, *pole, pole.* Jack and I and our two guides bunched closer together for warmth.

The terrain shifted again. We left the scree and stepped onto a steep rock face. No more rhythmic swaying, just fierce pushing up with the legs. Climb, push up, climb. Jagged boulders emerged, hideous, from the black night.

My legs quivered. I gasped for breath and felt the parka clawing at my face. Another gasp. No air. Panicked, I grabbed blindly at the fabric, ripping it back from my mouth, and sucked in half a breath. I stared at the moon perched on the ridge just above my head. So close now, so close. "Try, try," I whispered to myself.

I heard a voice in front of me. "Very close now," said Alouise. "Just a half-hour more."

My heart stopped. *A half-hour more! We should be closer!*

Suddenly, my legs were gone. The trail was just too steep. I stopped to lean on my poles as a flush of anger rushed over me. Anger at Jack. Anger at myself for being there, for telling everyone I knew that I'd gone off to climb Mt. Kilimanjaro. Anger because I knew if I didn't make it to the top, neither Jack nor I would ever forget it. I'd feel defeated and small, and that would come between us forever.

He's finally done it, I thought. *Taken things too far. I could die up here—and for what?*

I was paralyzed by anger, warmed by it, shaken by it, perched on the side of that endless mountain staring, exhausted, into the black face of failure.

Then I felt the faint outline of a hand brush the small of my back. Damás had slipped in front of Jack and stood behind me. His feathery touch sent a silent, confident signal: You can do it.

I *can* do it, I thought. I *will* do it. My paralysis melted. My right leg moved. Fueled by furious energy, it lifted onto the boulder ahead, pushed off. Climbed up to the next, pushed off. Time stopped. There was only effort in the ghostly moonlight. Effort beyond fitness or even desire. Climb. Push. Climb.

Ahead of me, mammoth boulders loomed, too high to step up. I had to claw and crawl. Alouise reached a hand down from above. *Try!* I told myself, extending my hiking pole; he pulled it forward as I scrambled toward him.

And suddenly, there was nowhere left to climb. The outline of the mountain fell dizzily away. I stood at the summit frozen in puzzlement, breath shallow, legs shaking.

It was, I learned later, 6:22 AM—eight minutes before sunrise. There I stood on the roof of Africa. Gilman's Point, 18,460 feet high.

The kid who flunked jump rope had climbed Mt. Kilimanjaro.

Alouise and Damás emerged from the shadows with congratulatory thumbs up. Jack appeared suddenly beside me, grinning, with the two Mooseheads dangling from his hand, frozen solid. Even through my exhaustion, I let out an astonished half-laugh. Steely one minute, bewitchingly romantic the next—that was Jack. His confidence was exhilarating. He was forever galvanized to adventure—and he wanted to share it all with me. The question was: What did I want for myself?

I paused in the gray half-light, breath slowing, legs steadier now.

We hugged and posed with unopened beers for victory photos. Just then, red-orange rays seeped onto the plain below and the sun rose in one glorious ball of African fire.

Jack was beaming, backslapping, doing high fives, taking pictures.

I was just breathing. Warmed by the sun and dawning reality. *I made it. Reached the top.* Hundreds of people a year make this trek, but this day was for us—for me.

It was a short victory.

"You know," Jack said, turning to me, "Gilman's isn't the very top. Uhuru is a few hundred feet higher—technically the summit. About an hour and a half to get there."

Expectation hung on the frozen air as Jack waited for my answer.

I breathed in. Breathed out.

"Then you should go," I said. "You'll be disappointed if you don't. But I'm not going. I'm done. This is good enough for me."

Jack paused, surprised. *He's waiting for me to cave*, I thought. *Not this time.* Damás, standing at my side, shot him a look.

"Oh," Jack said, registering Damás's concern. "O.K., then, I'll meet you afterward."

I waved him off with a smile and headed down the mountain with Damás as my guide. Breathing was easier then.

Would I do it again? Absolutely. On that mountain, I tapped into a hidden reservoir of will, and with that will I touched the moon.

Will I do it again?

No. I tumbled the word over in my mind and inspected it. Said it out loud. Let its unfamiliar texture roll off my tongue.

Once was enough. Good enough for me.

ॐ ॐ ॐ

Anne Sigmon washed out of high school and college PE. Exotic travel was the stuff of dreams until, at thirty-eight, she married Jack, took tea with erstwhile headhunters in Borneo, and climbed Mt. Kilimanjaro. Even after a stroke and autoimmune illness, she still travels to the wild, from Botswana to Syria, Iran, and Uzbekistan. Anne's essays and award-winning travel stories have appeared in national magazines and websites including Good Housekeeping, *GeoEx.com, BestTravelWriting.com, and in many anthologies, most recently Bradt Guide's* To Oldly Go, Deep Travel: Souvenirs from the Inner Journey, *and* Wandering in Cuba—Revolution and Beyond.

SIVANI BABU

ॐ ॐ ॐ

The House on KVR Swamy Road

The only constant is change.

*W*e push through waves of people and cows on the street, the dust and smog swirling red and heavy, giving the scene the hazy air of a vintage photograph. A calf chews languidly on a banana as flies buzz around its head. The tinny sound of temple music floats by, along with the aromas of everyday life: fruits, spices, incense, the musk of oxen, diesel, smoke.

Nearly two decades have passed since I last walked KVR Swamy Road, but I still remember the admonitions from grownups to keep the dust down by not dragging my feet. Now, a grownup myself, I laugh. *A drop in the bucket*, I think, but I pick up my feet anyway, hopping, jumping, leaping over puddles and pungent piles of cow manure.

I hold my memories close. I've missed this place. It was such a significant part of my childhood that it's hard to believe I've gone this long without returning. Emotions flit around like hummingbirds, constantly changing direction. I'm excited to see my uncles again after all these years, and nervous to meet their wives and children. I'm curious to see how the place has changed. And mostly, I'm hopeful that it hasn't really changed at all—that the memories, some long forgotten, will still be there, waiting for me.

My parents and I, flanked by my uncles, arrive at a narrow wooden door. *Has that always been there?* One of my uncles opens it, revealing a private alleyway that separates two buildings. Sunlight floods the space between the structures as gray water trickles through a narrow drainage canal running the length of the alley. I stoop down, step through the door, and slip off my shoes, the feel of cool cement on my bare feet plunging me into a memory.

Thwap, thwap, thwap, thwap. I was six years old and running across the room, trying to see how loudly I could slap my feet against the concrete floor. The sound was captivating—a novelty compared to my carpeted existence back home in California.

Outside, the heat was fierce, the sun relentless. Rickshaws, bicycle bells, car horns, and the mooing of cows all mingled in the familiar symphony I'd come to associate with summers in Rajahmundry, India.

Thwap, thwap, thwap.

"*Nimadhee!*"—gently—my mom chided as I ran by, lapsing into her mother tongue, a language she seldom spoke at home.

I slowed and softened my steps for a moment—just long enough for her to resume her conversation with her brothers and sisters. Then, buoyed by their raucous laughter at my back, I was off again, slapping away at full speed. I joined my cousins on the terrace, our own laughter blending with the chorus as we peered over the terrace wall and gazed at the scene below:

men on motorbikes dodging rickshaws and cyclists; women on foot balancing woven baskets atop their heads. I watched baskets full of eggplant, mangos, squash, and sapota go by.

The house on KVR Swamy Road didn't look like a house—at least not like the houses I knew. I was a child of California's Central Coast. Aside from the homes of my friends, which were a lot like my own, the only house I really knew was the stucco structure with the red tiled roof and fruit trees in the yard where the scent of the Pacific lingered on a westerly breeze. The floors were carpeted, my bedroom walls papered with delicate purple butterflies and posters of Magic Johnson, and the only people who lived there were my parents, my siblings, and me.

But the house on KVR Swamy Road was different. It was actually three concrete, whitewashed houses bought over several years. The individual buildings were connected on the lower levels in certain places, but by the third story—the top—the buildings were separate. The ground floor held my Thatha's—my grandfather's—print shop, and the family, immediate and extended, lived in the sixty-two rooms above, sharing one kitchen, one dining room, and a handful of squatty potties.

After marrying my mom, my dad jokingly started calling the house "Kothaval Chavadi" after the famous wholesale vegetable market that supplied produce to millions of people in Madras. The house was always bursting with people, not just family, but also friends, employees, and business associates. No one ever knew who was supposed to be in the house and who wasn't, so the assumption was that everyone belonged. Anybody could wander in off the street, and as long as they didn't act shifty, they'd be served a full meal and treated like the old friend they just might be.

We were the only branch of the family in the United States, so during the summer, my mom would take me and my siblings to Rajahmundry and we'd stay with family in the house that looked nothing like a house but was undoubtedly a home.

———

Sixteen years after my last childhood visit, I stand in a patch of sunlight between the buildings and look around. The din outside the narrow door fades. I was nine the last time I stood in this alley. After my grandparents died, my mom stopped bringing us back here. Most of the doors are closed. The alley is silent. I take a few steps. I want so badly for them to walk me back in time. Instead, they take me to my great aunt's room, to a woman I've always called "Big *Ammamma*"—Big Grandma.

I remember her as a woman who towered over everyone, but she no longer towers over me. Big Ammamma has been hunched by age, and also, I am not nine anymore. My five-foot seven-inch frame means that few people in India tower over me these days. But it's more than her height that's changed. She's quieter. Her voice is shakier. Her presence is more delicate.

"*Ela unnaru?*" How are you? I ask her in stilted Telegu, my words rusty from decades of disuse.

She laughs at my attempt, pulls me in and kisses my cheek, and then promptly asks when I'm getting married.

Once, on a solo trip to India, my dad told his entire family that I was engaged (I wasn't) just so he could avoid having a similar conversation. I briefly consider taking a page from his book. He's standing behind me and I'm certain he would back my play, but my mom is standing next to me, and she would never approve.

"We'll see," I say, and the conversation immediately comes to a lull.

I look around the room and then out to the alley and the closed door across the way. Something feels off. And all that's familiar is the scent of coconut oil in Big Ammamma's hair.

The whirs, bangs, and whooshes of the enormous printing presses reverberated off the concrete walls. I sat with Thatha in his office as he worked, the scent of tobacco and cloves drifting from his clothes. I'd made a habit of throwing out his cigarettes when he wasn't looking.

"You shouldn't smoke," I would say to him, filled with the indignance of a child.

"*A'unu, Amma*,"—yes, Mom—he would reply, smiling, his glimmering eyes framed by the thick, black rims of his glasses. He never got angry and never complained, but he didn't quit, either.

I'd been his tiny shadow all day long, splashing around as he filled barrels in the morning when the water came on for an hour, following him as he introduced me—his "granddaughter from America"—to some of the shop owners next door, sitting across from him as he taught me to play chess, and tagging along as he went down to the print shop.

Kalahasti, Thamma Rao & Sons had been in the book publishing business since 1882. Thatha and his brothers inherited the business from their father, and in the 1940s, as India moved toward independence, the family had taken great risks to print and distribute contraband, pro-independence literature. As the story went, they'd printed the contraband in broad daylight and at night, caught up on their normal publishing jobs. But even more surprising than the brazenness of the operation was its success. The British only ever became suspicious at night, and their nighttime raids proved fruitless.

A history of revolution was fine and good, but at six years old, I just wanted to play with the printing presses. And even when he should have, Thatha never really said no to me.

Work stopped as he picked me up and stood me on a stool in front of an organized box of typeset letters. All morning long, I'd watched the machine and the men who ran it. I knew what to do. I grabbed a handful of letters and set them into the printing press. My spoken Telegu was decent— honed out of necessity during these summer trips—but my ability to read it was nonexistent. I set complete gibberish and then, with Thatha's help, pulled a lever to ink and print it. It didn't matter that I'd printed nonsense. I had a huge grin on my face, and so did Thatha.

Now, as an adult, I'm back in the house, still trying to get my bearings. Where was the kitchen, and the stove where we heated water for our early morning bucket baths? Where was the dining room where I begged to sit on the floor and eat with the adults?

"Where was the print shop and Thatha's office?" I ask Thamma Rao Uncle, one of my mom's five brothers.

"It is no more."

I know what that means. The print shop was destroyed several years ago when the government demolished part of the building to widen the street.

"Is there anything left?" I ask, wondering if there might be books or a small piece of machinery I can take back with me. I know the answer, but I'm still saddened when another uncle, Dharma Rao, confirms it.

I try to hide my disappointment but am unsuccessful.

"*Chustanu*. For you, I will look," Dharma Rao Uncle offers.

I thank him, and I believe him, but I suspect there will be nothing left to find.

It was well past bedtime for me and the other children. The town had grown dark, and all of the oil lamps in the house had been extinguished. We'd wiled the hours away playing cards and carrom, laughter filling the night. Thatha had set up a row of cots on the terrace for all of the kids, and I climbed into mine, the once-scratchy canvas softened by time. Blanketed by the sweet scent of jasmine and camphor, I counted shooting stars, wishing on each of them as they passed overhead, until I fell asleep.

"What about the terrace?" I ask my mom, who in turn asks her brother.

I am desperate after all these years to find something that feels familiar, and so many memories are tied to that terrace: warm nights reading by candle and starlight, my uncles hammering a giant block of ice into small pieces to fill the cooler of bottled water and Thums Up cola they'd bought for our visit; sewing fresh flowers into sweet-smelling, colorful garlands; flying kites in the afternoon swelter, their neon colors shimmering in the heat as the concrete scorched the soles of my bare feet.

I look hopefully at my uncle and he gives me the head nod, the one that simultaneously combines the nod for yes with the shake for no and means whatever you want it to mean. I would laugh, except that I need to know the answer.

"No," he finally says. "It is gone. You can see where it was from the roof, but we cannot go up. It is locked." My uncle explains that they no longer have access to that part of the house; it doesn't belong to them anymore. After my grandparents died, it passed to a member of the extended family who keeps it locked and keeps people out.

I sigh and look at my hands in my lap. Eshwar Rao, my youngest uncle, stands abruptly and leaves the room. I wonder where he is going, but I sit and listen as the conversation moves on and then dies. This silence, too, is unfamiliar.

Why had I thought that after nearly two decades, this place would be the same?

When he returns to the room, Eshwar Rao Uncle has a key in his hand.

"Come with me," he says.

I stand and follow him up a narrow staircase. As we near the top, the staircase turns and there's a drop in the ceiling.

"Watch your—" he starts to say, but he's too late. I smack my head against the concrete, stumbling as bright golden dots swarm my vision like bumble bees. I blink a few times then reach up and rub my forehead, pleased to see my hand come away with only a dusting of chalky whitewash rather than a smear of blood. I never had to duck as a kid.

Eshwar Rao Uncle cringes and hisses. "Are you O.K.?"

I am, and we keep going.

I follow him up the remainder of the stairs and then down a walkway past more closed doors. Something is nagging at me. We reach another door, and I watch silently as he slips the key into the heavy metal padlock. Something is still bugging me. We step out onto the roof. "There," he points. When I follow his gaze, I find a brand-new building—one I've never seen before.

The key is still dangling in Eshwar Rao Uncle's hand, and I finally realize what's been bothering me. The doors.

There are no doors in my memories of the house on KVR Swamy Road. They were there, I'm sure, but no one ever closed them, and so it was as if they didn't exist. The closed doors came later—after Thatha, the last of the family's true patriarchs, died; after Kalahasti, Thamma Rao & Sons fractured and splintered; after the buildings were divided among quarreling extended family members; and after the government demolished so much of the home to widen the road below. That was the final blow. They sheared off half of the house and left the building unfinished—half-destroyed rooms open to the street, allowing the memories to escape until they were gone, just like the terrace where I once slept under a canvas of night that smoldered with embers from millions of miles ago.

How, I wonder, could there be nothing left?

I want to cry.

I want to hug Thatha.

"Will you come to our home?"

The voice surprises me. It belongs to Dharma Rao Uncle's oldest daughter, a teenage girl whom I've only just met. She skipped school to spend time with me, her cousin from America, and I've welcomed her company throughout the day. My once boisterous uncles have grown quiet with age, but she's filled the void created by their silence, and I am grateful for that. I didn't notice before, but she's followed

Eshwar Rao Uncle and me up to the roof, as have her parents. They all look at me expectantly.

"Of course," I say, turning back toward the door and the walkway and the stairs. Their home is in the building next door. "We will go this way," my uncle says, stopping me midstride and gesturing across the alley as I turn toward him. "Like when you were small."

I follow him across the roof.

I've spent the entire day looking for parts of the house that feel familiar, wanting to see the places and people that made my early stays in India so important. I wanted to see things that reminded me of my grandfather—to linger in the life of a man whose impact on me was disproportionately larger than the amount of time I spent with him before he died. I wanted to gather those memories like typeset letters and place them in my mind, pulling the lever to ink them indelibly.

But there is, it seems, nothing to gather. Thatha is gone. When I was nine, he suffered a stroke while my family and I were in the air, returning from what would be our last summer visit. My grandmother followed shortly after. The house was irretrievably changed after that. The people, too, in so many ways. And I am no longer a dewy-eyed child.

Still, I've carried this place with me. After those early chess lessons with my grandfather, I continued to study the game and grew into an accomplished young player, competing in my teenage years. As a photographer, I've traveled the world, sleeping under the stars on six continents, photographing the night skies from Patagonia to Siberia, and always recalling those evenings on the terrace. And, of course, throughout my life, whenever I've inhaled the scent of a brand-new book or run my fingers over gold-stamped spines and elegant typography, I've thought of Thatha.

Maybe that is the point: whether I realized it or not, this place is a part of me—like ink absorbed into paper.

I look over at Dharma Rao Uncle standing on the roof and remember how I used him as a human jungle gym in my youth. I smile at the memory and listen. I hear the laughter that once bounded off of the concrete walls and floors, and I smell jasmine and camphor, tobacco and cloves. I slap my feet against the concrete, grinning as we near the edge of the roof. How many times did I take this route between buildings as a child? Dozens? Hundreds? I steal one quick glance down at the alley several stories below.

And then, just as I have so many times before, I leap.

໑ ໑ ໑

Sivani Babu is the co-founder and co-CEO of Hidden Compass. She is an award-winning journalist and nature photographer who has contributed to numerous publications, including BBC Travel, AFAR, Backpacker, Outdoor Photographer, *and* Iron Horse Literary Review. *Her work has been recognized in the Best American Travel Writing series and has appeared in exhibits from San Diego to the Sorbonne. After working on a Supreme Court case and representing hundreds of indigent defendants in federal court, Sivani left her career as a federal public defender to sail across the most brutal sea on earth. Since then, she has chased storms through Tornado Alley, searched for polar bears in the Arctic Circle, and survived a broken neck and a concussion while sailing through a lightning storm in the Bermuda Triangle. She has more lives than a cat.*

SHANNON LEONE FOWLER

৵৵ ৵৵ ৵৵

A Rare-Colored Stone

A storm, a few pints of Guinness,
an amateur autopsy, and Irish luck.

I left my hostel in Killarney in bright sunshine, but twenty
minutes later the sky darkened and cracked open, and
it began to pour. I'd been planning a full-day hike around
the lakes in the national park and then through the Gap of
Dunloe. The forecast had been for sun, but this was Ireland.
In winter. It didn't look as if it would let up anytime soon, so I
turned back. But the hostel I'd just left was now fully booked
for the night. Cursing my own foolishness for not bringing my
waterproof trousers, I stuffed my things into a large plastic bag
and then back into my daypack, zipped my yellow rain jacket
to my chin, pulled up the hood, and set off once more.

It was 1998, and I was twenty-four years old. I'd graduated
from college in California the year before and was traveling
around the world by teaching SCUBA diving. After Central
America, the Caribbean, and Greece, I'd landed a job at an

outdoor sports store in Galway, where I spent my days off backpacking around Ireland. I was young, innocent, and optimistic. Getting a little lost was part of the pleasure of the journey. I depended on luck, and I expected people to be kind and everything to work out in the end.

But right then, things were not working out. I couldn't see much past the sheet of water dripping from my hood. I'd made it to the edge of town, where the Ring of Kerry road borders the national park, when the downpour turned into a deluge. *Crap crap crap,* I thought. *Maybe I should find another hostel and explore Killarney instead, spend the day inside St. Mary's Cathedral and the Museum of Irish Transport.* I turned back a second time and walked a few soggy steps. *But it might take hours in the rain, trying to find a bed for my budget.* I spun on my heel and headed again for the lakes, not that I'd see any of the scenery I'd heard so much about in this weather. I did this two more times—cursing, turning, and walking in different directions along the road. Unable to make up my mind and already cold and soaking wet, I stuck out my thumb.

The second car that passed, an ancient, battered station wagon, pulled over to the side of the road. I ran up to the car but couldn't make out anything through the fogged-up window. When I opened the door, the driver smiled up at me through a long dark beard, and I realized I'd opened the driver's side. I apologized and ran back around. Cahill, a name I had an embarrassingly hard time pronouncing, told me he could drop me off at the start of the Gap. He was tall and thin with a weathered face. Turned out he was a sheep farmer nearby, and I was surprised to learn we were the same age. Rain pounded the roof, and the windshield wipers worked furiously as we chatted along the dripping green, tree-lined country road. Inside the car, it was warm and humid, and I recognized the swampy scent of peat.

"Shout you a Guinness?" Cahill asked after a while. "This is pint-and-pub-fire weather if ever I did see it."

"How 'bout my shout in exchange for the ride?"

"Not having it. You're a guest, and on your tod." He looked over, winked, and grinned. "I'd be honored to show you a bit of the local *craic*."

The tiny old pub was filled with smoke and loud men. It smelled of wet wool and a wood fire. Sopping jackets and hats were piled onto tables and chairs. Cahill wound his way through the crowd and approached a group at the bar, pounding each man on the back before turning to the bartender.

"Story horse?" the bartender, a woman about my mum's age with dark hair and a smoker's voice, greeted him.

"Found this wee Yank out in the wet after it started bucketing down." Cahill nodded at me. "Two pints if you please, Sheenagh."

While we waited for the first pour to settle, Cahill introduced me to the group of men. I hopped onto a barstool, my daypack in a puddle at my feet, and answered the usual questions: *Your name's Shannon...like the river? What famous movie stars do you know out there in California? Do the kids surf to school? So what do you think of our green isle?* I'd already learned that describing myself as Irish American would only be met with a dismissive snort—*you and every other Yank who comes over on holiday*. And it seemed even less credible when I could hardly understand a word they were saying. I'd been living in Galway for months, but it still sounded as if they were using two completely different languages—one for me, and another to talk amongst themselves. As I sipped the creamy, malty beer, I tried my best to follow their fast-paced, singsong conversation. When I was completely lost, one of them would turn to me and, using slow, enunciated sentences, let me in on the punch line.

Another round of Guinness was set down on the bar in front of us. *"Sláinte!"* We raised the pints and clinked glasses, cheeks flushed from the warmth of the fire, the beer, and the company. I was still damp, but I no longer minded.

Only I *was* starting to get worried about the long walk I had to the hostel at the end of the Gap. Difficult to believe, but it seemed to be raining even harder now. I checked my wrist for the time; it would be dark in a couple of hours. My men's dive watch (the dive watches they made for women had buttons so tiny, they'd be impossible to work with neoprene gloves on) was not exactly discrete, and Cahill caught my eye.

"Where are you staying tonight, love?"

"Black Valley Hostel."

"You should have said! I live right by. I'll drop you. Stall the beans and settle in!"

So we ordered bowls of steaming-hot stew—thyme-soaked lamb, chunks of buttery soft potato and carrot, all mopped up with crumbly soda bread. Each time I tried to pay, for our stews, for another round, one of the men would push my wallet away.

"Your money's no good here." Sheenagh, the bartender, winked at me.

I scraped up the last bit of potato from my bowl, took a long sip of Guinness, and looked around the packed, noisy pub. I'd been surrounded by Cahill's friends at the bar and, perhaps because of the concentration required to try to follow their conversation, hadn't noticed the dead bird in the corner. I was pretty sure it was a pheasant. Its head hung crookedly over the side of a table, one upside-down yellow glassy eye staring in my direction.

Two sweaty, red-faced men stood over the bird, steak knives clutched in their hands. Blood pooled on the table and the floor at their feet. The men were arguing, but good-naturedly. Every so often, one or the other would plunge his knife into the pheasant's chest, push aside the tawny speckled feathers, point and gesticulate. The small group gathered around the table would lean in closer to see, before weighing in on the animated debate. The pub was too crowded and loud for me to hear anything they were saying from across the room, but their gestures were fervent. No one seemed to notice the occasional blood spatter from a waved knife.

Cahill explained. There'd been a hunting contest earlier that morning, and both men had shot the pheasant. Now they were performing an amateur autopsy to determine which of their two bullets had been the lethal one. A bar tab was at stake.

The best travel experiences are simple. They can't be planned. It's just a feeling of something genuine—knowing you're lucky to be in exactly that place at exactly that instant. Those ridiculous, magical, perfect, accidental moments of joy are still the reason I travel. All these years later, I carry the story of that rainy afternoon outside Killarney with me, like a small, rare-colored stone. Because, in hindsight, Ireland was the last time everything would really be O.K. in the end.

This was months before I met my fiancé at a hostel when we were both backpacking through Barcelona, years before he was killed by a box jellyfish while we traveled together in Thailand. Terrible things can also happen at home. But when they happen abroad, there's a heightened sense of loneliness, of not belonging, of bewilderment and confusion. Sean's death is another stone I carry with me. But I never would have met him if I hadn't been traveling, and I wouldn't trade the time I had with him for any other stone in the world.

When I look back on my travels in Ireland, it surprises me now that I wasn't even surprised then, when everything worked out at the end of each day. With all that happened after, those memories have become much more precious.

Late in the evening, when Cahill and I left that tiny old pub, the dispute over the dead bird had not been settled, but the rain had stopped at last, and thousands of pinpoint stars filled the huge black sky.

Cahill dropped me in front of the hostel at the end of the Gap, wished me well, and sped off into the night. The building was quiet, but I was too giddy from Guinness and the kindness of strangers to give it much thought. I rang the bell, and rang it again. Eventually an older woman wearing curlers, a tattered robe, and slippers appeared, looking cross. I asked for a bed.

"We're closed for the season," she replied.

I looked around. I was in the middle of nowhere in the pitch dark. There wasn't any other accommodation for miles and miles.

The woman sighed. "I guess we can give you a bed for the night. But there won't be any heat. We've shut it off for the winter, and we'll lose money running it for one person."

"No problem at all. Thank you so, so much."

"You'll be cold. I can't help that."

"I'll be fine. I really appreciate it. Thank you."

Relieved and exhausted, I washed my face and brushed my teeth. Shivering, I put on every item of clothing I had in my daypack, including my beanie. I could see my breath in the room. But I was so grateful to have a bed. I climbed under the covers and was just drifting off when I heard a metallic whir and a cough, and the heater by my bunk sputtered to life.

॰॰॰ ॰॰॰ ॰॰॰

Shannon Leone Fowler is a writer, marine biologist, and single mother of three young children. After her doctorate on Australian sea lions, she taught marine ecology in the Bahamas and Galápagos, led a university course on killer whales in the San Juan Islands, spent seasons as the marine mammal biologist on board ships in both the Arctic and Antarctic, taught graduate students field techniques while studying Weddell seals on the Ross Ice Shelf, and worked as a science writer at National Public Radio in Washington, DC. Originally from California, she currently lives in London and studies seabirds in Alaska. Since having children, she's conceded to booking ahead, but still leaves packing to the last minute. Her memoir, Traveling with Ghosts, *was published in 2017.*

ℬ ℬ ℬ

Come and See

Is it disaster tourism, if you're invited?

The key master died in Mount Merapi's 2010 eruption. Most of the villagers living on the volcano's slopes evacuated safely, fled in the middle of the night with only the clothes they happened to be wearing. But others, some following the key master's example, refused to leave their homes.

He is the volcano's spirit guardian, entrusted with the sacred duty to protect the kingdom of Jogjakarta—the sprawling Javanese metropolis nineteen miles south of one of Indonesia's most volatile volcanoes. More than one thousand years ago, the legend goes, the Sultan of Jogjakarta instructed the very first key master to eat an enormous egg, which transformed him into a giant and then, eventually, into the hill that lies directly between the volcano and the city. A geologic intermediary so perfectly placed that the legend seems believable.

Every key master since has lived atop or near this hill so that he can monitor the moods of the volcano spirits. But his primary job is attending to the giant within the hill, keeping it content with offerings of food and flowers so that it, in turn, will do its job: diverting the flow of lava around the city.

For those who live in Merapi's shadow, the question is never if, but when. In 2010 the eruptions were unusually destructive. The spirits were agitated. Mount Merapi didn't just erupt once; it sputtered and spewed for a whole month, issuing warnings throughout October until reaching its zenith five minutes after midnight on November 5th.

At least three hundred fifty villagers were killed. More than one hundred thousand displaced. And the key master, loyal to his post, died in the literal line of duty: on the hill between the volcano and the city.

I can't see the volcano the day we arrive in Jogjakarta. Even from the tiny balcony of our room at the Ministry of Coffee (a hostel we clearly picked for the name), elevated above rooftops, laundry lines, and snarled traffic jams, the horizon is a sepia-tone washout. It's a sticky afternoon, the city choking on the fumes of its motorbikes and taxicabs. My husband and I have heard of Mount Merapi, but not from legends or guidebooks.

We're traveling in Indonesia for only a month, but our friends had lived here—endured the torrential rains, the oppressive humidity, the dearth of wine, the cobra in their back yard, the constant threat of dengue fever. My husband's journalism buddy was freelancing while his wife taught at an international school, so in November 2010, as hot ash covered his back yard like a freak snowstorm and his wife and two-year-old daughter evacuated to the coast, he headed up the volcano to report on the eruption with his Jogjakartan fixer. Fajar slipped the news crew through checkpoints and translated interviews with villagers gathered in emergency evacuation camps. Then our friends moved promptly back to California. That was two years ago.

Rob uses the phone at the front desk. "Nobody knows Jogja better," our friend had raved, giving us Fajar's number before we left for Indonesia. Fajar insists on meeting us right away. He brings his girlfriend, a British girl named Yasmin with black hair sculpted into a cute bob and draped in a colorful scarf. Fajar is a small, sinewy guy with voluminous dreadlocks that add about one-third to his total human volume. They declare themselves our official Jogja hosts and brainstorm an itinerary for the next day while we sit in the lobby sipping small cups of strong coffee.

"Should we take them to Merapi?" Yasmin asks. I'm curious about the volcano that drove our friends away, but I don't say so. I'm embarrassed by my eagerness.

"We're up for anything," Rob says. But I know he wants to go, too. We didn't come to Java looking for a story, and we certainly didn't come to be disaster tourists. But we are both writers—my husband the bold journalist, unafraid of confrontation; me the quiet observer, composing sentences in my head—so maybe, subconsciously, we did. Because aren't writers always searching for something in the rubble?

Mbah ("grandfather") Maridjan was something of a celebrity mystic in Java. As key master, he had earned a reputation of defiance and bravery when he refused to evacuate during Merapi's 2006 eruptions, instead leading residents in a silent procession, circling local villages three times and making offerings of rice cakes to the angry mountain spirits.

Soon after, he starred in a commercial for an Indonesian energy drink—KukuBima Ener-G—with a national boxing hero. The ad opens with the key master in a lush field, gazing calmly at the fuming volcano, then cuts to the shirtless boxer in red track pants, throwing shadow punches and bouncing on his toes. Merapi sputters in the background and as the smoke plumes turn from gray to orange, the boxer takes off running through the woods. The music crescendos. Birds take flight. A deer bounds through the trees in the opposite direction. Purple bolts of lightning jag through the orange clouds as he reaches the key master in the field. The boxer takes a swig of KukuBima, erupting with strength in sync with the volcano behind him. Mbah Maridjan shakes his hand. They bow to each other, right hands balled to their chests in fists. The screen flashes: KUKUBIMA ENER-G!

The next morning, Fajar and Yasmin are waiting outside in a rental car. Merapi is still hidden, today behind a scrim of rain clouds, but Fajar doesn't trust his vintage VW Beetle to survive the climb if we do venture up the volcano. He weaves effortlessly through diagonal rain and knotted traffic, pointing out this temple compound and that excellent Sumatran restaurant.

Fajar is equal parts Bob Marley vagabond and Sumatran warrior, which makes him the perfect local guide. When he moved from Sumatra to Jogjakarta, he tells us, his mom found his box of weapons under his bed—twenty-five knives, swords, and brass knuckles—and gave them away to his friends. "They were so proud to have my swords!" He grins at us in the rearview mirror. As far as I can tell, "sword" is not just a funny translation.

We won't be able to see anything if we visit Merapi in the rain, so Fajar drives to the ancient Buddhist temples of Borobudur. We offer to pay their admission, but Fajar and Yasmin are happy to wait outside, holding hands, chain-smoking and drinking the free tourist coffee until we return. Back in the car, Fajar turns up the volume on his playlist of American pop songs, and he and Yasmin continue singing along. I don't know half the songs, but they know all the words. We still can't see Merapi even though the rain has let up, but as the playlist starts its third time on repeat, Fajar turns the music down.

"When Merapi erupted, these were full of ash and lava," he says, pointing out the dry riverbeds, sandy swaths of tree-less earth lined by squatty palm trees. We pass what looks like a school. "That was a bunker," Fajar says. Then a vacant lot that was a refugee camp. As we wind higher up the foothills, Yasmin stops humming. Fajar stops playing percussion on the steering wheel. One of them turns off the music.

"We were here the day of the big eruption," Yasmin whispers. They both peer straight ahead, as if watching the memory replay through the windshield. Charred tree trunks appear on a naked ridgeline. Saplings and bushes sprout up here and there, but they aren't tall enough to hide the crumbling foundations lining the road. Fajar tells us the legend of the key master—the egg, the giant, the hill—as we pass more skeletal houses.

"He wouldn't leave," Fajar says. "They found him in his home, buried by ash."

Mbah Maridjan was appointed key master by the Sultan of Jogjakarta in 1982. He lived four kilometers from the crater rim. He didn't have a car. He was eighty-three years old when he whispered his last prayer. Rescuers discovered him under the rubble, kneeling in the sujud position: forehead kissing the floor, prostrate in prayer. They say the batik fabric of his sari was fused to his skin. Twelve other bodies were found with his, presumably trying to convince him to leave.

It was the pyroclastic flow, most likely. "Pyroclast" comes from Greek: pyro for fire, clast for broken in pieces. No one knows how fast or hot it surged down the mountainside into the key master's home, but pyroclastic flows have been measured at temperatures reaching one thousand degrees Celsius and speeds up to four hundred fifty miles per hour. Hurricane Force is the highest rating on the Beaufort Wind Force Scale, for winds greater than or equal to seventy-four miles per hour. A pyroclastic flow defies comprehension.

What did the key master ask for with his last breath? Did he whisper his prayer or shout? Did he see the rocks rushing down the slope? Hear the trees snapping, the walls collapsing? Feel the hot ash bury him? And was he afraid?

I realize we've arrived only when we pull into a gravel parking lot full of old military jeeps the color of split pea soup. "The peak is about a mile away." Fajar points into the mist. A pack of jubilant young men in fatigue jackets materializes around us, yelling and joking, pushing the car back and forth. Someone opens my door and politely escorts me out. Two others do the same for Rob and Yasmin before locking Fajar inside. They continue the rocking, laughing hysterically. Fajar pounds on the window and flips them off with both hands.

There used to be a village here, but this close to volcanic ground zero, buildings basically disintegrated. Where houses once stood, there's now a strip of crudely constructed roadside stalls selling souvenirs, shoes, cigarettes, and sweet ginger tea. And where I imagine a bucolic scene of cows grazing in abundant fields, a herd of jeeps sits in a gravel lot waiting to be fed by curious tourists. But you wouldn't know this was tragic ground from the raucous mob of drivers buzzing with a scheme.

Fajar, now freed from the car, is quietly handing out eggs. Someone presses a plastic baggie of flour into my hand and another into Yasmin's. She cocks her head toward a driver leaning against a jeep. "It's his birthday," she whispers. "Once all the tourists leave on that big bus, we'll plaster him with eggs and flour."

The tour bus putters away. Someone gives the signal. Mayhem erupts. Flour bursts in festive plumes, eggs fly through the air and explode on the birthday boy's back, and we all squeal and dart around the jeeps. I lose track of Rob in the chaos. A driver nudges me, noticing I still have my baggie of flour. I gently empty it over the birthday boy's head and dash out of the fray, right before someone tosses a bucket of mystery liquid on him. It reeks of something so terrible that he sprints to a wooden outhouse and starts dry heaving. But

his retching stirs no mercy; his friends keep stalking the outhouse, throwing another egg or handful of flour whenever he
cracks the door open.

I thought this place would be solemn, like walking into a
stained-glassed cathedral or attending a funeral. There are
ghost stories here for sure, but there are also eggs and flour
and birthdays.

Imagine living on Merapi's slopes. Imagine the frequent rum-
bles, the plumes of smoke, the flares of lava. You could relocate, but your family has probably lived here for generations.
You might own land, a farm, some cows. You could live in
fear and anxiety, or you could find a narrative that explains
it all. And so you believe in the key master and the Javanese
spirit world. You believe that the spirits—those who roamed
and ruled Java until humans settled on the island—now
inhabit Merapi's crater.

Besides the fact that they live in a palace, their life inside
the volcano resembles your own in the village. Those clouds
of ash and gas? Regularly scheduled palace cleanings and
remodeling projects. That low rumbling? Just the echoes of
another palace procession, led by the head spirit's carriage.
Some believe that Merapi's big eruptions are punishment for
wrongdoing, but you trust what you've heard: to warn villagers of an eruption's magnitude, the spirits extend a special
thread from the crater. You also trust the key master. He will
read the moody mountain spirits. He will keep the giant in
the hill strong. He will tell you if it's time to flee.

But why should you imagine any of this? What good will
it do to try on someone else's reality? Is imagination just
another form of disaster tourism?

After the 2010 eruption, people were curious. They would
drive up the semi-paved road, the same road we've just
traveled, to see it for themselves. Fajar's friend Chris saw
these disaster tourists, and he saw men without jobs—men

who had been farmers or sand-truck drivers before Merapi scorched their farms, killed their cows, and filled the riverbeds with ash, burying the sand. So Chris bought an American World War II–era jeep and hired three drivers. Two years later, he tells us now over steaming cups of ginger tea, there are twenty-five guides in the Merapi Jeep Tour Community. He has to hire by lottery.

Despite the fog and impending dusk, Chris insists on driving us up the volcano—"Where we don't take the tourists!" He snuffs his cigarette in an ashtray and pulls out his keys.

"Only if you let us pay for it," Rob says, as we follow him to his favorite jeep, the first one he bought.

My husband sits up front next to Chris, his reporter instincts on high alert, tapping some quick notes into his phone. I squeeze into the back seat, devoid of seatbelts, with Fajar and Yasmin. We pause at a roadside stall, where a woman pours a jerry can of gas through a funnel held by her daughter, and then we're off, lurching over rubble in the open-top jeep, maneuvering around huge boulders that weren't here two years ago. The fog adds dramatic effect to a scene that doesn't need embellishment: an old military jeep rolling through the quiet devastation of a war zone.

"Tours usually visit the key master's grave," Chris says, grinding through the gears. "But it's getting dark, and you have to see the museum."

This is what disaster looks like: You stand awkwardly in front of the husk of an incinerated house, shivering slightly. It's that time of day when the wind picks up just as the last bit of sunlight leaks from the sky. As if the space it took up insists on being filled. The full skeleton of a cow is assembled on the ground where a front door should be. An old woman the size of a child appears. Her face is all wrinkles and a toothy smile. Nobody else is here. This is the solemn cathedral you expected.

The woman's name is Ibu Wati, and she doesn't live here anymore. She lives down the mountain now and walks up here every day. She shakes your hand with intense sincerity, wrapping knobby fingers around yours, and invites you to walk among her memories—to tour her loss. She is the sole curator of this museum. You notice the dirt under her nails.

Ibu Wati speaks no English, but she accompanies you through the rooms. Cement stumps that suggest where walls once stood now display what remains of her belongings. You try to pause at each item, even when you can't tell what it is, to pay some sort of respect. But what does that mean? If you look long enough, will it alleviate her loss?

Some objects take a few seconds to recognize: melted coins and silverware, blackened shoes and crispy books, the charred frames of a tricycle and a motorbike. A table and four chairs sit alone in one room, scorched, as if waiting for their owners to finally sit down to dinner.

She points to what used to be her little studio; she used to teach dance here. You ask about the box of melted black rectangles. Cassette tapes. The reel of tape that once produced music is a solid black clump, the notes trapped inside. A few tapes are still intact, but most are warped into odd shapes, like an avant-garde art project or a science experiment gone awry.

A cracked clock with a partially melted face is mounted on one of the only walls still standing. The black hands are paralyzed at twelve and one, the red second hand just above the eight. Five minutes and forty seconds after midnight. Two cow jawbones hang on either side, a frame of bone and tooth. Underneath, on a scorched piece of wood, the date of the eruption is painted in white: 5 November 2010.

You feel paralyzed, too. You didn't realize it until this moment: today is November 5th.

Ibu Wati is asking you a question. Do you want to take your picture in front of the clock?

Unnamed emotions bloom in your chest. They crawl up your throat, flush your face. You feel like an intruder, a voyeur, but she wants you to take the picture. She comes here every day so that people like you can see the remnants of a life like hers.

Somewhere a muezzin is chanting the evening prayer, but the fog smothers the words into a single muted minor tone, like one black piano key held down too long. Ibu Wati gestures toward your husband's camera, then to her disaster shrine. Her eyes shine in the twilight. You put a few rupiahs in her donation box and shake your head no. This is her story, not yours.

Should I even be telling it to you?

"My job is to stop lava from flowing down," the key master told *The Jakarta Globe* in an interview before the 2010 eruption. "Let the volcano breathe, but not cough."

Mbah Maridjan defied government evacuation orders. He ignored the warnings of Java's head volcanologist and the pleadings of friends. To one such friend, *The Jakarta Globe* reported, he said, "My time to die in this place has almost come, I can't leave."

Mbah Maridjan's son succeeded him as the next key master—the fourth generation of spirit guardians. Shortly after the eruption, KukuBima Ener-G mixed a new commercial with images of an erupting Merapi and a praying key master, memorializing Mbah Maridjan as a spiritual daredevil.

Later that week, Fajar picks us up at the Ministry of Coffee. We're going back to Merapi so Rob can interview some of the drivers for a story. Rubbing his bloodshot eyes, Fajar tells us someone broke into an apartment in his complex the night before. "Who breaks in at midnight?" he laughs. "Any good thief knows that's too early!" He and some friends took off after the culprit—armed with their swords. They spent a good part of the early morning hours searching for the thief.

"What would you have done if you caught him?" Rob asks.

"Kill him," Fajar replies, without pause or bloodlust. I believe him. I catch Rob's reflection in the rearview mirror. My eyes are wide, but my husband doesn't flinch.

An hour later, we sit together with a handful of drivers on wooden benches in front of the jeep office. The wall next to me is plastered with photos of bikini-clad women sprawled across jeep hoods. I sip my sweet ginger tea and try not to breathe in too much secondhand smoke. Each time the drivers find an inroad for a dirty joke, they take it. The punch line usually has to do with cows. Fajar translates the jokes as well as the answers to Rob's questions, which he now focuses on Tri, who is soft-spoken but still more talkative than the others.

After the eruption, Tri's seven cows became sick and skinny and he had to sell them. He was one of the first jeep drivers, he says, and his tour route goes past the remains of his house. But if he doesn't mention it, his passengers don't know. Like Ibu Wati, he returns day after day, while people who don't live in the volcano's shadow take pictures and imagine the drama.

"Where do you live now?" Rob asks. Fajar translates: In one of the "plastic houses"—shorthand for the temporary government housing for the tens of thousands displaced by the volcano. Two years have passed, and Tri and his family are still waiting to receive notice that their permanent government housing is ready.

"He wants to know if you'd like to see his plastic house," Fajar says.

I look over at Rob. Is it disaster tourism if you're invited?

This is what survival looks like: After showing you his home of bamboo poles and blue tarps in the displaced camp, Tri wants to make one last stop. His eyes gleam with mischief, or maybe pride. His sister has a half-melted television that still works. She isn't supposed to be living in her house, he explains. It's within the government boundaries still deemed unsafe for habitation, but so far nobody has checked.

The first thing you notice is the gauzy lattice of spider webs across the semi-scorched rafters. It's dark in the house, but you quickly and easily make out hundreds of spiders. Panic scampers up your throat. This fear of yours feels ridiculous here, and you compose yourself while Tri fiddles with the TV. The back of it has indeed melted into a strange plastic crater. The electricity isn't working, so he carries the TV to a different room while his sister rummages around for the antenna. You stand next to your husband in the dim room, everyone staring expectantly at the blank screen. Suddenly, as promised, it flickers to life.

Tri and his sister smile triumphantly, faces beaming in the electric glow.

Before dropping us off at our hostel, Fajar takes us to his favorite Sumatran restaurant for sheep curry. While we eat, he tells us that he gave almost all of his money to the search and rescue effort after the eruption. "I'd just spent my last rupiah on gas for my motorcycle and a few cigarettes to share with Yasmin when your friend called me to help him report on the eruption." With the money he earned helping with that story, Fajar paid the rest of his college tuition and finished his degree. He's never told our friend that, but this, I understand, is why he's been such a dedicated guide.

"I would do anything for a friend," Fajar says solemnly. "My goal in life is for the most people possible to cry when I die." I can't help thinking of the key master.

Rob tries to swipe the bill when it comes, but Fajar is quicker. "You can bring me a pair of American cowboy boots the next time you come to Indonesia!"

Back at the Ministry of Coffee, Fajar gets out of the car to say goodbye. I hug him and realize that he really is no bigger than me. Then he and Rob exchange the embrace of men—a handshake pulled into emphatic back pats.

Visiting Merapi is not like other volcanic sightseeing. At Volcanoes National Park in Hawaii, you can safely watch the natural wonder of lava bubbling and churning. At Pompeii, the ancient Italian city buried by the pyroclastic flow of Mount Vesuvius, you can tour the ruins, imagine lava coursing through the streets. But at Mount Merapi, it's all there: the evidence of natural disaster, the daily lives of those who survived, the ghosts of what did not, and the pressing inevitability of next time. You can see it, smell it, touch it. You can taste it in the ashy grit on your teeth.

Here is the uncomfortable truth of disaster tourism: We want to get close to danger without actually being in danger. But maybe there's something more. Maybe it isn't the tragedy that we are really drawn to. Maybe what we crave is evidence of human resilience. We want to see it with our own eyes, hope it exists within us should we ever need it. Maybe that's the allure of the key-master legends, the ferocity in Fajar's friendship, the story that the residents of Merapi want to share.

Come, Tri's eyes sparkle. You must see our miraculous melted TV!

Come, Ibu Wati implores, her crow's feet crinkling as she smiles. Take my hand. Tour my disaster. Walk among my rubble.

See my survival.

❧ ❧ ❧

Kaitlin Barker Davis is a writer from Portland, Oregon, where she lives with her husband and daughter. Her essays on place, travel, and motherhood have appeared in Nowhere Magazine, Narratively, The Rumpus, The VIDA Review, *and elsewhere. She has an MFA in Creative Nonfiction from Seattle Pacific University, and you can find her at kaitlinbarkerdavis.com.*

TANIA ROMANOV AMOCHAEV

෫෨ ෫෨ ෫෨

Not a Stranger

A fortuitous accident and a forever
altered notion of family.

A fierce banging interrupted my hard-won sleep. I
fought off the noise, drugged with the pill I'd finally
been unable to resist after long days of travel on Bhutan's
rugged roads. But the pounding persisted, the door rattled
on its hinges, and footsteps raced heavily on stairs and down
hallways.

"Get up, Tania! Get up! Now!"

I staggered toward the sound of Tandin's shouting and
fumbled with the light. The switch didn't work. I wrestled the
door open onto an equally dark, empty hallway. Tandin stood
there, a giant form in the blackness, flashlight in hand.

"There's a fire. Grab something warm and wait here for
me. We have to get out! I'll be right back."

He tore down the hallway, banging on doors, shouting.
Terrified, I found my headlamp and grabbed my glasses.

I threw on my black down jacket and pushed my feet into heavy trail shoes. I could hear fire crackling. I smelled smoke.

Tandin ran back, encircled me with his arms, and pulled me toward the stairs directly across from my room. Flames lit up the back window of the stairwell, our only path out.

It wasn't the first time Tandin and I had faced peril.

Fourteen years earlier, in 2000, my husband Harold and I had trekked for twenty-three days through the mountains of Bhutan, a Buddhist kingdom deep in the Himalayas. It was an intense expedition that included climbing over several mountain passes above fifteen thousand feet. Tandin was our guide, a young man on break from school in Darjeeling.

About a week into the trek, after hiking past villages unreachable by car, then past the infrequent dark-gray tents of yak-herding families, we were at the stage of the journey I always love most. My daily world of business, the bustle of city life, cleaning and cooking, cars and traffic, all receded beyond consciousness. Here there was only the present.

One morning as dawn approached, I crawled to the front of our tent. The ground was white. Everything was white. As my eyes adjusted, I slowly discerned large, lumpy animal shapes, like so many fallen snowmen. I realized with relief that they were our yaks, those giant bovine beasts, sleeping in the meadow. Ponies had carried our gear from the lower elevations, but they'd gone back down to replenish their oxygen. Up here, only yaks had lungs truly adapted to the environment, so now they carried everything for us. It was a delicate dance, for yaks couldn't survive below twelve thousand feet—the air was too rich for them—and ponies couldn't carry heavy weight above that elevation.

But our yaks had escaped the previous evening, and their herders had still been searching late into the darkness. Now they were covered with the overnight snowfall, their breath billowing around them. I headed back to my sleeping bag to wait for the young porter I knew would soon appear with cups of hot instant coffee.

Harold woke briefly, and I snuggled against him, ensuring not an inch of space came between us. I wanted to memorize the feel of his body, intimately familiar after twenty years of marriage. I didn't know how many more such mornings we'd have. The white wisps of our breath mingled in the tent as he drifted back to sleep and I listened to the quiet sounds of camp waking up.

Meanwhile, one question occupied my mind: Would I be walking out of here?

It wasn't just the snow worrying me.

Yesterday we'd climbed for hours along increasingly steep trails, and as we approached the final stretch of a pass that crested at almost sixteen thousand feet, my confidence edged on cockiness: I was in my early fifties and proud of the fact that I was stronger than I'd ever been.

When we reached the top, it was too windy to rest, so we headed down a steep, narrow trail. At first, each step was a challenge, but then the decline eased, and frightening cliff exposures faded into memory. My pace was strong, hiking poles in cadence with my stride, weight centered, breathing smooth. I had acclimated to the elevation and was past the headaches, sleeplessness, loss of appetite, and general inertia that plagued me the first few days. I glanced back toward the pass, relieved to see our yak train following behind.

That's when it happened. My foot slipped out from under me. Suddenly I was sliding on my back, then skidding to a halt.

No big deal, I thought. *Get up, sweep the dirt off my rear, continue.*

But no sooner had I initiated that maneuver than I found myself back on my butt. Excruciating pain shot through my left leg.

"Are you O.K.?" Harold caught up just in time to see my failed attempt to stand.

"I'm sure it'll be fine," I said, putting my head between my knees and breathing deeply. "I just need a minute."

I was desperate for it to be true. But when I put my hand on my ankle, I flinched again.

"Take off your boot," Harold suggested, kneeling beside me. "Let me look."

The rest of the hikers sat, welcoming the break we'd skipped at the pass. My world was shrinking, focused on a small spot in my lower left leg. My ankle had already started swelling, and soon I could barely get it back in my boot. No way was I walking.

My mind kept moving between pain and fear. The alternatives were few. The yaks were out of the question—I had seen their antics, the herders trying desperately to get them under control—and our single remaining pony was long gone, somewhere two thousand feet below us.

Our young guide squatted beside me. Tandin was tall and large-boned. His features were chiseled onto a long narrow face, and he looked as if he could stride a Mongolian plain with an eagle on his arm. But his rugged face was comforting, exactly what I needed at the moment.

"I will carry you, Tania."

He spoke quietly, with a confidence I didn't expect in someone so young.

I looked around. No one had a better idea. Our break had stretched out, and it was still a four-hour walk to camp. Harold helped me stand and took my things. Tandin moved his daypack to his chest and prepared to lift me onto his back. Then, holding one arm under my left knee so my ankle wouldn't bounce, he started down the mountain, every foot-plant landing firmly—as if we were in Central Park, not on the side of a Himalayan peak. I clung to him like a giant breathing backpack. At first each step was jarring, but either the Advil or exhaustion soon mellowed me out.

For the two hours it took to reach the base of the slope, Tandin entertained me with stories about his childhood. I don't remember the scenery, but I remember that Tandin played basketball with the crown prince—now king—of Bhutan. That he participated in archery contests. That his father had left when he was very young and remained estranged from the family, and that his mother still lived in the remote village where she was born, though the rest of his family had moved to the capital, Thimphu.

After a long descent, we finally reached the pony, but it had no saddle. It would be impossible to ride it. My choice was clear: After a brief rest, Tandin would have to carry me for another two hours, all the way to camp.

During those two hours, Tandin shared more of his life with me, telling me all about his grandfather, the patriarch of his clan and a devout Buddhist. In Bhutan, Tandin explained, it's the husband who moves in with his wife's family, rather than the other way around, as in China and India. Grandfather had six daughters, and he had to provide housing for all of their families.

That evening, my ankle had swelled far beyond the size of my boots. Our medicine kit consisted of Advil and Arnica gel, and I had never heard of the latter.

"It's a special healing cream—it reduces swelling," said my friend Jean, as she sat on Harold's cot in our tent. "I never go anywhere without it. Can I put some on your ankle?"

The thought of anyone touching my ankle was unbearable, but Jean warmed her hands, spread the cream evenly on them, and then, as if coddling a newborn baby, gently caressed from my toes to my knees. She performed that ritual three times a day, and by the second evening, the swelling had reduced to nearly normal.

Just after dawn on our second morning at camp, the porter arrived, calling, "Hello, Sir!" as always. That meant me, I knew. Everyone was "Sir." He stood in his flip-flops in the snow outside the tent and poured steaming hot liquid into a banged-up metal cup, which was, at that moment, more exquisite to me than the finest china.

We'd already spent an unplanned extra day in camp. Between two major mountain passes, we had no radio signal and no way to call for a helicopter. The nearest road was many days' walk away, and we were less than halfway through one of the most challenging trips in Bhutan.

After coffee, washing, and packing, Harold lifted me out of the breakfast tent and helped me onto a rock. Jean gave me a final Arnica treatment, and I put on thick socks and eased into my heavy leather boots, tying the laces firmly to hold my foot steady. Harold and Jean each gripped me under an arm as I came to a standing position. Everyone stood in a broad circle, watching me again. A lot was riding on this moment.

Slowly, I put weight on my left foot and concentrated on my thigh muscle, on carefully lowering my knee, on the toe of my boot touching the ground, on exerting the tiniest amount of weight. I screamed, obliterating the silence. Excruciating pain tore through my body. Tears streamed down my face. Harold and Jean held on tightly, afraid to jostle me. I stood on my good leg, desperate to do anything but give up.

I looked over at Yves, Jean's husband and the organizer of this expedition, and remembered our first meeting. He'd wanted to make sure Harold and I were prepared. Yves was tough; he'd served in the French Foreign Legion in Algeria. He suffered no wimps.

Six months earlier, I'd taken Harold helicopter skiing in Canada for his sixtieth birthday, and I'd fallen on the first run. Harold kept skiing while I was helicoptered out. My ACL was torn; it required surgery and at least half a year's healing time.

I'd had to convince Yves that I would be ready for this trek. I'd told him I was as tough as he was. Now I had to prove it.

But there was a more important reason for my desperate determination. Five years earlier, Harold had started fighting an aggressive prostate cancer that didn't disappear post-surgery, as it should have. He was given a two- or three-year life expectancy. I quit my job, and we started on all the adventures we never had time for while working and raising children. Harold was doing well, but the periodic treatment sapped his energy. It was no small miracle that he could still do this rigorous hiking.

I was as determined to continue for him as for myself, because we never knew how much longer he would be walking.

I breathed deeply, looked Harold in the eyes as he wiped my face with his hand, and said, "I can do this."

Harold asked the others for a moment alone, and they walked away.

"You know we can figure something out," he said, "some way to get out of here."

"No, it's really O.K. I can do this."

"Baby," Harold said, "are you thinking about me or yourself?"

It was hard to even understand his question. Without realizing it, Harold and his illness and I had merged into a single unit. Something precious and unbreakable.

"I'll do it, sweetheart. Really."

I'd always believed I had a high pain tolerance. That belief was about to be tested.

I will never know how I did it—how I continued hiking on a broken ankle (which was confirmed when I returned to the U.S.)—but I do know that for the next twenty days, my only medication was Advil and the thrice-daily tender, almost ritualistic, application of Arnica gel, a miracle medicine I've never been without since.

We didn't just stroll. We were above fourteen thousand feet most of the time, crossing three more passes that were higher than the tallest mountain in the U.S.

A cultural trait of Bhutanese people, it seems, is an inability to say anything negative. No matter how often we asked, the guides replied that the destination was "not too much farther," even though some days we hiked more than fourteen hours. Our longest day ended in a blinding snowstorm, and the next morning we woke to two feet of snow on the tents. Level surfaces didn't exist; we were either climbing or descending. Some of our fellow travelers came close to giving up. I persisted.

Through all this, Tandin was never far from my side.

Some days after my fall, Harold and I sat alone on a boulder above the trail. The mountains glistened; we had just passed wild sheep clambering in the rocks. It was a moment that reminded us why we always pushed ourselves to the limit instead of sitting on a beach in a fancy resort. I leaned between his open knees, feeling the warmth of his chest, daydreaming, until his words brought me back.

"We should have Tandin come to school in California," he said. "Maybe live with us."

"Really?" I was surprised—but only because I'd been thinking the same thing. Still, after two decades together, this happened often. "That sounds lovely, but do you think we can handle something like that? I thought we wanted to be free, you know, to do stuff."

"Of course I still want that, but something in me also wants to do something for him. If it weren't for Tandin...." Harold's voice dropped off. "I don't know where we would be right now. Don't tell me you haven't been thinking the same thing."

He knew me too well. Perhaps he also saw illness limiting his days, his ability to share.

Near the end of our trek, Tandin led us through remote, steep villages that might as well have been in the Middle Ages. Behind curved fields of golden rice, forests rose, capped by snow-covered peaks. In one field, a young woman stood atop a large pile of rice sheaves. She wore a long skirt with a rich violet print, and a bold brocade jacket over a green blouse. She stared at us, curious. But then Tandin came into view and—as everyone did upon meeting him—she smiled. The villagers gathered around him, laughing and joking. He played with the children, flirted with the young women, teased the grandmothers. Even the dogs came to play with him.

"Tandin, do you know these people?" Harold asked, mystified.

"Oh, no." He gave a delicate nod. "I've never been here."

But he'd grown up in a similar place. "You cannot imagine how hard these people work to achieve this day of harvest," Tandin said. "Everything is done manually: clearing the terraces, plowing, planting, tending the fields. And the continual worry about the pigs."

I had stopped to look at a small raised platform over a terrace.

"That's where children spend nights," he said, "trying to stay awake, hoping to scare away the pigs."

Back in California, we were used to neighbors who shot wild pigs. Here, children were planted to scare them. But the Buddhist tradition of nonviolence made it difficult to deal with the pigs, even though they ruined 25 to 30 percent of the crop each year.

"For a while we tried putting firecrackers on a string, so we wouldn't have to stay up all night," said Tandin. "But the pigs quickly figured out there was noise but no real danger and learned to ignore them."

I thought of the hand-powered flashlight Tandin used in camp, whose quiet clattering reminded us that batteries were both expensive and hard to dispose of in this still-unpolluted land. To me, this trip was a glorious glimpse into a kind of life that had disappeared in most of the world, buried under layers of technological evolution. It was easy to romanticize the artful terracing, the black oxen pulling hand-carved wooden plows, the grain flying and glowing in the sunlight as women stood on mats, winnowing rice through woven straw trays.

As seductive as a seventeenth-century Vermeer canvas brought to life, it touched the Russian peasant roots inside me. I wanted to sink into the rice at my feet and absorb the experience. And, on a level I couldn't be proud of, I was also grateful that I was only passing through; that when cold, dark winter came in this deep valley with no amenities, I would be back in my life full of luxury and ease.

"Tandin, is this what your village looked like?"

"Oh yes." Another gentle nod.

"And did you spend nights on these pig-watching platforms?"

"Oh yes. When I would come home from my school in Thimphu, I would have to do this." He paused. "But it is better for someone more serious, who is not so tired from school, who wouldn't fall asleep, to be the one guarding the fields."

I smiled, and he grinned sheepishly.

Tandin had intimate knowledge of life in the village, but he'd already started putting distance between himself and it. Around the fire the night before, we'd asked if he would sing for us. Expecting some romantic Bhutanese ballad, we were surprised to hear Eric Clapton. The outside world was seeping into Tandin; it was a spigot that would be hard to close.

Now he grew serious. "As hard as these people work, they will give away much of this rice, very quickly," he said. "They will finish the harvest, and then it will be time for their *putscha*. To gain face with neighbors, they will make as grand a feast as possible and send everyone home laden with gifts. When it is over, much of what they have worked for all year will be gone, and they will have to subsist on what is left for the rest of the year."

Tandin was clearly troubled by the practice. He told us that farmers showed their wealth by leaving rice stacks in the fields for a long time, to advertise their lack of imminent need for it—even though it could start rotting. And some wealthier farmers, he said, even served and ate old rice left over from previous harvests, rather than the fresh new grains, to boast of abundance.

We Americans had our own "keeping up with the Joneses" issues. Harold and I knew that if Tandin came to California, our customs would seem as strange to him as eating old rice to prove superiority seemed to us. We envisioned translating American behavior for him, just as he'd opened up Bhutan for us.

As we grew to know Tandin better, he learned about our lives, too. Harold and I had both been successful computer business executives. To Tandin, the freedom to do what we wanted now, in retirement, spoke to the benefit of studying technology. Before we realized what had happened, one day he announced that he, too, wanted to study computers. We suspected his skills lay elsewhere, in his ability to captivate and lead, but we were reluctant to discourage his newfound mission.

"Tandin," Harold asked one day as we walked through a forest whose trees had orchids growing from their trunks, "what would you think of going to college in America?" I'd been hanging back, entranced, but now we all stopped and looked at one another.

" Oh…that would be amazing, but I do not believe I would qualify," he replied, each word carefully considered. "My grades were not so great, and my test scores are not high. And I could not afford it without a scholarship."

But we could see the raw desire in his eyes.

By the end of the trip, when we returned to Thimphu, we were anxious to meet Tandin's grandfather. We wanted to present our idea, and we wanted his blessing.

Grandfather was a man of dignity, strength, and calm. Slight of stature, he was slim and straight as the bamboo arrows he, too, had shot in his youth. His wrinkles were like the bark of a tree, but his eyes sparkled, and he smiled easily. His gnarled fingers never stopped moving over his prayer beads. He didn't say much, but he listened.

Even seated on a floor mat, Harold towered over everyone in the room, but for some reason my husband seemed the supplicant as he explained our idea.

Grandfather eventually spoke, with Tandin translating. "I understand how my family might benefit from your offer," he said. "I understand how Tandin might benefit."

Tandin paused, clearly worried about what came next. "But how do you benefit from bringing my grandson to America and sending him to college?"

Everyone stared at Harold. While fighting for his life since the cancer diagnosis, my husband had developed a wisdom that could still surprise me. "I am a relatively new student of Buddhism," he said. "But I like what it teaches about releasing goodness into the universe and seeing how it circles, perhaps returning when you don't expect it."

Grandfather grinned. Then he exchanged a few words with Tandin, who turned to us, chagrined. "Grandfather wants you to know I have not always been a model student. Or the most obedient son."

"Tell him we already figured that out."

We agreed to set up an email account for Tandin. He'd use the computer at a café in town to communicate with us. We left Bhutan believing we would soon have a student in our household again.

A lot changed in the aftermath of the comparatively innocent days when we'd hiked the Himalayas with our young guide. The 9/11 Twin Tower bombing in New York eliminated any possibility of the U.S. granting Tandin a visa to study in California. A scholar heading for Stanford or Harvard, maybe. A young man headed for Santa Rosa Junior College, no way. After extensive letter exchanges with congressmen and consulates and colleges, we realized we'd hit a dead end. While

314   TANIA ROMANOV AMOCHAEV

we struggled to come up with an alternative, Tandin got
accepted to a college in Bangkok. We consulted with his family, then agreed to send him there to study computer science.

At first, Tandin sent regular letters and reports, but in the
second year, communication dropped off. He was half the
world away, so it was hard to feel personally involved, to help.
Less than eighteen months into it, we learned he had failed
out of the program. He was simply unsuited for it. But we
heard nothing from him.

Were we pouring money down a rat hole? Or supporting
a promising young man, struggling but worth our continued
commitment? Was Tandin likely to stay connected with
two people in distant America? Or had he already disappeared, another undocumented immigrant we'd inadver-
tently launched into the world?

It was fortunate that he reminded us of our own son. Brad
had struggled through school, yet eventually earned two master's degrees. Whenever he ran into problems, he retreated,
became uncommunicative. We knew this scenario. So we
held onto our faith.

When Tandin realized we weren't giving up on him even
though he'd failed, he found another program that would let
him work year-round and finish in three years.

"You won't regret this, I promise you," he emailed.

Despite starting over at a new school, in just over four
years, he graduated from Bangkok University with a bach-
elor's degree in Hospitality and Tourism Management. By
then he had also met and fallen in love with Chhimi, a fellow
Bhutanese student. Harold wasn't well enough to attend the
graduation ceremony, but he kept the announcement tucked
in with family photographs.

In 2011, I lost Harold to the cancer he'd battled so daringly
all those years, long past any predictions. We had a memorial in his beloved redwood grove at our home in Healds-
burg. While friends and family spoke about this wonderful

man—my sweetheart, lover, and fellow walker through the world—Tandin lit 108 yak-butter oil lamps in a small temple in Thimphu to ease Harold's passing into his next life. He wanted me to come and do the same.

Three years later, I did.

I flew to a country still familiar, yet modernizing rapidly, with signs of construction everywhere. Tandin's aunt had just passed, and we spent days with monks, family, and friends, observing their traditions of mourning and remembrance. I sat for hours listening to chanting that brought Harold back to me more easily than I could have imagined. Grandfather was older and more delicate, but welcoming. When I asked if he'd let me record his praying, he pulled me close, his voice rising and falling in a prayer he had probably performed millions of times. In many ways, the trip was a homecoming, a return to something vaguely familiar, no longer odd and foreign.

One afternoon, Tandin and I visited the small temple near the family home, where a monk ushered us into a small altar room filled with rows of yak-butter lamps. They left me alone, and with soft chanting in the background, I lit 108 lamps. At first, it seemed an enormous task. But as I neared the last lamp, I slowed down. It felt as if Harold was there with me. I wished, then, for 108 more, or maybe to never stop.

During my visit, we spent much of the time in Thimphu, but Tandin and I also traveled to some areas we had previously trekked together. On our way to Bumthang, in the east, we had an unexpected meeting with his father in the mountains near his remote village. We shared yak-butter tea near the new packed earth home he was building, and I was invited to pound dirt into one wall. As we drove farther along those harrowing mountain roads, Tandin's phone rang. It was his mother, calling from Thimphu. He pulled over, spoke with her briefly, then beamed at me. "I have never spoken to my mother and my father in the same day before! And you are here with me as well. It is a most auspicious day."

—————

It was late that same night in Bumthang when the hotel we were staying in caught fire.

As Tandin grabbed my arm and pulled me toward the stairs across from my room, I could see the fire was behind the stairwell, and I froze. It was the only exit path.

Once again it was Tandin, and me, and few alternatives.

But now I trusted he would save me. Somehow, his confidence became mine.

We raced down the stairs, the sound of breaking glass driving me faster, the smoke filling my lungs until I could barely breathe. I stumbled out though the deserted lobby, but Tandin immediately turned around and sprinted back up the same threatened stairway. An older man staying down the hall from me was still in his room. I stood outside, shivering and shocked, terrified that Tandin was headed back into those flames. While I waited, other hotel guests appeared, exiting the building wrapped in blankets, dazed and scared. But no Tandin.

Finally, I saw him emerge from the now dense smoke, nearly carrying the confused gentleman whose life he had saved. "I think we got everyone out," he said.

An ancient piece of firefighting equipment bounced noisily toward us along the pitted dirt road from Bumthang, and we watched as a group of men jumped from the truck and sped by us to fight the fire. With minimal protective gear, they tore into the flames, shooting water from their hoses, seemingly fearless. I couldn't watch for long.

Fate or luck had kept Tandin awake that night, talking to a fellow guide. Tandin had smelled the smoke, raised the alarm, and saved everyone in the hotel, including me.

As I grow older, I find fewer rational explanations for the pain and blessings fate showers upon me. The mathematical precision of the logic I studied in college has been tempered with life's impossible curves. I do, however, often return to Harold's conversation with Grandfather. I can see them both sitting in that intimate room, cups of yak-butter tea between them, figuring each other out, deciding how much to trust. Deciding to believe in each other.

On this second trip to Bhutan—before the temple visit, the lighting of candles, the father-son reunion, the hotel fire, and another heroic rescue—I walked into Tandin's married home for the first time. I met his mother-in-law and was greeted joyously by his wife Chhimi, whom I knew from Bangkok. As we hugged, I saw two small people hiding in the doorway. The older and braver boy pulled his sister forward. They both stood before me—a complete stranger from far away. Certain they'd run to their mother, I stepped back so they wouldn't be frightened. Instead, big smiles broke out on little Palbar and Dechen's faces. I was not a stranger.

"Hi Granny!" they shouted, and soon they were hugging me, too.

જી જી જી

Tania Romanov Amochaev is the author of One Hundred Years of Exile: A Romanov's Search for her Father's Russia, Mother Tongue: A Saga of Three Generations of Balkan Women, *and* Never a Stranger, *a collection of travel essays. She is a Solas Award winner, and her work has been featured in multiple travel anthologies, including the Best Travel Writing series. Born in the former Yugoslavia, Tania's family fled the country, and she spent her childhood in a refugee camp in Trieste, Italy, before immigrating to the United States. Tania attended San Francisco public schools and grew up in the city's Russian community. After graduating from the University of California at Berkeley, she forged a successful business career in high tech, serving as CEO of three companies.*

Acknowledgments

This was a bizarre time to edit a book about travel, but I was exceedingly fortunate to have the support of many wise and generous people.

First, thank you to Dolly Spalding and Paulette Perhach, who voluntarily read hundreds of essays and helped me make some tough decisions. I can't express how much I appreciate all the time, hard work, and keen insight you gave this project. Giant thank-you hugs also go out to Emilie Staat Strong, Laurie Weed, Jen Castle, Blake Spalding, Kyle Keyser, Marcia DeSanctis, Colleen Kinder, Christina Ammon, Erin Crane, Ava Menin, Peauxdunque Writers Alliance, Abbie Kozolchyk, and Dan "Pencils Down" Prothero, for various acts of editorial support and encouragement. This book wouldn't be the same without your guidance, and I love y'all.

Thank you to Aislyn Greene and Jennifer Flowers of *AFAR* and to Sivani Babu and Sabine Goldman of *Hidden Compass* for taking the time to nominate essays for the collection. And thanks to Niesha Davis, Sensitivity Reader Extraordinaire, for sharing your knowledge and expertise. Thanks to Howie Severson for your great design work. *Shukran* and a hand on my heart to Deep Travel Workshops for inviting me to teach in Fez so I could become wondrously lost and found!

Larry Habegger and James O'Reilly of Travelers' Tales, you are infinitely patient, kindhearted, and smart, and I thank my luckiest stars for a decade of collaboration with you two extraordinary gentlemen. (Can this really be the seventh book we've put together!?) Your vision is inspiring and your dedication to championing women travel writers legendary. Thank you for everything you have done and continue to do.

And to the spectacularly talented Colette Hannahan, who illustrated and elevated this anthology with her exquisite paintings, thank you does not suffice! I dedicate (at least) thirteen lifetimes' worth of gratitude practice to you.

Finally, to all of you curious, intrepid, passionate women who lived and wrote the 1300 travel essays submitted this year, thank you for sharing your journeys with me. It was a profound honor to lose myself in your stories. They stay with me, like new maps written on my heart.

———

"In the Presence of Boys" by Marilyn Abildskov originally appeared in *Sonora Review* in 1997. Reprinted by permission of the author. Copyright ©1997.

"A Family Project" by Faith Adiele published with permission of the author. Copyright ©2020

"Convivencia" by Christina Ammon published with permission of the author. Copyright ©2020

"Not a Stranger" by Tania Romanov Amochaev published with permission of the author. Copyright ©2020

"The House on KVR Swamy Road" by Sivani Babu originally published online at *GeoEx* and *Travelers' Tales Editors' Choice* in 2019. Reprinted by permission of the author.

"Meeting Joy" by Jennifer Baljko published with permission of the author. Copyright ©2020

"Come and See" by Kaitlin Barker Davis originally published in *Nowhere* in 2017. Reprinted by permission of the author.

"You Don't Have to Be Here" by Anne P. Beatty originally published in the Fall 2018 issue of *Creative Nonfiction*. Reprinted by permission of the author.

"Stolen Tickets" by Naomi Melati Bishop first published as "My Father's Journey Around the World with Stolen Plane

Tickets" online at *Vice* in 2016. Reprinted by permission of the author.

"Our Ravaged Lady" by Erin Byrne first appeared in *Hidden Compass* in 2020. Reprinted by permission of the author.

"Casi Loco" by Anita Cabrera first appeared in *Away* in 2020. Reprinted by permission of the author.

"Headlights" by Marcia DeSanctis originally published in *Entropy* Magazine as "On Weather: Tempest" in 2017. Reprinted by permission of the author.

"A Rare-Colored Stone" by Shannon Leone Fowler first published in *Pilgrim Magazine* as "Kindness of Strangers" in 2020. Reprinted by permission of the author.

"Half Dome" by Alison Singh Gee first published in *Sierra* magazine as "Explore Yosemite's Mist Trail—and the Park's Chinese American Legacy" in 2018. Reprinted by permission of the author.

"Key Change" by Rahawa Haile originally appeared in *AFAR* in 2019. Reprinted by permission of the author.

"Call of the Sirens" by Colette Hannahan published by permission of the author. Copyright ©2020

"A Strange Ambition" by Eva Holland originally appeared as "Get Schooled in the No-Nonsense Art of Survival" in *Outside* in 2018. Reprinted by permission of the author.

"Traveling Queer and Far" by Sally Kohn first appeared in *AFAR* in 2020. Reprinted by permission of the author.

"Making the Rounds" by Abbie Kozolchyk first published in *Saveur* in 2018 as "The Peruvian Town is Obsessed with Their Sweet Bread Loaves." Reprinted by permission of the author.

"The Godfather Town" by Ann Leary published by permission of the author. Copyright ©2020

"A Bedtime Story" by Diane Lebow published by permission of the author. Copyright ©2020

"Single Woman Traveling Alone" by Jacqueline Luckett published by permission of the author. Copyright ©2020

"Save the Date" by Martha McCully published by permission of the author. Copyright ©2020

"Journey Proud" by Toni Mirosevich published by permission of the author. Copyright ©2020

"Why I Took My Daughter to Auschwitz" by Peggy Orenstein originally appeared in *Condé Nast Traveler* in 2018. Reprinted by permission of the author.

"Zooming in on Petra" by Susan Orlean first published in *Smithsonian Magazine* in 2018. Reprinted by permission of the author.

"Wingmom" by Suzanne Roberts first appeared in *Bad Tourist* (University of Nebraska Press) in 2020 as *"My Mother is my Wingman."* Reprinted by permission of the author.

"Tracking a Ghost" by Jill K. Robinson first appeared in *The San Francisco Chronicle* in 2017 as "Quest for the Gray Ghost: Tracking the snow leopard in Ladakh." Reprinted by permission of the author.

"Wade in the Water" by Alexandria Scott first published in *Hidden Compass* in 2019. *Reprinted by permission of the author.*

"Good Enough" by Anne Sigmon published by permission of the author. Copyright ©2020

"Frangipani" by Mathangi Subramanian first published online at Powells.com in 2019. Reprinted by permission of the author.

"To the Travelers Watching Reality TV" by Anna Vodicka first published in *Off Assignment* as "To the Roomful of Travelers Watching American Reality TV" in 2019. Reprinted by permission of the author.

"Finding El Saez" by Alia Volz first published in *Nowhere* Magazine in 2017. Reprinted by permission of the author.

About the Editor

Lavinia Spalding has edited five previous editions of *The Best Women's Travel Writing*. She is the author of *Writing Away* and the co-author of *With a Measure of Grace* and *This Immeasurable Place*, and she introduced the e-book edition of Edith Wharton's classic travelogue, *A Motor-Flight Through France*. Lavinia's work appears in such publications as *AFAR, Tin House, Yoga Journal, Longreads, Sunset, San Francisco Chronicle, The Guardian, Ms.,* and *Post Road*, and has been widely anthologized. She is also a public speaker and teacher. When she isn't leading writing workshops around the world, Lavinia lives with her family in New Orleans and on Cape Cod. Visit her at laviniaspalding.com.

About the Illustrator

Colette Hannahan is a painter and illustrator based in San Francisco. She believes that every landscape and skyscape deserve a portrait, so she's going for it, one by one. You can see her artwork (including the full-size color renderings of the illustrations in this book) on her website colettehannahan.com or follow her on Instagram @colettehannahan.